How to STEM

Science, Technology, Engineering, and Math Education in Libraries ·

Edited by Vera Gubnitskaia and Carol Smallwood

THE SCARECROW PRESS, INC.
Lanham • Toronto • Plymouth, UK
2014

Published by Scarecrow Press, Inc.
A wholly owned subsidary of The Rowman & Littlefield Publishing Group, Inc.
4501 Forbes Boulevard, Suite 200, Lanham, Maryland 20706
http://www.scarecrowpress.com

Estover Road, Plymouth PL6 7PY, United Kingdom

British Library Cataloguing in Publication Information Available

Library of Congress Cataloging-in-Publication Data

How to STEM : science, technology, engineering, and math education in libraries / edited by Vera Gubnitskaia, Carol Smallwood.
  pages cm
Includes bibliographical references and index.
ISBN 978-0-8108-9273-6 (pbk. : alk. paper) -- ISBN 978-0-8108-9274-3 (ebook) 1. Science and technology libraries--United States. 2. Science--Study and teaching--United States. 3. Technology--Study and teaching--United States. 4. Engineering--Study and teaching--United States. 5. Mathematics--Study and teaching--United States. 6. Library orientation for science students. 7. Libraries--Special collections--Science. 8. School librarian participation in curriculum planning--United States. 9. Academic libraries--Relations with faculty and curriculum--United States. 10. Libraries and education--United States--Case studies. I. Gubnitskaia, Vera, 1960- editor of compilation. II. Smallwood, Carol, 1939- editor of compilation.
  Z675.T3H59 2014
  026'.5--dc23
  2013025036

♾™ The paper used in this publication meets the minimum requirements of American National Standard for Information Sciences Permanence of Paper for Printed Library Materials, ANSI/NISO Z39.48-1992.

Printed in the United States of America

To the family of Vera Gubnitskaia, and to the contributors

Contents

Tables and Figures

Foreword

Paula M. Storm

In *How to STEM: Science, Technology, Engineering, and Math Education in Libraries*, the contributors have provided a cornucopia of ideas on how libraries can engage youth in the crucial subjects of science, technology, engineering, and math. The twenty-five chapters cover exciting ideas for this engagement, ranging for those applicable for preschoolers to those for college students. Written by a diverse group of authors from public libraries and academia, these chapters will persuade readers into incorporating some of these ideas into their library's events and services.

The book contains eight parts, each emphasizing a different aspect of how to accomplish this incorporation. The chapters contain specific, practical ideas complete with instructions, required supplies, related educational standards, and reading lists.

The chapters in part I emphasize how hands-on activities that are both fun and educational can be used to further science, technology, engineering, and math (STEM) awareness. Ranging from Christner's science activities for preschoolers through partnership programs featuring LEGO® to animation workshops for teens, the authors describe such interesting ideas that surely readers will want to plan similar activities at their home institutions.

Parts II and III contain chapters on the uniting of STEM with information literacy. Kirchner, a former K–8 teacher describes how libraries can provide a science lab to homeschooling families, whereas Petralia and Turner explain how to customize a for-credit information literacy class for STEM disciplines. A similar theme is addressed in chapter 8 by Mattson and Hannan on reaching gifted high school STEM students. "Kidventions" in chapter 9 focuses on students using the US Patent and Trademark Office database to foster ideas for inventions of their own complete with the budget, marketing, and evaluation information necessary for the program. Johnson and Russell established a Math Emporium at F. D. Bluford Library on the campus of North Carolina Agricultural and Technical State University. The Math Emporium is known for successfully improving the math scores of non-STEM students. Another LEGO® activity to foster interest in STEM is described by Krueger in Chapter 11.

Innovative collection development ideas are discussed in part IV. In chapter 13, Bramwell describes how the Mount Prospect Public Library received a grant from the Institute of Electrical and Electronics Engineers (IEEE) to purchase science kits for K–6 students. These kits circulate and are also used in some library programs. In chapter 14, Hughes and Pinkston advocate the purchasing of STEM-related graphic novels to pique the interest of older students.

Part V focuses on research and publishing and begins with Alvin Hutchinson's description of how the Smithsonian Libraries developed the Smithsonian Research (SRO) program. This program compiles and maintains the published research output of Smithsonian scholars, thus providing a valuable service to their scientists. Another way to help scientists is described in chapter 16 by Rauh and Galloway. They advocate that librarians help guide the research and publication process for STEM faculty by facilitating literature reviews and suggesting journals in which to publish.

Outreach is the theme of part VI, and the programs described in these chapters offer an array of ways to connect with students of all ages. The section begins with Hopwood's advice to non-STEM librarians who want to create science-related programs. She suggests the use of social media to connect with STEM experts and using readily available materials for the activities so as to keep costs low. The next chapter focuses on how to get girls excited about science, followed by McAuliffe's essay on designing a geographic information systems (GIS) day program for students and adults. Finally, Lauritsen from the Robert E. Kennedy Library at California Polytechnic State University in San Luis Obispo describe the Cal Poly Science Café that features expert-led interactive programs on STEM-related subjects.

In the section on partnerships, Badia from McGill University addresses the sometimes-frustrating problem of getting students to attend library workshops. She gives very useful, practical hints on how to provide university STEM students with relevant, interesting workshops that will help them in their coursework. This is followed by chapters highlighting the role libraries can play in STEM career exploration and how STEM librarians can better serve the faculty in these subject areas.

Of course, all of these exciting ideas require an investment of time or money; most take both. Many books and other materials for the sciences are not inexpensive and today many libraries are already financially strapped. Therefore, the final section of *How to STEM: Science, Technology, Engineering, and Math Education in Libraries* addresses the funding of these programs. Cordell and Rogers give excellent advice on grant writing for STEM in chapter 24 and Wright describes inexpensive programs and experiments that will not task a library's budget.

The importance of STEM to our future cannot be overly stressed. Many future careers will rely heavily on these skills and it will be crucial that average citizens of the near future be aware of how science and technology will affect their lives. Libraries can and should play an active role in bringing STEM awareness and education to students of all ages. *How to STEM: Science, Technology, Engineering, and Math Education in Libraries* is an excellent way to begin that process.

Preface

During the past few years, groups like the President's Council of Advisors on Science and Technology, Center for Education have been placing great emphasis on the significance of STEM (science, technology, engineering, and math) education. The curricula have been revised in many educational institutions and school districts across the country. It is clear that for STEM to be successful, other community organizations, including libraries, need to be closely involved in the process. Library staff realize the importance of getting involved in STEM education, but many have difficulty finding comprehensive information that will help them plan and successfully implement STEM direction in their organization.

How to STEM: Science, Technology, Engineering, and Math Education in Libraries is by and for librarians who are involved in contributing efforts into advancing these subjects. The anthology is divided into eight parts: I. Range and Scope; II. Teaching; III. Information Literacy and Educational Support; IV. Collection Development; V. Research and Publishing; VI. Outreach; VII. Partnerships; and VIII. Funding. A total of thirty-four authors from a variety of library, science, technology, and instructional fields in the United States and Canada contributed twenty-five chapters in which they described specific projects that will spark the interest of librarians regardless of their professional concentration. It was exciting for coeditors to discover the richness of ideas, creativity, and quality of material submitted for publication. We greatly appreciate the enthusiasm of the contributors and their willingness to share their work.

Vera Gubnitskaia and Carol Smallwood

Acknowledgments

Sharon Britton, library director, Bowling Green State University-Firelands, Huron, Ohio

James B. Casey, retired director, Oak Lawn Public Library, Oak Lawn, Illinois

Su Epstein, library director, Saxton B. Little Free Library, Columbia, Connecticut

Beth Nieman, youth services librarian, Carlsbad Public Library, Carlsbad, New Mexico

Mark Aaron Polger, instruction/reference librarian and information literacy instructor, College of Staten Island, CUNY, New York, New York

Ann Paietta, director, Essex Free Library, Essex, Vermont

Anna Ercoli Schnitzer, disability issues librarian, Taubman Health Sciences Library, University of Michigan, Ann Arbor

Leigh Woznick, library media specialist, Bridgewater-Raritan Middle School, Bridgewater, New Jersey

I

Range and scope

ONE

WonderWorks: Preschoolers Playing with STEM

Carissa Christner

Craft and story programs for young children have long enjoyed widespread popularity in public libraries, but programs rooted in science, technology, engineering, and mathematic (STEM) skills for preschoolers are a relatively new idea. One of the reasons for this preference for arts-based programming is a perception that lessons from the STEM disciplines tend to have predetermined "right" and "wrong" answers and arts lessons have more loosely defined guidelines for success, making them more accessible to a wider audience. Is it possible to design STEM programs for young children that engage them in playful exploration at the library?

In December of 2012, a new program called WonderWorks premiered at the Madison Public Library in Madison, Wisconsin. This class teaches STEM skills to three- and four-year-olds through play. Each week during a four- or six-week series, fifteen children meet for a forty-five-minute class dedicated to exploring one aspect of science, technology, engineering, or math. The class begins with a welcome song and book related to the topic of the day. Then the children (and their adult caregivers) are invited to try out several stations set up around the room with different experiments, games, and exploration areas. They can play at each station for as long as they like, moving on to another when they are ready. No one is required to try all the stations, and if only one station piques their interest that week, they can stay at that station the whole time, or go home whenever they are done. Although the class is still relatively new, many lessons have been learned along the way, and some fantastic resources have been discovered.

LESSON #1: MANY BOOKS ABOUT EARLY STEM SKILLS ARE WRITTEN FOR PRESCHOOLS

Most of the projects described within books rely on teachers having repeated, prolonged, almost daily contact with the children they are teaching. This allows for longer and slower experiments (like growing seeds) and also for more natural following of the children's own interests and curiosity. For instance, if a preschool teacher overhears a child wondering why leaves turn colors in autumn, they can follow that line of thought with a whole series of explorations and discussions about seasons and trees and colors and the child will be more likely to engage because it's a topic in which they have a personal interest.

In library settings, we don't usually have that sort of contact with children. At best, we might see them for an hour once a week. Therefore, we either must choose projects that can be explored within the timeframe available or the ones that can travel from the library to home to extend the learning.

One of the benefits of library programming as compared to the preschool ones is that an adult caregiver generally stays with the children at the library. The lessons taught in WonderWorks benefit adults as well as children. Many of the projects can be easily replicated at home in order to continue the learning process beyond the hour at the library. Our favorite projects are the ones that fully engage the thinking of both the adults and children working together.

LESSON #2: BOOKS ABOUT SCIENCE AND MATH FOR PRESCHOOL AGE CHILDREN ARE EASIER TO FIND THAN BOOKS ABOUT ENGINEERING AND TECHNOLOGY

Science and math are more traditional areas of study (especially in early education) than engineering and technology. However, many books about science and math may actually include engineering and technology projects (these STEM skills are all very intertwined, after all). For example, the book *Science Is Simple* (Ashbrook 2003) contains chapters about pumps, siphons, wheels, and rocket ships—all topics related to engineering and technology.

Here are a few examples of what a science-focused lesson might look like.

Science — Shadows

Read: Hall, Pamela. 2011. *Follow It! Learn About Shadows*. Mankato, MN: Child's World.

Supplies:

- Shadow puppet theater (premade or DIY, see below)
- Dark paper
- Plastic drinking straws or wooden skewers
- Tape
- Lamps (a variety of sizes and light bulb strengths)
- Flashlights
- Disposable clear plastic container large enough to fit around head of a flashlight
- Large roll of white paper or sidewalk chalk

Activities:

- Create a shadow puppet theater and some shadow puppets (search online for "DIY shadow puppet theater"). Children can either help to create the puppets and the stage or, you can prepare these items before class and offer children the opportunity to play with the puppets, learning how they work best and performing impromptu puppet plays.
- Play with shadowgraphy. Shine a bright light against a blank wall and use your hands to create animal-shaped shadows on the wall. Teach students one or two simple hand shapes to try for themselves. (Search online for "hand shadow puppetry" for helpful diagrams or for "shadow puppets by Olive Us" for a well-made video demonstration of making hand shadows.)

Create classic silhouettes:

1. Tape a piece of dark paper to the wall.
2. Have someone sit down in front of the paper (sideways, in profile).
3. Shine a light on them, casting their shadow on the wall.
4. Trace their shadow on the paper with a pencil.
5. Cut out the shadow and glue it to a lighter sheet of paper.

- Cut a hole in the bottom of a disposable plastic container. Insert the head of a flashlight into the container and tape the flashlight to the container to secure it. Decorate the (clear) lid of the container with stickers or cut out paper shapes and shine it on a wall to see the shape shadows.
- Create full-body shadow drawings. Place a large piece of paper on the ground outside and have a child stand so that their shadow is cast on the paper. Trace their shadow on the paper (or draw directly on the sidewalk with chalk), then have them lie down on the

paper and trace around their body in a different color and compare the shapes.

- With each of these activities, experiment with the light source being closer or farther away from subject. How does that affect the shadow? What if the light is high vs. low? Bright vs. dim? Write down your observations or discuss them with classmates or adults and see if they agree.

Science—Static Electricity

Read: Inkpen, Mick. 1990. *The Blue Balloon*. Boston: Little, Brown.
Supplies:

- Balloons
- Tissue paper (scraps are fine)
- Confetti
- Feathers
- Crisp rice cereal
- Plastic bottles
- Plexiglas
- Wool sweaters (or scraps of polar fleece fabric)

Activities:

- Blow up a balloon and rub it on your hair to make it stand on end.
- Blow up a balloon, rub it on wool or fleece to charge it with static, then hold it near scraps of tissue paper, feathers, crisp rice cereal, or other lightweight objects and see which ones can be picked up using the power of static.
- Search online for "Snap, Crackle, Jump" for a fun experiment with static and crisp rice cereal.
- Put scraps of tissue inside plastic bottles and rub it with a wool sweater. The papers will stick to the sides where you've rubbed the sweater.
- Hold a static-charged balloon near a stream of running water and watch the stream bend toward the balloon.

For more science activity ideas written in a library-friendly format, read the book: *Science Is Simple: Over 250 Activities for Preschoolers* (Ashbrook 2003).

LESSON #3: WHAT DOES TEACHING "TECHNOLOGY" TO A PRESCHOOLER MEAN?

Although we began this project with a more mainstream mindset about technology (iPads! Digital cameras! Cell phones!) it quickly became apparent that preschool children need no instruction in how to *use* today's very intuitive technological gadgets. They were too young to write software or tackle other complicated technology skills. Our library also couldn't afford to buy class sets of new gadgets each time the series was offered and so the question arose—what are the goals of teaching technology to young children?

After consulting local science educators, it became clear that for this age group, "technology" simply refers to "tools." Any tool that helps us learn or complete a task is technology. This opened up a wide variety of class topics and made technology lessons more attainable. After designing a few lesson plans around this new understanding of technology, a planning pattern emerged:

1. Choose a tool to feature.
2. Gather as many different examples of that tool (in child-safe varieties) as you can.
3. Create open-ended activities that explore different ways to use that tool and give students ample time to experiment and practice using the tool.

Here are a few suggested technology topics and activities to explore:

Technology—Tweezers and Tongs

Read: Schwartz, Amy. 1999. *How to Catch an Elephant.* New York: DK Publishing.

Supplies:

- Tweezers
- Tongs (as many sizes and types as you can collect. Invite participants to bring some from home!)
- Practice chopsticks (the kind that are attached at the top)
- Objects to pick up (pom-poms, cotton balls, feathers, cotton swabs, fabric scraps, Styrofoam peanuts, wooden blocks, etc.)
- Containers in which to transfer objects (egg cartons, muffin tins, paper cups, bowls, empty tissue boxes, etc.)

Activities:

- Pick up a variety of objects with different sizes of tweezers and tongs. Which ones work best for which objects?
- Can you use the tools to place the objects in specific compartments (like the holes in an egg carton)?
- Bonus math/science skill practice: can you sort the objects by color or type? (sharpens sorting and classification skills).

Technology—Scales

Read: Willis, Shirley. 1999. *Tell Me How Much It Weighs*. New York: Franklin Watts.

Supplies:

- Scales
- Coat hangers
- String
- Things to weigh
- Pencil and paper to record weights

Activities:

- Compare digital vs. analog scales—do they record the same weight?
- Try weighing things on a small (kitchen) vs. large (bathroom) scale. Which scale gives more accurate numbers for heavy objects? For light objects?
- Make a simple balance scale using a coat hanger hung on a doorknob with strings tied to each of the bottom corners. Tie different objects onto the strings to see which are heavier or lighter by watching which way the hanger tips. How do you know which object is heavier?

Technology—Scissors

Many children, when they first begin to use scissors, start by snipping "fringe" around the edges of a piece of paper, then cutting paper in half, cutting straight lines, cutting curved lines, then cutting out shapes. The children in your class might be at different stages on this developmental path, so be sure to offer a variety of scissor activity options.

Read: Lionni, Leo. 1982. *Let's Make Rabbits: A Fable*. New York: Pantheon Books.

Supplies:

- Scissors (both child-safe and decorative-edged)
- Play clay
- Paper (a variety, including both whole sheets and scraps)
- Sandpaper
- Craft foam sheets
- Paper plates
- Plastic drinking straws

Activities:

- Cut play clay with blunt scissors.
- Snip straws into short lengths. (Bonus: these short tubes can be used as beads, strung together on a length of string or yarn or threaded onto a wooden skewer or uncooked spaghetti.)
- Try snipping cardstock, craft foam sheets, sandpaper, construction paper, paper plates, small paper cups, or other papers. Which ones are easier to cut? More difficult? Try using the decorative edge scissors—how do those compare?
- Search online for instructions on making a "paper plate hedgehog."
- Search online for "scissor skills" to find printable practice pages with straight lines and curved lines.
- Cut scraps of paper for a collage.

Technology—Hole Punches

Read: Merriam, Eve. 1995. *Hole Story*. New York: Simon & Schuster Books for Young Readers.

Supplies:

- A variety of hole punches (standard, three-hole punches, shaped craft punches)
- A variety of papers (construction paper, cardstock, fine-grain sandpaper, thin craft foam sheets, old file folders, whatever you have on hand)

Activities:

- Punch holes in paper (this alone might be enough to keep children engaged for the entire class time). To extend the play aspect, you can pretend that the papers are train tickets or frequent-buyer punch cards and set up an area of the room like seats on a train or like a shop.
- Lace yarn or ribbon through the holes children have created.
- String several punched pages together (with a binder rings or ribbon).
- Create artwork with the punched paper or the "confetti" results.

Technology—Eye Droppers

Read: Weeks, Sarah. 2000. *Drip, Drop*. New York: Harper Collins.

Supplies:

- eye droppers, turkey basters, bulb syringes
- water
- food coloring

- coffee filters or thick paper towels
- baking soda
- vinegar
- muffin tins, ice cube trays, Styrofoam egg cartons

Activities:

- Drop colored water onto coffee filters or paper towels. Bonus science activity: Discuss how the colors mix when they bleed into each other. What new colors are created?
- Drop colored vinegar onto baking soda.
- Transfer water from one container to another (e.g., from a cup into an ice cube tray).
- Experiment with each of the different types of droppers. Which ones are easier to use? Which ones pick up more water?
- Try blowing bubbles in the water using the droppers.

Technology — Staplers

Read: Hanlon, Abby. 2012. *Ralph Tells a Story*. New York: Marshall Cavendish Children.

Supplies:

- Staplers in a variety of sizes
- Staples (include colored staples if available)
- Paper (scrap paper, colored paper, gift wrap, wallpaper samples, etc.)
- Felt, polar fleece or craft foam sheets

Activities:

- Staple papers together to create books.
- Staple felt, polar fleece, or craft foam sheets together to create pockets or purses.
- Staple strips of paper into rings to create crowns or paper chains.

LESSON #4: WHAT DOES TEACHING "ENGINEERING" TO A PRESCHOOLER MEAN?

After exploring technology and discovering it to be a larger field than originally imagined, we turned the same question to engineering (the other field of STEM study not fully explored in preschool education literature). Instead of studying only how things are built, engineering can be presented as an exploration in problem solving, tinkering, or figuring out how things work. The formula for these classes can begin with a question, but don't be surprised if children simply play with the materials and do not do structured experiments to find the "best" answer to the question. Even if their play looks unstructured, they are still learning basic engineering concepts in a natural, hands-on way that will help them when they study these same concepts more formally in school. They may also frame questions of their own, following their own interests and strengthening their natural curiosity about engineering.

Next are a few ideas for engineering topics.

Engineering—Balancing and Fulcrums

Read: Walsh, Ellen Stoll. 2010. *Balancing Act.* New York: Beach Lane Books.

Supplies:

- Blocks, including cylinders, semicylinders, and triangles
- Wooden rulers (plastic ones bend too much), or similar wood scraps
- Objects to balance (toy cars, coins, other blocks, etc.)
- A board sturdy enough to support the weight of adults (a scrap of 2"-x-4" lumber works fine)
- Pipe (PVC or metal, about 4" to 6" long and about 1" in diameter)

Activities:

- Balance long pieces of wood or blocks on top of flat or curved blocks. Try to find the center of balance. Which works more easily? Curved, flat, or pointed fulcrums? What could you adjust to make balancing easier or more stable?
- Create a simple "rola bola" by balancing the sturdy piece of wood on top of a cylindrical block or pipe and (holding on to a table or chair) standing on the wood and trying to balance.

Engineering—Sink vs. Float

Read: Burningham, John. 1970. *Mr. Gumpy's Outing.* Harmondsworth, England: Puffin Books.

Supplies:

- Foil
- Craft foam or Styrofoam
- Waxed paper
- Tubs or bowls of water
- Coins, marbles, pom-poms, cotton balls, other things to load into your "boats"

Activities:

- Build a boat from foil and see how much weight you can put on it before it sinks.
- Try floating different materials (Styrofoam, craft foam, waxed paper, etc.).
- Try different boat shapes (round, triangular, diamond-shaped, square).
- Try different weights (flat things like coins vs. round things like marbles).
- What boat shape holds the most weight? What material holds the most weight?

Engineering—Catapults

Read: Landry, Leo. 2005. *Eat Your Peas, Ivy Louise!* Boston: Houghton Mifflin.

Supplies:

- Plastic spoons
- Rubber bands
- Wooden craft sticks
- Clothespins
- Pom-poms, marshmallows, cotton balls, or other soft ammunition

Activities:

- Build a simple catapult (search online for "spoon catapult" or "clothespin catapult").
- What object flies the farthest?
- Can you hit a target on the floor?
- What do you need to do to make the object fly higher? Farther?

Engineering—Pulleys

Read: Dahl, Michael. 2006. *Pull, Lift & Lower: A Book about Pulleys.* Minneapolis, MN: Picture Window Books.

Supplies:

- Lace-up shoes
- Miniblinds
- Empty thread spools
- Small pulleys
- String, yarn, rope
- Rolling pins
- Heavy objects with handles or otherwise easy to tie a rope to

Activities:

- Practice tying shoes or at least tightening the laces (shoelaces through the holes are pulleys).
- Create pulleys with string or rope over spools or rolling pins and lift heavy objects. Compare to lifting the object without a pulley. Which is easier?
- Let kids raise and lower miniblinds (with adult supervision).
- Have pulleys and string at one table and just let kids play around with them.

Engineering—Blast off!

Read: Mitton, Tony. 1997. *Roaring Rockets*. New York: Kingfisher.

Supplies:

- Small paper cups
- Rubber bands
- Paper
- Bicycle tube
- PVC pipe
- Empty (disposable) plastic drink bottle
- Tape
- Paper-wrapped plastic drinking straws

Activities:

- Tear off most of the paper cover from a plastic straw and blow through the uncovered end to send the last piece of the paper cover flying through the air!
- Search online for "DIY stomp rockets." Whose rocket launcher sends the rocket highest?
- Search online for the instructions to make "jumping cups." Can you make them jump higher?

LESSON #5: GAMES ARE AN EFFECTIVE (AND SNEAKY) WAY TO TEACH MATH

Sally Moomaw has written a number of books about teaching math to preschoolers using simple games made from common office and library supplies. In addition to counting and number recognition, early math skills include shapes, patterns, comparisons (more/less, bigger/smaller, etc.), and sorting. All of these concepts can be interpreted in a game.

Here are some math lesson plan suggestions.

Math—Same vs. Different

Read: Marthe, Jocelyn. 2009. *Same Same.* Toronto: Tundra Books.

Supplies:

- Assorted buttons
- Memory games (there are many free printable versions online)
- Foam alphabet letters (in both upper and lowercase)
- Blocks
- DIY sound- and texture-matching games
- Plastic eggs
- Super Glue
- Balloons
- Things to fill the eggs and balloons (seeds, grains, flour, salt, beans, buttons, coins)
- A funnel

Activities:

- Sort a collection of buttons by a variety of factors (number of holes, size, color, shape, etc.)
- Play memory games
- Sort wooden blocks by size, color, shape
- Sort alphabet sets by color, whether upper or lower, curved lines, straight, or a mix
- Search online for "egg shaker matching game" and match by sound
- Search online for "tactile matching game" for several ideas (some with fabric, some with filled balloons)

Math—Patterns

Read: Murphy, Stuart J. 1996. *A Pair of Socks.* New York: HarperCollins.

Supplies:

- Buttons
- Paper
- Yarn
- Cereal, pretzels, or other snacks with a hole

Activities:

- Tape buttons to a strip of paper in a pattern and have students recreate that same pattern on their own strip of paper.
- Practice aural patterns by clapping a rhythm or tonal pattern and having students repeat it back to you.

- Arrange people in the room in a pattern (adult, child, adult, child, etc., or alternating between people wearing blue jeans and people wearing something else).
- Weave strips of paper into a sheet of paper with slits cut into it to create a pattern.
- Create snack necklaces by stringing foods onto a piece of yarn in a pattern.

Many more ideas for simple, DIY games that incorporate early math skills can be found in: *Teaching Mathematics in Early Childhood* (Moomaw 2011b) or at the website http://www.mathatplay.org. Also recommended: *Math Arts* (Kohl 1996) and *More than Counting* (Moomaw 2011a).

The primary goal of WonderWorks is to plant an early seed of interest in the STEM skills in children so that they have positive associations with these disciplines. One parent in the class pointed out that she had enrolled her daughter in WonderWorks because she felt unqualified to create STEM activities at home. She agreed that after attending a series of the classes, she was beginning to see many more opportunities in everyday play to incorporate STEM skills in a nonthreatening and fun way. This experiment in library STEM skills programming has been a success.

WORKS CITED

Ashbrook, Peggy. *Science Is Simple: Over 250 Activities for Preschoolers.* Beltsville, MD: Gryphon House, 2003.

Kohl, MaryAnn. *MathArts: Exploring Math through Art for 3 to 6 Year Olds.* Lewisville, NC: Gryphon House, 1996.

Moomaw, Sally. *More than Counting: Whole Math Activities for Preschool and Kindergarten.* St. Paul, MN: Redleaf Press, 2011a.

Moomaw, Sally. *Teaching Mathematics in Early Childhood.* Baltimore: Paul H. Brookes Publishing Co., 2011b.

TWO

Creating STEM Kits for Teen Programs

Kelly Czarnecki

Many public library branches are part of a larger system. While we might be geographically spread out, there are many ways that we share programming resources with one another. We might send out an e-mail with helpful tips or include a URL with instructions. We may have an internal database with step-by-step information on hosting a particular program. Many public libraries might even receive support at the state level, from hands-on training to try out a program with staff before offering it to patrons to borrowing equipment including laptops, projectors, or even gaming consoles and games. It is this model, the sharing of physical resources across branches, that we're going to address in this chapter.

Because most libraries were affected by the economic downturn in 2010, we are learning to do more with fewer resources, and therefore, need to be a bit more creative with our money and our time. Sharing resources so that a program may be replicated from one branch to the next can be a great way to be prudent with resources and more efficient with our time since we're not reinventing the same program each time we offer it at a different location.

Teen Take Out (TTO) kits have been a part of how the Charlotte Mecklenburg Public Library teen services offers a convenient and efficient way to deliver programs. The kits are centrally located at a downtown branch and are shipped out through internal delivery. There are close to fifty kits that are available for shipment, and many of them are focused on STEM subjects. We made the shift to more science-based kits in 2011 due to several factors. One was a change in our entire system's programming focus. Each program had to fit into three strategic priorities: educational success, workforce development, and literacy. This allowed us to focus on what we offer to the community and to better articulate the outcomes of our programs and services. The programming kits needed to align with these priorities. The other factor was community needs, particularly local public school system needs. As a public library, we often host visits from local school groups. Developing programs that fit the library focus as well as the schools' need to develop STEM skills was a perfect fit.

In addition to circulating kits among our branches, we provide them to our outreach department so that they might take a kit to a site with populations that aren't able to come to the brick-and-mortar library. Anyone from youthful offenders to after school clubs can receive the benefits of the kits at their location.

The infrastructure for the kits is set up on the staff Intranet using Drupal open source web-development platform. Staff fill out an online form, which is then sent to the Teen Take Out team. Once the team approves the kit, which is largely based on the kit's availability, they select the "approved" radio button and it automatically populates the calendar on Drupal, which anyone can access and view. The team members can add new kits to the online system, populate the fields with links to additional resources, or upload instructional sheets. They can also add comments from the evaluation forms that staff filled out. While it is the team's responsibility to organize and maintain this tool, it's really the expertise of the staff that use it that ensures the system's development and growth.

Let's look at seven examples of STEM kits that are used in the system. The main purpose of the STEM kits is to serve as conversation starters or an introduction to a concept, perhaps even a reiteration of principles being taught in school. Since we're public librarians and are not taking on the role of teachers, we don't focus on stocking the kits with curriculum and lesson plans. The majority of teens who come to our library are not looking for a school experience. With that said, a teacher who brings a group for a field trip or a homeschool parent or group can borrow the kits and use them in the library. Some of the kits automatically come with curriculum, which will be mentioned below. In that case, we modify it depending on the audience.

DIGITAL DRAWING AND ANIMATION

Computer-assisted drawing and animation software packages are available to allow young learners to create and develop graphics. They also serve as excellent STEM tie-ins when we need to address a variety of complex topics, such as physics, the illusion of motion, measurement, and timing, among many others.

We created a tie-in to our physical collection by pairing this kit with our Comic Creations kit, which contains instructional drawing books and tracing paper.

The software used for this kit is Anime Studio Debut 7 and Manga Studio Debut 4 by Smith Micro Software, Inc. The software allows users to create digital 2D movies, cartoons, anime, and cut-out animations. Because this software requires enhanced graphics ability, we installed it on our Alienware laptops, which were purchased in 2006 and previously used as our gaming computers. The company offers a thirty-day trial on both the anime and manga studio software, which allows you to test your own and your audience's interests before you decide to make a purchase.

Video tutorials and manuals that illustrate steps to a movie or cartoon creation are included in the kit. Users can draw their character and scan it into the software and then illustrate it using the color palette and digital tools that come with the program. Because you have to limit your audience who can simultaneously work on computers based on the number of the software licenses you purchase, having the option to hand draw the graphics and incorporate them into the software allows larger groups to participate.

The kit itself travels in two separate tubs with a carrying bag for the laptops. There is a binder with handouts printed as well as tutorials saved on the desktop screen.

READYANIMATOR

Another great kit for digital drawing that adds the component of animation is called the ReadyANIMATOR. While the system itself is unique because it has a moveable arm and flat surface where a white board (or other background) lays on top for creating animated movies, it works with the iPod Touch. There are many apps available at little or no cost that run on this device to enable animation, from hand-drawn objects to animation using clay or other materials. The app we use is called iCanAnimate. Videos created on the iPod Touch can be uploaded to YouTube or iMovie for further edits. While children as young as five can pick up the basics of creating an animated short, the use of additional software brings a new level of sophistication to the end product through music, title slides, and transitions. You can explore many technology, science, and engineering concepts with stop motion animation, from animating a complex process such as the birth of a butterfly to understanding how math is used for sequencing and timing of a video. Several people can work with the ReadyANIMATOR at once, particularly if various roles are assigned to group members, such as the artist, director, sound engineer, and so forth. It can also be conducive to crowds who form an assembly line and add one or two frames to one project, move to the back of the line, and continue the process until it's completed or someone determines that it is finished through a timed program or end of story.

The kit travels in a plastic tub and contains dry/erase markers, an eraser, and objects to animate including foam letters. There are also white board cutouts called supports which are inserted horizontally (i.e., standing up) on top of the white board base. Paper can be fastened to the supports to look like trees or even a city skyline. The ReadyANIMATOR is easy to use, portable, and works well both in and outside the library as an outreach activity.

BUILD ROBOTS: CUBELETS

Cubelets are magnetic color-coded cubes that can be snapped together to make a variety of robots. The cubes are already programmed to do certain things such as move forward, sense light, make a noise, or turn around. The order in which they are snapped together and which side of the cube is against another also determines what the robot does.

This is a great kit for all ages but particularly for those who might find visual or textual programming a bit of a challenge. Because there are no small parts like in other robotics kits, such as LEGO, it's more difficult to lose or misplace. Users get programming experience by figuring out what the blocks do when they are put together. Youth take pretty quickly to this easy-to-use set and are usually willing to experiment.

While Modular Robotics, LLC, the company that developed the Cubelets, does provide a beginners' manual, they also encourage an approach of experimentation, or in other words, seeing what works as a result of snapping the blocks together.

FLASH DRIVES WITH FREE SOFTWARE INSTALLED

There can be many challenges to having software installed on library computers, particularly if you don't have administrative privileges to do so and need to depend on others to do it for you. One solution we've found that works well is to install portable apps or other software on flash drives. These flash drives, eleven total, travel in a plastic kit and can be used in any computer lab throughout our library system. The software is free and integrates a variety of technology and programming skills. This can also be a more affordable alternative if your library is unable to purchase an iPad or a similar tablet. Flash drives are a more portable alternative to a laptop and can easily be plugged into a desktop computer in a computer lab setting, which would be conducive to teaching a group of people in one location.

The Take Out Team has also developed instructional sheets for each software to help get people started. These sheets are available on our

Intranet. Some of the software includes game design, such as GameMaker Studio, Scratch, Kodu, and Alice ML. Other software installed is related to graphic design, such as GIMP, Inkscape, and KompoZer. Portable apps is a free and open source site with software that works on any portable storage device, such as a USB flash drive, memory card, iPod, or portable hard drive. Software is chosen based on the file size and anticipated audience interest.

You can build a program based on this software in a variety of ways. You can choose to focus on one program per class, unless the goal is to give participants a wide range of familiarity with free downloadable software. Having a goal, such as creating a specific product can make the user experience more meaningful. For example, rather than advertising that people can learn how to use Scratch, let them know they can animate a digital greeting card. While they are learning how to use Scratch, their focus isn't on mastering the software but on creating a product. In that context they are picking up some skills along the way so that they can use the program on their own in the future. If software from the kit attains a positive response from attendees, you may consider having it permanently installed on your desktop computers. Depending on your configuration, it's also important to have an idea of how often updates are generally required, as this can be a barrier to IT in installing it.

FLY TO LEARN

X-Plane is a flight simulation software with accompanying curriculum for both students and teachers which include handouts and tutorials. Through the short lessons, participants are able to virtually explore everything from potential and kinetic energy, force, weight, lift, and more. Although it might be too much like school to delve deep into each lesson, a library might decide to approach the learning in several different ways. If groups visit your library, it can be a fun activity to span across several visits. Perhaps a class is currently studying related topics and would welcome a visit to the library where they can further test their skills in a participatory and fun way. The software was provided for free to the library along with educator training, which was supported by a community grant given by Time Warner Cable. Because of the support materials that accompany the software, it's well worth the investment. This software is installed on the Alienware laptops as well as in our computer lab. Teens have taken well to the lessons and definitely relate to the graphics of flying their plane if they are familiar with videogaming. Alternate between letting them explore on their own and focusing on a particular lesson. This can keep them moving forward. Activities such as building small wooden planes or having a contest across other library branches can also be a way to motivate the participants and help them understand some complex processes in a fun way.

THE NEO CUBE MAGNETIC PUZZLE

The Neo Cube is a great introduction to geometry, math, and physics principles, which of course are tested on through most of the college entrance exams. They are magnetic balls that can create an infinite number of shapes and patterns. We first introduced this kit during the library's annual Teen Tech Week celebration in March. We purchased eight sets so several libraries could use the kit at once. Along with The Neo Cube, the kit included an instructional sheet for ideas on what to design and a resource guide on numbers in nature which talks about complex structures in the natural world. Typically, in a library setting, conversations around science and math principles are casual and can be used as spring boards for further discussions while constructing various shapes. Because the individual balls are very tiny and easy to lose track of, especially if they're not connected to one another, we recommend this program for the older ages. We also post a disclaimer on the kit that because of choking hazards this is intended for a teen audience only. So far there have been no safety issues. Other library branches have incorporated instructional videos alongside using The Neo Cube, so that participants can see and follow along with what different shapes can be constructed.

POWER HOUR: MAKING A SOLAR-POWERED COOKER

This kit was part of a larger set that used the Power House developed by Thames and Kosmos to explore energy sources. While the hype has somewhat passed, the solar-powered cooker was a great tie-in to exploring the *Hunger Games* trilogy by Suzanne Collins. It's usually a hit with most kids, regardless of a tie-in because it involves cooking food. The kit contained cardboard boxes with a flap cut out at the top. Teens would cover the bottom with newspaper and black construction paper. The flap would be covered with a clear transparent top such as plastic wrap. Tinfoil then acted as a reflective surface for the heat and was added to the box. Although most of the materials in the kit needed to be replenished from one use to the next, parts of the materials could be reused if they were not damaged in any way. Many examples of how to build a solar-powered cooker using a cardboard box exist online. It's best to try it out first before having your program. S'mores, which are graham crackers with melted chocolate and marshmallows, are usually a crowd favorite, and it doesn't take too long to heat. Because it was an overcast day when we held the program for the first time, we improvised and used high heat lamps we happened to have at the library, which worked well. This is also of course a practical program in which kids can learn some skills in how to provide for themselves if they'd have the opportunity to go camping or as part of a Boy Scout or Girl Scout activity. Discussion on how the sun's rays are converted to cook the food as well as how other solar power based systems work can be a great springboard into discussion about energy principles.

RETRO WEAPONRY

This kit also lends itself to a tie-in with the *Hunger Games* trilogy, and has connections beyond the story as well. It has two wooden trebuchets and catapults from ThinkGeek. Participants can build the structures and then refer to an accompanying discussion sheet to talk about the concepts of acceleration, gravity, physics, and energy. Most participants enjoy launching objects once they build their retro weapons. Marshmallows work great! Several staff who have worked with this kit suggested being familiar with how to tie large knots first as a group since the assembly wasn't necessarily intuitive. Another staff shared that she had a friend who brought a larger catapult for the teens to use as part of the library program. It fired tennis balls more than 150 yards. The flexibility in the arm allowed teens to aim at and hit targets they marked in the parking lot. This kit can also provide great curriculum tie-ins for those who might be studying medieval times.

STEM kits can be a great way to engage young learners in important topics as well as reaffirm the concepts they're studying in school. Hands-on activities, discussions, and plain fun are great ways to demystify complex concepts and light the spark of a young mind to continue their own exploration through this growing field. There's a lot of flexibility in what you want the kit to consist of as well as how to utilize it. The kit itself is a constant living and growing organism that can be tweaked as it is tried out in the library. Don't be afraid to experiment and continue to develop the kit as needed. Be sure and share your successes with your colleagues!

THREE

Digging into Reading: A Worm's Perspective

Barbara Fiehn and Jeanine M. Huss

Reading promotions are an attempt to catch the attention of patrons and encourage new engagement with library materials. Imagine a library growing 500 silkworms in a display case at the library entrance. That is just what the library at the Kansas City Arts Institute did in conjunction with the Fibers Department to highlight library holdings about fibers topics. Other libraries have participated in community wide sustainability programs by hosting vermicomposting workshops for children and adults, including the building of worm farms.

Many libraries use the concept of "bookworms" to encourage reading by building a community bookworm with patrons adding segments with the titles read. Taking the worm concept further nurtures interest in science, recycling, vermicomposting, worm farming, as well as reading. A worm farm displayed in the library creates a variety of patron reactions. Accompanying the worm farm should be a display of fiction and nonfiction books. Add collaboration with a science teacher or county extension agent for hands-on activities.

BEGIN PLANNING THE WORM ACTIVITY

- Identify location of the display. This will determine the size and type of worm habitat you will use. Red wigglers prefer temperatures between 55 and 80 degrees Fahrenheit.
- Locate a community resource person knowledgeable about vermiculture.

- Do additional research about building worm habitats.
- Select dates and outline activities.
- Determine your primary and secondary audiences.
- Arrange for speakers such as local gardeners, master gardeners, science teachers, extension agents, or horticulturists. Possible activities include making your own worm habitat, reading books about worms at story times, or showing movies about worms.
- Determine and construct publicity vehicles. Alert local news media.
- Make supply lists.
- Construct or purchase a worm habitat at least one month before events.
- Collect books and other media display items.
- Plan for recycling the worm farm when finished.

CREATING A WORM ENVIRONMENT

A variety of containers can be used for worm bins, including large plastic storage bins, large plastic microwave containers, self-created wooden crates, wooden barrels, store-bought vermicomposters, two-liter bottles, small shadow boxes, built containers using wood with Plexiglas sides, or glass jars. The most important consideration when choosing a container is the cost and space in the library for viewing. Transparent containers allow patrons to view the burrowing red wigglers. To keep the worms happy, cover transparent areas with black cardstock or material so the worms will burrow near the outside of the container. The worm container needs a lid. Removing the covering from the container's sides reveal the worm tunnels and with luck, a worm or two for viewing by patrons.

Worms, as all living things, have the basic requirements of air, food, water, and a moderate temperature for survival. Holes should be placed in the lid and sides of the container to allow aeration since worms receive oxygen through their moist skin. Drilling holes in the bottom of the container allows excess water to leave the container. Place the bin on bricks to allow for water collection underneath. Worms will not leave the comfort of their home through the holes at the bottom unless their home is too wet or dry.

One librarian used a large clawed bathtub for his worms with a large shower curtain underneath. The only caution in this would be the possible mess and that kids will need to dig in the soil to see their worm friends.

If you would like to host a workshop on making vermicompost containers at the library, ask patrons to drop off empty and clean two-liter Sunny D (with the lid) or Hi-C bottles for converting into worm homes. Several YouTube videos offer suggestions in building vermicomposting containers. Search for "mini vermicomposting bins" or "vermicomposters." Several of the resource books at the end of this chapter also suggest ways to build vermicompost containers.

Worms of all types can be ordered through Carolina Biological Supply Company, Uncle Jim's Worm Farm, or several other businesses that specialize in red wigglers. Many resources suggest red wigglers as best for indoor worm habitats.

HARVESTING YOUR COMPOST

Keeping the worm habitat for over two months necessitates harvesting the compost. After two to three months, the bin will have improved soil and double the worm population. At least every six months, depending on the size of your worm habitat, harvest the new soil. Reduced bedding and more compost means it is time to harvest. Harvesting means removing the finished compost from the bin. After several months worms need to be separated from their castings, which at high concentrations create an unhealthy environment for them. Here are several methods for harvesting.

Divide and Dump

Most of the uneaten food, bedding, and worms will probably be in the top third of the bin. Remove this material, worms and all, and put it aside to start a new bin. Remove the remaining material for use as compost. Put the uneaten food, bedding, and worms back in the bin, and resume feeding and maintaining the bin.

Worms Sort Themselves

This method works only in bins large enough to provide space. Move the contents of your worm bin to one side, place fresh bedding in the empty space, and bury your food wastes there for a few months. Harvest the other side after most of the worms have moved into the new food and bedding.

Dump and Sort

Spread a sheet of plastic out under a bright light or in the sun. Dump the contents of the worm bin and build a few cone-shaped piles on the sheet. Gently remove the top layer of each pile until you see worms. To escape the light, the worms will dive deeper into the piles. After repeating the process every twenty minutes for a few hours, a wiggling pile of worms will remain. Save the compost and return the worms to their bin and fresh bedding immediately.

The Mesh Bag

Do not feed the worms for ten days to two weeks. Prepare a small onion sack, laundry bag, or other mesh bag with holes large enough for worms to crawl through. Fill bag with some of worms' favorite foods, such as apples, melon peels, and kiwis. Bury the bag with food in a corner. After two days, the worms will migrate into the bag. Remove the bag and set in a covered container. Leave air venting.

Put down a plastic sheet or bag in the harvest area. Beginning in the corner opposite where the bag was buried, start pulling out handfuls of the finished compost and dump it into an empty bucket. A few worms should remain. Place found worms into the covered bucket with the bagged worms.

Rebuild the bed with moistened leaves, newspaper, and a couple of handfuls of dirt. Bury the bag of worms and any stragglers in a corner. In a week or a little less, depending on how much food was in the bag, feed the worms in the opposite corner. In a few days, lift the mesh bag out of the first corner and shake it free of castings. The worms should have moved to the next feeding area and voila, you have just harvested your bin! By having all your worms in a bag, it is easier to estimate the worm population and divide the population if necessary to start another worm bin for yourself or a friend.

Regardless of which method you choose, the compost harvested will most likely contain a worm or two, cocoons, and baby worms. If you are using the compost outdoors, there is no need to worry—the worms will find a happy home and the food scraps and bedding will eventually decompose. If you are using the compost indoors, remove old bedding and food scraps. Though the worms will not harm plants, they may not like living in a small pot. To remove the worms and baby worms, place a melon rind, a good size peach, a pear piece, or apple core on the top of the container in which you have placed your compost. Place a piece of cardboard over the top of the entire surface. This will bring the remaining worms to the top for removal.

USING WORM COMPOST

Vermicompost benefits soil by

- improving its physical structure
- enriching soil in microorganisms
- attracting deep-burrowing earthworms already present in the soil
- improving soil capacity to hold water
- enhancing germination, plant growth, and crop yield
- improving root growth and structure

Use compost immediately or store it and use it during the gardening season. Mix compost directly with potting or garden soil as a soil amendment, which helps make nutrients available to plants. The compost can be used as a top dressing for indoor or outdoor plants.

Using the compost will help your plants thrive by adding plant growth hormones, beneficial microorganisms, humus, and nutrients to the soil. Vermicompost is lumpy and clay-like when removed from the bin. Let it sit in a plastic bin or bag away from rain and sun for 1–4 months; it will transform into a fine-grained product.

Rich with phosphorus, nitrogen, and many other nutrients and trace minerals, worm compost is an excellent organic fertilizer. In the garden, use compost in planting and as a top dressing for flowerbeds. Brew a liquid fertilizer or "compost tea" by placing some compost into a pantyhose leg, tying the opening tightly, and steeping the "tea bag" in your watering can.

FEEDING THE WORMS

Feeding the earthworms or red wigglers is simple. Leftover fruit and vegetables are perfect. Do not add meat or cheese to the containers. Worms spend most of their time eating! They love fruit and vegetables like carrots, lettuce, cabbage, celery, potato peelings, apple peelings, banana peels, orange rinds, and grapefruit cut into small pieces. They also like cornmeal, oatmeal, coffee grounds still in the filter, tea bags, and crushed eggshells. Eggshells help maintain a good pH and should be added weekly. Nonbiodegradable materials should not be added to the bin. Stinky vegetables, such as broccoli and onions will take some time for worms to break down and may cause the bin to smell. Collect waste products from the library, including shredded paper to feed the worms. The only caution in shredded paper is to use only black ink. Colored ink and excessive citrus peals are toxic. Maintaining a feeding chart near the worm habitat helps patrons visualize feeding schedules, amount and type of food, action taken during the feeding time, and observations made while feeding the worms. Allow young patrons to assist in feeding and recording new data.

BENEFITS OF WORM CULTURE

Red wigglers are beneficial animals. They help aerate the soil and can provide up to two inches of soil per acre in one year. By weighing the food placed in the worm habitat, a person can calculate their reduced ecological footprint. Vermicomposting can take place in small apartments as well as urban and rural homes.

- Worm bins can be placed under kitchen sinks or in garages.
- Household organic trash is broken down in the worm farm. No greenhouse gasses are released into the atmosphere. This means a worm farm helps stop global warming.
- Household food waste becomes 100 percent natural fertilizer from worm castings.
- Worms decompose food waste, reducing the amount of space needed at the local landfill.
- Vermicompost bins are easy to maintain and worms do not need daily walks.
- Vermicomposting can be inconspicuous and less upsetting to neighbors than large unsightly compost heaps.
- Worms are self-propagating.
- Worm castings (poop) make great compost.
- Worms eat half their body weight in one day.
- A worm farm teaches children how to care for the environment.

WORM ACTIVITIES

Library programming with worms can easily include a number of simple science experiments. Plan activities to fill the time it will take for the experiments to work using construction of personal worm habitats, discussions, book talks, craft activities, or story time between the beginning of the experiment and checking on the results. Kids of all ages like to touch worms and learn simple ideas about them. Have hand cleaner and paper towels available to use following worm handling.

- *Warm or cold climate to test preference.* Place a cookie sheet on top of a bucket of ice that covers half the worm environment and place heating pads underneath the other side of the cookie sheet.
- *Dry or wet environment to test preference.* Place a damp paper towel on one side of the cookie sheet and a dry paper towel on the other side of the cookie sheet.
- *Dark or light environment to test preference.* Place worms inside plastic containers, like sour cream or cottage cheese containers, with a sheet of paper with a slit in the middle for worms to move through. Cut the lid in half and place on one side of the container only.
- *Charting food recycling.* Allow patrons to feed the worms small pieces of fruit, vegetables, cereals, grains, pieces of straw, leaves, pulverized eggshells, or coffee grounds. Reinforce science skills by having patrons complete a data chart when they add food or water to the worm habitat.
- *Patron observations.* Encourage patrons to write or draw either what they see in the worm habitat, or what they read about in a book at this center. Add some magnifying glasses or containers and draw-

ing tools to your table, so that patrons can write and draw what they see and learn.

WORM FUN FACTS

- In one acre of land, there can be more than a million earthworms.
- Worms are ectothermic animals, which means they depend on their external environment for heat.
- If a worm's skin dries out, it will die.
- A worm has no arms, legs, or eyes.
- Earthworms cannot regenerate when cut in half.
- Worms have a mouth but no teeth.
- Worms and birds both contain gizzards to grind their food.
- Worms are hermaphroditic, meaning each worm contains both eggs and sperm. However, it still takes two worms to reproduce.
- Baby worms are not born. They hatch from cocoons smaller than a grain of rice.
- A cocoon holds the baby worms until they are ready to hatch.
- Charles Darwin wrote an entire book on earthworms.

TREATS AND ACTIVITIES FOR CHILDREN

A quick search of the Internet for "worm snacks for kids" or "worm activities of kids" will lead to a plethora of information for your library program. Choose ones that meet the needs of patrons' ages, time available, and library resources. A few favorites follow:

- Gummy worm treats.
- Worm snack—add gummy worms to a favorite cereal-based snack mix.
- Core apples, fill with peanut butter, and stick a gummy worm coming out of it.
- Worms and fruit with mud: Make strips of string or other cheese. Soften cheese until pliable. Wrap cheese around peaches, strawberries, plums, or slices of cantaloupe or apples. Dribble with caramel or fudge sauce and serve.
- Birds eating worms: Cut pipe cleaners into smaller pieces and shape them to make several "worms." Place the worms on a brown carpet square (this represents the dirt). Children use a clothespin or plastic relish tongs as a bird beak and catch the worms with their beak. As they catch worms, they place them in a basket until all of the worms have been collected.

- Sing the song, "Nobody Likes Me, Everybody Hates Me." Various versions can be found on the Internet and in children's and camp-fire songbooks.
- Draw pictures of what worms like to eat.
- Use gummy worms to measure surfaces in the room. These worms should not be eaten.

DISPOSING OF THE WORM BIN

Generally, red wigglers are meant to be inside pets. They should not be released into a forested or natural area because they are not native to states formerly under glaciers. Some worms can survive in the garden. Worms do not move very quickly on their own, but humans have helped them spread to areas where they are rapidly altering and creating imbalances in forest ecosystems. They have damaged peat moss areas in the Canadian forests and American hardwood forests. Red wigglers are least likely to survive a winter in the United States.

- Contact elementary school teachers about taking over the worm farm.
- In the southern parts of the country, put the worms in the garden. They may not survive in northern areas where the ground freezes.
- Contact Cooperative Extension to find a Master Gardener or local composter.
- Give to an angler.
- Distribute worms at a "make and take" worm habitat making workshop.
- Donate to a local gardener.
- Place them in a paper bag and place in the garbage as a last resort.

STANDARDS FOR USE OF LIVE ANIMALS

Worms are live animals; as such, they should be treated in a humane manner. Patrons should be informed about how to safely interact with the worms in your habitat. For a "build your own worm habitat" event, be sure to include care and treatment information. The National Science Teachers Association recommends teachers and others using live animals adhere to the following guidelines:

- Learn safety and responsible use of animals in the classroom.
- Make sure your purchase is from a reputable dealer and handle animals properly so both students and the animals stay safe and healthy during all activities.

- Follow local, state, and national laws; policies; and regulations when live organisms, particularly native species, are included in the classroom.
- Integrate live animals into the science program based on sound curriculum and pedagogical decisions.
- Develop activities that promote observation and comparison skills that instill in students an appreciation for the value of life and the importance of caring for animals responsibly.
- Instruct students on safety precautions for handling live organisms and establish a plan for addressing such issues as allergies and fear of animals.
- Develop and implement a plan for future care or disposal of animals at the conclusion of the study as well as during school breaks and summer vacations.
- Stress the importance of not conducting experimental procedures on animals if such procedures are likely to cause pain, induce nutritional deficiencies, or expose animals to parasites, hazardous/toxic chemicals, or radiation.
- Shelter animals when the classroom is being cleaned with chemical cleaners, sprayed with pesticides, and during other times when potentially harmful chemicals are being used.
- Refrain from releasing animals into a non-indigenous environment. (National Science Teachers Association 2008).

PUBLICITY

Promotional phrases are often needed for bookmarks, brochures, and other advertising. The following are a few we came up with and have used:

- Early bird gets the worm
- Where the bookworm eats the worm
- Worms eating my trash
- Worm your way through a book
- Burrow into good reading
- Worms: the best library pets because they don't make a sound
- Close encounters of the bookworm kind
- Double your fun and lessen your waste with worms

Hosting a worm-themed program can be an exciting learning event for library staff and patrons. Careful planning and creativity can bring both current and new patrons to the library. Remember this is a fun experience, so if hesitant, start small. Expand into a larger event in the future. Be prepared for circulation increases in all areas of sustainability materials.

RESOURCES FOR WORM ACTIVITIES

Appelhof, Mary. 1997. *Worms Eat My Garbage*. Kalamazoo, MI: Flower Press.

Grant, Tim, and Gail Littlejohn. 2001. *Greening School Grounds: Creating Habitats for Learning*. Gabriola Island, BC: New Society Publishers.

Grant, Tim, and Gail Littlejohn. 2004. *Teaching Green: the Middle Years: Hands-On Learning in Grades 6–8*. Gabriola Island, BC: New Society Publishers.

Hand, Julia, and Carolyn Peduzzi. 1995. *The Wonderful World of Wigglers*. Montpelier, VT: Common Roots Press.

Ingram, Mrill, and Amy Kelley Hoitsma. 1993. *Bottle Biology: An Idea Book for Exploring the World Through Plastic Bottles and Other Recyclable Materials*. Dubuque, Iowa: Kendall/Hunt Pub. CO.

Kneidel, Sally Stenhouse. 1998. *Creepy Crawlies and the Scientific Method: More Than 100 Hands-On Science Experiments for Children*. Golden, CO: Fulcrum Pub.

Hillen, Judith, Arthur J. Wiebe, and Dave Youngs. 1989. *Critters: K–6 Life Science Activities*. Fresno, CA: AIMS Education Foundation.

National Science Teachers Association. 2008. "NSTA Position Statement: Responsible Use of Live Animals and Dissection in the Science Classroom." Last modified 2008. Accessed February 7, 2013. http://www.nsta.org/about/positions/animals.aspx.

Nolan, Andrea J. 1999. *Understanding Garbage and Our Environment*. New York: Learning Triangle Press.

Wood, Mike. 1995. *Magnificient Microworld Adventures*. Fresno, CA: AIMS Education Foundation

CHILDREN'S BIBLIOGRAPHY

Arnold, Caroline, and Mary Peterson. 2007. *Wiggle and Waggle*. Watertown, MA: Charlesbridge.

Brendler, Carol, and Ard Hoyt. 2009. *Winnie Finn, Worm Farmer*. New York: Farrar Straus Giroux.

Dixon, Norma. 2005. *Lowdown on Earthworms*. Markham, Ontario: Fitzhenry & Whiteside.

Pfeffer, Wendy, and Jenkins, Steve. 2009. *Wiggling Worms at Work*. Paw Prints.

Runton, Andy. 2011. *Owly & Wormy, Friends All Aflutter!* New York: Atheneum Books for Young Readers.

Trueit, Trudi Strain. 2010. *Worms*. New York: Marshall Cavendish Benchmark.

WORK CITED

National Science Teachers Association. 2008. "NSTA Position Statement: Responsible Use of Live Animals and Dissection in the Science Classroom." Last modified 2008. Accessed February 7, 2013. http://www.nsta.org/about/positions/animals.aspx.

FOUR

The Maker Movement, STEM and Libraries: How Libraries Large and Small Can Support Hands-on Math and Science Learning in Their Communities

Cynthia Houston

THE MAKER MOVEMENT

A new social movement called the "maker movement" is creating a stir in the library and educational communities. The maturation of the first generation of digital natives into young adulthood has given rise to a new breed of do-it-yourself (DIY) aficionados, or "makers," who use open source design software and low-cost desktop manufacturing tools to develop innovative products. Librarians and educators are intrigued because makers create community-based informal learning environments called "makerspaces" or "hackerspaces," and engage in activities that focus on the application of important skills in the science, technology, engineering, and math (STEM) areas. These new community centers provide the space, tools, and technical expertise for creating new products, some of which have commercial potential. At this moment, there are makerspaces in almost every community, with makers of every age collaborating on projects as simple as a LEGO robot or 3D-printed object, to 3D prototypes of cutting-edge products.

Digital natives, who were raised in a virtual world of Internet gaming and social networking, have transferred their youth culture of collaborative creativity into more "grown-up" domains such as home improvement and high-tech hobbies. Tips and techniques for young adults to enhance their domestic environments using easy-to-find, affordable, and recyclable materials now dominate the pages of hobby magazines, particularly the DIY periodicals such as *Make* and *Craft*. As digital natives are inclined to share their ideas, their natural next step is to find physical spaces for their DIY activities. In recent years, the maker movement has given rise to the creation of local community centers, called "makerspaces" where makers regularly gather at "meetups," coordinated through online social networking tools, such as Facebook or Meetup.com.

The editor-in-chief of *Wired* magazine, Chris Anderson, documented the maker movement in his book, *Makers: The New Industrial Revolution* (2012). He states that the maker culture exhibits three important characteristics:

1. use of digital tools to create designs and prototype them
2. a collaborative culture in which designs are shared
3. standardized files so that designs can be easily shared, modified, or incorporated into other designs

According to Anderson (2012), this approach to innovation means that makers are doing something new:

> First, they're using digital tools, designing onscreen, and increasingly outputting to desktop fabrication machines. Second, they're the Web generation, so they instinctively share their creations online. By simply bringing the Web's culture and collaboration to the process of making, they're combining to build something on a scale we've never seen from DIY before. (20)

No matter what item is being created in a maker community, be it a digital movie, a robot, or a knitted talking sock monkey, the use of new technologies for designing, building, and sharing projects is an important element of every product. This is because the maker movement owes its growth and popularity to the revolutionary desktop manufacturing technologies such as the Arduino microcontroller and the "Thingomatic" 3D printer, which allow makers to design and prototype their projects at very low development costs. The social network, which is part and parcel of the Web 2.0 world, also makes it easier for makers to find resources, share their ideas, and distribute their products online. According to Cory Doctorow, science fiction writer and author of the fiction work *Makers*, the maker philosophy is one of openness and sharing, with the goal of creating a more democratic, less corporate controlled, consumer society (Anderson 2012, Borman 2013, Doctorow 2010).

THE MAKER MOVEMENT AND STEM LEARNING

Concern about economic competitiveness in the area of science and technology has sparked national interest in improving education in STEM fields. As innovation in the twenty-first century is driven by new discoveries, STEM curricula emphasize the problem-solving mode of inquiry, with the goal of engaging students in exploring STEM-related concepts in a hands-on environment. (Fulton and Britton 2011; National Research Council 2011).

Educators working in the STEM disciplines view makerspaces as ideal student-centered informal learning environments for STEM-related activities. As makerspaces provide tools, materials, and technical expertise in many STEM areas, they are places where young people can be encouraged to explore ideas and develop projects that cater to their interests. Many educators believe that informal environments like makerspaces support deeper, more meaningful learning in STEM disciplines, as opposed to receiving information through a textbook or formal lecture (Gershenfeld 2005). Because activities in makerspaces focus on technical application of science and technology concepts, STEM learning is made less abstract and easier to understand—potentially attracting a wider population of young people to these fields (Britton 2012).

The federal government has recognized the power of the maker movement to spark interest in STEM careers. In 2012, the Defense Advanced Research Projects Agency (DARPA), in partnership with O'Reilly Media's Maker Division, launched a program to implement makerspaces in 1,000 schools in the United States as part of the Manufacturing Experimentation and Outreach (MENTOR) program. The MENTOR program's primary initiative is to develop and implement physical and digital workspaces for collaborative design and manufacturing in high schools (Dougherty 2012). At the international level, the Clinton Global Initiative STEM Learning Working Group is currently funding a Maker Education Initiative and the development of a "maker corps" of college students to serve as peer mentors in makerspace communities.

MAKERSPACES, LIBRARIES, AND STEM

The 2013 January/February edition of *American Libraries* featured stories on the maker movement and the rise of makerspaces in libraries, with tacit acknowledgement that the notion of library as place is evolving from a passive "warehouse" model to a more participatory "programming space" model. Library makerspaces as centers for collaboration, exploration, and "making" are being implemented in a number of public, academic, and school libraries across the country. Many librarians believe that makerspaces in libraries can transform the perception of the library from a storehouse of information to a space of "co-creation," where patrons can design and build things, and then share their creations with others in the community (Britton 2012). Library makerspaces can be especially important to low-income patrons who often use the library for access to technologies that they are not able to afford themselves. According to Cleveland Public Library's CEO Felton Thomas Jr., makerspaces have the potential to "make libraries the center of learning where technology is provided that levels the playing field for the disadvantaged" (quoted in Good 2013, 45).

Through creative programming and strategic partnerships, libraries large and small can support makers of every age as they create, invent, and explore practical STEM applications. For example, the STARnet libraries are a partnership between the Space Science Institute's National Center for Interactive Learning and the American Library Association. The goal of the project is to bring STEM learning into libraries with hands-on interactive programs, travelling exhibits, and training in STEM curricula. Many STARnet libraries have added makerspace activities to their existing programs because of the strong connection to STEM learning. As another example, Indiana's Allen County Public Library partnered with a local maker organization, TekVenture, to open a portable makerspace on their library grounds.

Significant funding opportunities are available for libraries and museums who are interested in participating in the library makerspace movement. Most significantly, the Institute for Museums and Library Services (IMLS) partnership with the MacArthur Foundation Learning Labs in Libraries and Museums sponsors support for the planning and design of up to thirty Learning Labs (IMLS, 2011). So far, twelve labs focusing on developing twenty-first century digital technology skills among youth have been funded, eight of which are in libraries across the country.

MAKING ROOM FOR LIBRARY MAKERSPACES

As librarians consider the possibilities for programming in their physical spaces, they should consider becoming players in the Maker movement. There are currently a number of makerspaces in public libraries in small towns and urban areas across the country. As each makerspace is developed to meet the needs of the community, their characteristics differ, but all provide open access to tools and materials, technical assistance, and training in cutting edge technologies. Although not every library has the space or resources to fully implement a makerspace, there are a number of ways libraries can be involved in the maker movement and support STEM learning activities. Different levels of library involvement in makerspace activities are outlined below in increasing degrees of participation and resource requirements:

Level 1: Collection Development

All libraries should engage in collection development of materials in a variety of formats supporting the maker movement and STEM learning. Collection development efforts should fit the needs of the community the library supports, but should maintain a focus on the nuts and bolts of starting a makerspace, include guidebooks for projects in the STEM areas, and any related materials in multiple formats that occupy the 500, 600, 700 sections of the library collection.

Level 2: Community Outreach

Makerspaces in libraries have been widely touted as an effective means to attract youth who do not normally visit the library. However, involvement of librarians in community makerspaces has not been widely discussed. Regular visits by library staff to local makerspaces with information related to the library's collection of maker resources and programming have the potential to develop a successful partnering of resources, expertise, and facilities. A booth at a local maker faire, where makers gather to show off their projects, would also be a means to communicate how the library supports the Maker community. As part of community outreach, libraries can assemble kits and portable programming materials to offer "pop-up makerspace" activities in schools and community centers in the service area.

Level 3: Library Makerspaces

If your library has space and resources to build and staff a makerspace, attracting a new population of patrons to use the technologies inside the space and participate in programming activities is an easy task. Makerspaces in libraries range from monthly "pop-up" programs in community rooms to dedicated spaces for digital media production or desktop manufacturing. Maker programming in libraries can transform libraries into spaces to "create, build, construct, do, and express all kinds of both personal and collaborative products" (Loertscher 2012, 45). A more radical idea offered by Phillipe Torrone (2011) of *Make* magazine is a complete retooling of libraries into Techshops, where tools and expertise for making things is the focus of library activities as opposed to distributing books and information.

CHALLENGES AND OPPORTUNITIES FOR LIBRARY MAKERSPACES

As makerspaces chart new territories in library services, there are some serious issues to consider when wading into new waters. Primarily, libraries should consider the liability involved with housing potentially harmful manufacturing equipment, the expertise required to maintain it and train patrons in its use, how to develop an environmentally sustainable makerspace, and finally, how to program STEM-related makerspace activities so that they effectively introduce STEM concepts and spark interest in STEM careers. Here are suggestions and resources for addressing some of these important issues:

- Liability: Many libraries currently housing makerspaces have rules for participation and liability waivers that each participant must sign. Examples of these waivers can be found on most of the library makerspace websites.
- Staffing and expertise: Before commitments are made to implement a library makerspace, plans should be developed for staffing the space with knowledgeable librarians, employees, or volunteers. Most library makerspaces have limited operating hours due to their staffing requirements. Sometimes there are experienced makers on staff who are funded by existing budgets or grants; other libraries use volunteers or partner with a local makerspace. Some libraries have makers-in-residence who provide the programs for the makerspaces.
- Materials: Cory Doctorow (quoted in Borman, 2013) suggests that library makerspaces take advantage of the mountains of "e-waste" generated by the information age. However, e-waste often contains toxic materials so libraries must be knowledgeable about what kinds of e-waste are safe to handle and which are not. If this expertise is not available, there are a number of maker kits that can be purchased. Although these items may not be environmentally sustainable, they are safer to use in library programs.
- Programs: The primary focus of a library makerspace should not be on the glitz and glamour of new toys and tools, but on the participatory nature of the space and involving patrons in an engaging learning activity. If the focus of the makerspace is going to be on supporting STEM learning, than it is essential that STEM-related concepts be introduced and supported along with hands-on learning activities. For example, the makerspace at the Westport Public Library in Connecticut offers workshops on basic circuits and solar power, which are characteristic elements in a STEM curricula, as well as how-to classes for operating their 3D printers. Makerspace projects that involve only equipment training and procedures for

making things, may spark interest among community members, but may not include basic STEM principles underlying the projects.

IF YOU CAN IMAGINE IT, YOU CAN MAKE IT!

Library makerspaces supporting STEM initiatives have the potential to disseminate interest in science, technology, engineering, and mathematics to a wide audience, including minorities and youth from low-income families who are underrepresented in these highly skilled fields. Libraries have been identified as ideal locations for makerspaces because of their long tradition of serving the education and information needs of communities, and providing free programs and services for all. There are many ways to support makerspaces and STEM learning, from stocking library shelves with books and magazines, visiting makerspaces and maker faires, to housing a full-fledged makerspace in the building. Given the financial, physical space, and staffing needs of makerspaces, what is required is for libraries to imagine the different possibilities for supporting makerspaces and STEM-related programming in their own communities.

WORKS CITED

Anderson, Christopher. 2012. *Makers: The New Industrial Revolution.* New York: Crown Business.

Borman, Laurie. 2013. "Cory Doctorow on Making." *American Libraries 44*(1–2): 45.

Britton, Lauren. 2012. "The Makings of Maker Spaces, Part 1: Space for Creation, not Just Consumption." *The Digital Shift.* http://www.thedigitalshift.com/2012/10/public-services/the-makings-of-maker-spaces-part-1-space-for-creation-not-just-consumption/

Doctorow, Cory. 2010. *Makers.* New York: Tor Books.

Dougherty, Dale. 2012. "DARPA Mentor Award to Bring Making to Education." http://blog.makezine.com/2012/01/19/darpa-mentor-award-to-bring-making-to-education/.

Fulton, Kathleen and Britton, Ted. 2011. *STEM Teachers in Professional Learning Communities: From Good Teachers to Great Teaching.* Washington, D.C.: National Commission on Teaching and America's Future. http://nctaf.org/wp-content/uploads/2012/01/NCTAFreportSTEMTeachersinPLCsFromGoodTeacherstoGreatTeaching.pdf

Gershenfeld, Neil. 2005. *Fab: The Coming Revolution on Your Desktop—From Personal Computers to Personal Fabrication.* New York: Basic Books.

Good, Travis. 2013. "Three Makerspace Models that Work." *American Libraries 44*(1/2):45.

IMLS. 2011. "National Competition Selects 12 Libraries and Museums to Build Innovative Learning Labs for Teens." *News & Events.* http://www.imls.gov/national_competition_selects_12_libraries_and_museums_to_build_innovative_learning_labs_for_teens.aspx

Loertscher, David. 2012. "Maker Spaces and the Learning Commons." *Teacher Librarian 39*(6): 45–46. EBSCO Host databases.

National Research Council. 2011. *Successful K–12 STEM Education: Identifying Effective Approaches in Science, Technology, Engineering, and Mathematics.* Washington, DC: The National Academies Press. https://download.nap.edu/catalog.php?record_id=13158.

Torrone, Phillip. 2011. "Is It Time to Rebuild & Retool Public Libraries and Make TechShops?" *Makezine.* http://blog.makezine.com/2011/03/10/is-it-time-to-rebuild-retool-public-libraries-and-make-techshops/

SELECTED LIBRARY MAKERSPACES

Allen County (IN) Public Library TekVenture Maker Station

(http://tekventure.org/maker-station/)
Founded in 2011, this makerspace is a unique partnership between the library and nonprofit makerspace organization, TekVenture. The maker station is located in a 500-square-foot trailer and expands to an adjacent tented area in good weather. The space is staffed by TekVenture volunteers, is open two days a week, offers weekly "meetups," and a variety of workshops including 3D printing, inventing, "circuit bending," and basic electricity. The space houses PC and Mac computers, design and machine control software, CNC router, CNC milling machine, metal lathe, EggBot and OstrichBot, 3D printers, laser engraver, injection molding and vacuum forming prototypers, power tools, and electronics tools.

Carnegie Library of Pittsburgh The Labs

(http://www.clpgh.org/teens/events/programs/thelabs/)
This makerspace houses computers and equipment for digital media production. It is staffed by full-time mentors who assist patrons on a drop-in basis and also offer monthly workshops.

Cleveland Public Library Tech Central

(http://www.cpl.org/TheLibrary/SubjectsCollections/TechCentral.aspx)
Founded in 2012, this library makerspace occupies 7,000 square feet, is staffed by a team of trained library assistants, offers weekly technology skills programming and houses computers, 3D printers, a "tech toy box," and Internet access. Monthly programs include: Making Panoramic Images, Custom Cookie Cutters, Picture Slideshows, and Digital Abstract Art.

Detroit Public Library H.Y.P.E. Teen Makerspace

(http://dplhype.org/hype/hype-makerspace)
Founded in 2012, this urban makerspace offers weekly workshops and STEM summer camp. The space houses soldering tools, digital vinyl cutter, electronic prototyping equipment, color printing, sewing machines, and bike repair tools.

Fayetteville (NY) Public Library Fablab

(http://www.fayettevillefreelibrary.org/fablab)
Founded in 2011, this makerspace sponsors many "maker" programs for students and teens such as the STEAMpunk Club, Creation Club, and the LEGO and Pinterest Clubs. The creation lab contains a 3D printer, digital media production equipment and software, and is currently housed in a community room/tutoring center, but is in the process of expansion.

University of Nevada Reno, DeLaMare Science and Engineering Library Makerspace

(https://www.facebook.com/dlmlib?fref=ts)
Founded in 2011, this university library makerspace occupies 18,000 square feet of space with electronic prototyping equipment, large format and 3D printers and scanners, and maker kits. The space is staffed with full time librarians, three full time staff, and student workers. The library partners with groups in the community including the local makerspace for events and workshops.

Westport, Connecticut Public Library Makerspace

(http://www.westportlibrary.org/services/maker-space)
Founded in 2012, this makerspace occupies over 2,000 square feet of library space that is staffed by volunteer teens and paid teen staff who are managed by a team representing all areas of the library. The space offers monthly programming and has a regular "maker-in-residence." The library sponsors an annual mini-maker faire. Equipment includes 3D printers, computers, and woodworking tools. STEM activities include creating circuits with resistors; making solar bugs; making "brushbots"; Nintendo rehab; embedding LED lights in fabric; and solar power workshops.

SELECTED RESOURCES ON STEM, MAKERSPACES, AND LIBRARIES

Websites and Organizations

Dl2sl.org/—Digital Libraries to School Libraries (DL2SL)

Resource library and cataloging tool for adding Internet resources into the library catalog; DL2SL has more than 2500 science resources and over 600 technology resources that can be easily added to any OPAC via the MARC record.

Hackerspace.meetup.com

Social networking site for hackerspace and makerspace communities.

Instructables.com

How-to lessons on practically any subject, including projects for ma-kerspaces.

Makered.org/makercorps/

Official website for the Maker Corps, part of the Maker Education Initiative.

Makerspace.com

Blog devoted to reporting significant activities in the maker commu-nity, it also provides a directory of makerspaces and online forum for members.

The ALATechsource Webinar on Makerspaces

Four-part series on makerspaces in libraries.

STEMconnector.org

A one-stop shop for STEM information.

YALSA STEM Resources

An up-to-date list of resources catering to youth and STEM; the guide is located in the technology category of this wiki (http://wikis.ala.org/yalsa/index.php).

Periodicals

O'Reilly Media

Publisher of resources in print and electronic formats related to tech-nology at all age and ability levels. This corporation produces magazines such as *Make* and *Craft* that were the catalyst for the maker movement (http://oreilly.com/).

Make Magazine

O'Reilly Media—projects of all types for the maker community.

Craft Magazine

O'Reilly Media—craft projects of all types.

Books

Barron, Natania. 2012. *Geek Mom: Projects, Tips, and Adventures for Moms and their 21st-Century Families*. New York: Potter Craft.
This handbook describes projects families can do together.
Denmead, Ken. 2010. *Geek Dad: Awesomely Geeky Projects and Activities for Dads and Kids to Share*. New York: Gotham Books.
Projects families can do together.
The Editors of *MAKE*. 2008. *Best of Instructables Volume I*. Sebastopol, CA: O'Reilly Media, Inc.
The best projects published on the Instructables website.
Frauenfelder, Mark. 2007. *The Best of Make*. Sebastopol, CA: O'Reilly.
The best projects published in *Make* magazine.
Griffith, Saul, Dragotta, Nick, and Bonsen, Joost. 2007. *Howtoons: the Possibilities are Endless*. New York: Collins.
Comic book format for how-to-do-it projects.
Larsen, Elizabeth Foy, and Glenn, Joshua. 2012. *Unbored: the Essential Field Guide to Serious Fun*. New York: Bloomsbury USA.
Manual for hands-on projects and activities for families.
Makerspace Playbook. 2012. http://makerspace.com/wp-content/uploads/2012/04/maker-spaceplaybook-201204.pdf
Manual for getting started with developing a Makerspace.
Pakhchyan, Syuzi. 2008. *Fashioning Technology: a DIY intro to Smart Crafting*. Sebastopol, CA: Make:Books.
Projects for integrating electronics into clothing design.
Sarafan, Randy. 2010. *62 Projects to Make with a Dead Computer*. New York: Workman.
Handbook featuring projects that use recycled computer parts.
Tulley, Gever, and Spiegler, Julie. 2011. *50 Dangerous Things (You Should Let Your Children Do)*. New York: New American Library.
Guide for hands-on projects and activities for families.

MAKER KITS

www.adafruit.com/

Unique and fun DIY electronics and kits from Adafruit Industries.

www.makershed.com

Make magazine's retail outlet for books and kits.

www.sparkfun.com/

Online retail store for electronic products from Sparkfun.

www.makerbot.com/

Source for 3D desktop printers.

www.lego.com

Source for electronic controls for LEGO Mindstorms robotic construc-
tions.

FIVE

The *STEM Kids* program and the *FIRST* LEGO League (FLL) at the Grand Forks Public Library

Aaron Stefanich and Laura Munski

The Grand Forks Public Library (GFPL) Children's Department began a partnership with the Dakota Science Center (DSC) in 2010. DSC is a liaison between the community and the University of North Dakota (UND). Over the years DSC has helped the library connect with the university faculty and student organizations. Dr. Laura Munski, executive director of DSC, and Wendy Wendt, director of the GFPL, agreed to a partnership that involved both grant writing and programming in 2010. It was through this partnership that science, technology, engineering, and math (STEM) education was added to the children's library program. Grant monies from the North Dakota State Library have been used to purchase an IXL learning–web based math educational subscription (http://www.ixl.com). IXL is the math component of the *STEM Kids* program and covers pre-K to algebra math curriculum aligned with the state standards. Up to thirty students can access IXL through the library. A personal login allows individualized learning. The *STEM Kids* program also offers youth inquiry-based activities and supplemental DVDs and books that enhance their understanding of the engineering process and the importance of STEM education.

There is a strong library patron interest in STEM education programs. Grant monies from IEEE-Chicago (Institute of Electrical and Electronic Engineers) and the North Dakota State Library were used to purchase print, audiovisual materials, and STEM teaching kits. The *STEM Kids* program was launched in the summer of 2012. The STEM teaching modules developed for the summer program included: Early Simple Machines (LEGO), Early Structures (LEGO), Simple Machines (LEGO), Electronics, Straw Rocket Launcher, and Electricity with a Van de Graaff Generator. Each teaching module was placed in a separate storage bin that was barcoded and put into the library's online catalog. Currently, the modules each have an inventory list of materials, the kits, and the lesson plans and are available for teachers to check out.

The *STEM Kids* program would not have been possible without the library's partnership with the Science Center that provided the teacher's expertise to develop lesson plans and help with the logistics of *STEM Kids*. It was very time consuming to make educational modules from the kits. The kits provided how-to instructions but little or no background material or content correlation. Each kit activity needed a lesson plan developed for it, and the kits had to be augmented with additional materials in order to complete the lessons. Each module was matched to national and state science standards. DSC master teacher volunteers wrote, reviewed, and edited the lesson plans. The lesson plan format included grade level, instruction time, material list, objectives, teacher's introduction to the material, student instructions, skills, and vocabulary. The master teachers added laminated table-top vocabulary sheets which served as review tools for STEM concepts. The teacher was able to refer to the vocabulary sheet as the students constructed and tested their projects. Engineering process worksheets were developed for any activity where students would design and redesign to meet specific criteria. The worksheets helped the students use the eight steps of the engineering process for the activity: (1) identify the problem, (2) determine criteria and constraints, (3) brainstorm solutions, (4) select an approach, (5) build a model, (6) test the solution, (7) communicate the results, and (8) refine the design. The first two steps of the engineering process were specified on the worksheet for that particular activity and the students worked from there.

The lessons plans were the key to a successful program. In their feedback, parents and teachers commented that the lesson plans gave the program educational merit. Volunteer teachers stated that the ready-to-go lesson plans made them feel comfortable with the material. The lesson plans will facilitate the recruitment of the university student and parent volunteers to teach the sessions in the future.

The *STEM Kids* program also promoted engineering careers by purchasing the American Society for Engineering Education *Dream up the Future. Engineering: Go for It* (eGFI) materials. The teacher's kit includes two packs of engineering career cards, one engineering career poster, a six-page teacher guide, and twenty eGFI student magazines. The poster and career cards can be purchased separately and are especially helpful to encourage youth to pursue engineering careers. The Science Center developed lesson plans to accompany the materials and will share the lesson plans upon request (Dakota.Science@gmail.com). To extend learning beyond the *STEM Kids* summer session, we gave students a handout of the engineering career cards and a list of available STEM print and audiovisual materials at the last session.

To generate interest in *STEM Kids*, the library contacted local media about the program and had a few short articles published in the *Grand Forks Herald* newspaper. The newspaper also listed *STEM Kids* in their weekly events calendar. *STEM Kids* had its own page on the library website, and the program was listed in the library's summer reading program brochure. *STEM Kids* was advertised on the DSC website, and information was sent out to parents on the DSC e-list. The program was also promoted through word-of-mouth.

STEM KIDS PROGRAMMING

The Grand Forks Public Library hosted seven *STEM Kids* programs during the summer of 2012. Each topic-based session lasted one hour.

- *STEM Kids K–2* was held for three consecutive Tuesdays in June. The same eight children attended all the sessions and were placed in four groups of two children, based on grade level. Children learned the engineering design process while using Early Structures and Early Simple Machines kits. Each group used one kit. Each presenter taught one age group, with the aid of the lesson plans, for the one hour session. The lesson plans were designed in a logical progression from one session to the next.
- *STEM Kids 3–6* was held for four consecutive Tuesdays in July. The same eight children in third grade through sixth grade participated each week. Children were divided in four groups of two based on their grade level. Participants used Early Simple Machines, Simple Machines, Electronics, Straw Rocket Launcher, and Electricity with a Van de Graaff Generator.

Participation in each series was limited to eight children per program to ensure hands-on experience. The library had four LEGO kits of each type. We randomly selected and preregistered eight kids for each program. Children who were not selected were put on a waiting list to be contacted in the fall when *STEM Kids* would be offered again. The library plans on hosting many more *STEM Kids* programs during the school year and hopes to use the STEM educational modules for years to come.

WHAT WORKED AND WHAT DIDN'T WORK

Parents and instructors completed evaluations of the program. Parents reported that they were pleased with the *STEM Kids* program and would encourage their children to check out the STEM-related books and DVDs. Parents commented that their children enjoyed the program and learned the concepts presented in the lessons. They felt that room and class sizes were suitable for this type of program.

Groups of two children worked well for Early Simple Machines and Early Structures kits. Having two children working with one Simple Machines kit did not work as well; individual kits would have been better. The Electronics, Straw Rocket Launcher, and Electricity with Van de Graaff Generator modules were designed for eight children to work together. Except for the Van de Graaff Generator and Straw Rocket Launcher, it is important to purchase enough kits. Additional kits would need to be obtained if a library decides to conduct classes with larger-sized audiences.

A different facilitator was needed for each group of two children because each grade level worked on different lessons. A teacher could have a class of eight children from the same grade level. However, the individual attention provided to a pair of children enhanced learning. In the future, the *STEM Kids* program can be offered to one grade level at a time, with one teacher and additional helpers. Extra helpers would also cut down on the time needed to inventory module contents at the end of each lesson.

Meeting once a week over the summer had the drawback of some children missing sessions due to other commitments. The sessions were designed in logical progression so consistent attendance was important. For future *STEM Kids* programs the sessions will meet for three or four consecutive days or on consecutive weekends to address this issue. Sessions for grades K–2 work best when lasting forty to sixty minutes, while sessions for grades 3–6 could last two hours with a break in the middle.

The Electronics module includes an Electronic Projects Lab, an Energy Lab, eight Snap Circuits Jr. kits, and a Snap Circuits Green kit. The Electronic Lab was too complicated for the targeted age group. The small solar panels of the Energy Lab and the Snap Circuits Green kit did not work outside at the latitude of Grand Forks and did not work with a lamp. Only Snap Circuits Jr. kits were used for the *STEM Kids* program.

As part of the electricity module the Science Center developed a lesson plan for electric circuits. Dr. Fazel-Rezai (UND Electrical Engineering) made a list of the materials needed, which were ordered from the DigiKey Corporation. Since the LED lights burned out easily, the library should have ordered more than two per student.

A ROBOTICS TEAM IN THE LIBRARY

In 2011 a structured robotics program was added to the *STEM Kids* program - *FIRST* (For Inspiration and Recognition of Science and Technology) LEGO League (FLL). The *FIRST* family of programs consists of Junior FLL for ages six to nine, FLL for ages nine to fourteen, *FIRST* Robotics Competition for ages fourteen to eighteen and *FIRST* Tech Challenge for ages fourteen to eighteen. *FIRST* and LEGO formed a partnership in 1998 and founded the FLL. The *FIRST* family of programs has steadily grown. According to the coaches' handbook, in 2012 there were about 20,000 FLL teams in over sixty countries.

GFPL sponsored its first FLL team in 2011. The children's librarian, Aaron Stefanich, served as a coach, and DSC provided a team mentor, an engineering student from UND. Teamwork is an integral part of the engineering profession and is the foundation of the *FIRST* family of programs. The youth make the decisions for the team, but the coach must ensure that every team member experiences each aspect of the program.

Ordering FLL Materials

To sponsor an FLL team, the coach will need to go online and search "FIRST LEGO League United States" in the browser. Through the FLL website, the coach can register the team and order materials online. The first year the coach needs to purchase the FLL robot, a field set-up kit, and a FLL team registration. The robot is a one-time expense. Each year the coach will need to purchase a new field set-up kit and complete the FLL team registration.

The new challenge is released each year in mid-August. Teams can register from the time that the challenge is released until the registration deadline date in September. Registered coaches are notified of the new challenge via e-mail each year.

Starting a Team

The FLL team can have up to ten children ages nine to fourteen. The number of youth interested in joining the team may exceed the team member limit. Depending on the number of youth beyond the initial ten, the coach may register additional teams or may have the youth attend team meetings and the tournament as alternates. Once the team is entering the second year, the coach will have access to previous field mats and field kits that can be used to teach new team members.

To promote the program the GFPL advertised FLL through its website, brochures, and word of mouth. An informational meeting was held in mid-August. The coach and parents decided on dates and times for team meetings. To complete the FLL Challenge, a lot of work is required in a short period of time. FLL recommends two-hour team meetings twice a week for eight weeks. Scheduling team meetings is challenging. Out of the five sets of parents that attended the informational meeting, only two had their children join the team.

Parental involvement with the team is essential. The team is required to have at least one adult coach. The GFPL children's librarian was the registered coach for the team, and two parents of team members served as additional coaches. FLL provides training for the team coach and on-line support. The *Coaches' Handbook* reviews the responsibilities of a coach. As a first year team, it is important to take things one step at a time. Even with the *Coaches' Handbook* and mentor support, the GFPL coach often felt overwhelmed with all of the work that needed to be done.

The GFPL team was sponsored by the public library and met at the library. The library designated a special space where the team could meet and where the FLL materials could be stored undisturbed. Even though the challenge was released in mid-August, the GFPL team was not orga-nized until after the start of school in early September. The team started meeting once a week in mid-September and consisted of five boys and two girls. As the tournament approached, the team had to meet more often in order to complete the FLL Challenge.

It was necessary to have a team mentor, especially for a rookie team. A good mentor is someone who has been through an FLL season and knows how to program the robot. A professional engineer or technology person may be able to guide the youth as they work on the challenge. Invite an engineer to attend a team meeting at the start of the season to teach the youth the engineering process. The youth will follow the steps of the engineering process as they design and program the robot.

DSC recruited an engineering student and a computer science student from the university to be GFPL team mentors. Without these mentors, the GFPL team could not have accomplished as much as it did in so short a period of time. If a mentor with programming experience is not available, an NXT Video Trainer 2.0 DVD can be purchased from the LEGO Educa-tion website.

The FLL Challenge

Every year, a new FLL Challenge is released. The challenge is based on a theme, and consists of the Robot Game, Project, and FLL Core Val-ues. The *Coaches' Handbook* does a great job of laying out the season, and suggesting steps to take in order to complete the challenge.

Each team must download the challenge document which is posted on the FLL website. This document describes the project, the robot game field set-up, the robot game missions, and the robot game rules. The project is the research part of the program. The youth learn about an aspect of the theme and present their findings at the tournament. It is recommended that teams present a short skit describing the problem and their solution.

Much work needs to be done before the team can start programming the robot. The robot game takes place on the field that is set up on a competition table. The table must be built following FLL instructions which can be found on the FLL website. For storage purposes, the GFPL team found it best not to build the "official" FLL table, but to build a stowaway table that can be folded in half. Each year a new field mat is made to reflect the theme of the challenge. Before the team can set up the field, it must build the LEGO objects called "mission models." The building of the mission models is the first activity the team works on for the season.

The field set-up kit is only good for one season's theme. However, it is important to save the field mat, mission models, and building instructions. The mat, mission models, and challenges can be used again and again for out of season LEGO robotics programming. Summer and after-school robotics sessions can be offered for children that are unable to make the FLL team time commitment.

Community Outreach

Each year the GFPL has a public robotics event at the library. The UND computer science department and the College of Engineering and Mines provide inquiry-based activities for the event. The GFPL FLL team shares their robotic challenge with the public at this event. The library takes this opportunity to promote additional STEM library programs.

The GFPL robotics program is featured each year at the DSC Super Science Day, a regional community hands-on STEM event held in April. The GFPL FLL team shares their robotics challenge with the public at this event. Even though the Super Science Day takes place after the FLL tournament, robotics team members may choose to put photos of the event in the team scrap book to show that they remain a team out of season. The summer library STEM programs are also promoted at this event.

Grant monies from the North Dakota State Library have been used to purchase additional educational materials in robotics and engineering so that GFPL can offer a robotics program to the children that are not on the FLL team. GFPL purchased additional robots so that first-year youth can work with past year challenges to gain experience.

The FLL Tournament

At the end of each season, FLL tournaments are held throughout the United States and the world. In order to have a full FLL experience, it is important for each team to participate in a tournament. They are a great opportunity for teams to share what they have learned and accomplished. The tournament is open to the general public. Parents enjoy watching their children share what they have learned. Tournaments are often the highlight of the team's season because they provide an action-packed day of fun. There are teams from all over the region, and it is exciting to meet the other teams and see the various robot designs and programming.

The GFPL team competed in the North Dakota FLL Championship Tournament hosted by the UND College of Engineering and Mines (January 28, 2012). The tournament marks the end of the FLL season for most teams. It is recommended that the team holds a final meeting after the tournament to celebrate the season's accomplishments. After the tournament, the GFPL team had a pizza party. The end of the FLL season does not need to mark the end of STEM programming at the library. The FLL Robot and field set-up kit can provide many STEM programming opportunities outside of the season.

SUMMARY

Dr. Wayne G. Sanstead, North Dakota state superintendent, officially signed adoption of Common Core State Standards (CCSS) on June 20, 2011. The first full school year for the state to implement the CCSS will be 2013–2014. The new standards strengthen student skills in STEM education. Offering STEM programs at public libraries will help students excel at school and provide an opportunity to explore various STEM fields. A partnership between the library and DSC facilitated STEM programming by providing an educational backbone, access to master teachers, and UND student/faculty volunteers. This ongoing partnership will continue to develop new modules not only for library programming but also for teachers to borrow and use in their classrooms. The FLL robotics program brings excitement to the children's library. The STEM programming at the library garnishes community support which is a valuable asset.

WORKS CITED

FIRST LEGO League. *FIRST* LEGO League Coaches' Handbook. 8th ed. Manchester, NH: *FIRST* LEGO League, 2012.
"2012 Senior Solutions Challenge," accessed September 7, 2012, http://firstlego-league.org/challenge/2012seniorsolutions.

II

Teaching

SIX

Animation Programs at the Evansville Vanderburgh Public Library

Michael Cherry

In 2012, the Evansville Vanderburgh Public Library (Evansville, IN) was awarded a grant by the Young Adult Library Services Association (YAL-SA) and the Dollar General Literacy Foundation to design an outstanding summer reading program. The program focused on a series of animation workshops that would encourage young adults to study the history of animation. Two underlying histories were explored. The first examined the history of early animation toys including zoetropes, thaumatropes, and other optical devices. The other history, a more recent and popular one, explored the emergence of Pixar from George Lucas to Steve Jobs.

In addition, students learned the art of stop-motion animation. Through various workshops, they experimented with sand, light, clay, and other formats. Over the course of ten weeks, twenty-five programs were held at the central library, including outreach programs with the Girl Scouts, YMCA, and Media Ministries Dream Center. The programs were intended to teach students science, technology, engineering, and math (STEM)-related skills by focusing on the science of visual perception and digital literacy.

GETTING STARTED: PARTNERSHIPS, MARKETING, AND SCHOOL VISITS

The animation programs at the Evansville Vanderburgh Public Library (EVPL) were part of our annual summer reading program. The program, supported by the Public Library Friends, encourages participants to keep track of their reading over the summer. Books are recorded on reading logs and prizes are awarded for log entries and program attendance. The teen services portion is handled by five librarians who specialize in young adult programs. They design the teen summer program and market it at local schools.

Young adult librarians visited sixteen K–8, junior high, and high schools throughout April and May in 2012. They highlighted the summer animation workshops and promoted the workshops through the teen Facebook page and a blog on the library's homepage. The library's marketing department designed posters for animation programs and distributed them to our branches. Program calendars were included in the reading logs, which students could pick up at our summer program kick-off or any time after that.

While the summer program is supported by the Public Library Friends, additional support for activities must come from grants and outside organizations. The YALSA and the Dollar General Literacy Foundation award $1,000 minigrants for outstanding summer reading programs for teens. Applications can be found on YALSA's website (www.yalsa.org). The EVPL received this grant in February 2012 and purchased eight Stop Motion Pro software licenses and a Canon Digital Power Shot camera. The remaining funds were spent on five HD Microsoft LifeCams. Two additional software licenses were purchased through the library's teen programming budget and additional webcams were borrowed from staff members. Ten Stop Motion Pro software licenses were installed on ten portable laptops at the central library. Ten webcams and the digital camera accompanied the software licenses.

The laptops functioned as a portable animation lab that could be set up and taken down to accommodate our programming schedule. We do not have a dedicated lab at the Central Library and many of our programming rooms are used for other activities. The portability of the lab allowed for flexibility in the programming schedule. Other portable equipment included stands for the laptops and the media needed to create animation videos.

In June 2012, stop-motion animation programs were held at the central library. These consisted of three sets of four-program workshops open to all students in the city. Students were encouraged to register for all four programs. They would be learning about animation and creating their videos over the course of four weeks, meeting once a week. Other programs in June included light animation labs open to registered participants, and outreach programs with the Girl Scouts. Outreach programs with the YMCA and Media Ministries Dream Center followed in July. A four-week open studio animation that did not require registration also took place in July. Each program was limited to ten students, with the exception of the Girl Scouts and YMCA, where students worked in larger groups. Class size was restricted due to the available equipment, as well as a preference for smaller, more focused workshops.

The goals and objectives of the programs included teaching students digital literacy skills, digital content creation, video editing, and the science and optics of moving images. Students gained a basic understanding of Stop Motion Pro software and the history and different types of animation. While no formal evaluations were conducted, the program's goals were accessed by the overall attendance, community involvement, and the excitement of the students participating in media-rich programming. We will first look at the content of these programs beginning with the history of animation.

THE HISTORY OF ANIMATION: FROM ANIMATION TOYS TO PIXAR

The animation programs at the EVPL began by teaching students the history of animation toys. While animation is traditionally regarded as an art form, it also deals with visual perception. Its history coincides with developments in modern cinema and optics. In the past, zoetropes were featured in advertisements by opticians. Originally called the "Wheel of the Devil," zoetropes consisted of a drum, filmstrip, and slits (Solomon 1994, 8). The drum could be spun to create the illusion of movement.

Various examples of early animation toys can be found in Charles Solomon's (1994) book *Enchanted Drawings: The History of Animation*. The chapter, "Precursors and Experiments," includes an optician's advertisement for a zoetrope. The chapter details early experiments in animation technology including the invention of the kineograph, praxinoscope, and phenakistoscope, among other optical devices. Solomon's book introduced students to changes in animation technology. Teens created simple devices such as flipbooks and thaumatropes, and filmed them using a digital camera. A zoetrope was constructed by staff and participants created poster board strips for the drum.

In his article, "Integrated Learning: Zoetropes in the Classroom," Chris Merrill (2002) describes how zoetropes might be used to connect students to science education involving technology, motion, and basic geometry. He argues that in order to fully understand the zoetrope, we need to understand how the biology of the human eye works. Merrill's article is a useful resource for connecting animation with STEM education. Staff referred to it in their discussion of zoetropes and visual perception.

In addition to the activities and related readings, students explored books on the topic of optical illusions, including Al Seckel's *Optical Illusions: The Science of Visual Perception* (2008). Further discussions focused on cel animation, Disney, and Pixar. Students were surprised to learn that Buzz Lightyear may have actually come from a galaxy far, far away!

While students may have seen Pixar films, they often lack an understanding of its cultural history. Pixar began as a small computer division within Lucasfilm. In 1979, they were known as the Graphics Group. Early projects with Lucasfilm were made with Industrial Light & Magic. One early example included the animation short *The Adventures of Andre and Wally B* (1984). This animation short was shown to students at the EVPL and includes credits to Lucasfilm (*Pixar Short Films Collection* 2007).

George Lucas sold the Graphics Group to Steve Jobs in 1986. The company was renamed Pixar after the Pixar Image Computer, which had been the major invention of the Graphics Group. It enabled users to create 3D surfaces on a computer interface. Students were shown images of the Pixar Image Computer and staff explained Jobs's role in inventing iPads, iPhones, iPods, and other popular technologies used today.

In addition, we discussed the Pixar Image Computer as it relates to Pixar's early animation shorts such as *Luxo Jr.* (1986). This is considered the first animation film by the company and involves the lamp that would eventually become the company's logo. After watching *Luxo Jr.*, staff addressed storytelling as it relates to animation shorts (*Pixar Short Films Collection* 2007). This was important because the lengths of the students' videos would also be short but would require storytelling through the medium of technology.

Teaching young adults the history of Pixar is important for several reasons. It allows them to see how different inventions bring about changes in technology and animation, and it connects the optical inventions of the nineteenth century with popular culture today. It also shows how pioneers like Steve Jobs and George Lucas revolutionized the film, music, computer, and cell phone industries, which all play an enormous role in the digital lives of teenagers.

Furthermore, with an understanding of history students can form a more critical relationship to their culture. Many of them are surprised to learn that the same people who gave us Yoda, the iPhone, and the iPod are largely responsible for the creation of Pixar. As educator Renee Hobbs (2011) argues, the study of popular culture is a critical component to the study of digital and media literacy today.

With an understanding of animation history, students were now ready to begin work on their own videos. The following sections describe how youth librarians might teach animation to improve digital literacy and promote STEM learning. Suggestions for equipment and various types of animation are described.

STOP-MOTION ANIMATION

An excellent book for novice animators is Mary Murphy's (2008) *Beginner's Guide to Animation: Everything You Need to Know to Get Started.* It helped us design the content for our summer programs. It serves as a great addition to the young adult collection and offers ideas on constructing capture stations, light boxes, and puppet armatures. Most important, it suggests the types of hardware and software available for librarians interested in animation.

The author advises using iStopMotion or FrameThief for Macs and Stop Motion Pro for Windows-based PCs. Below is a list of potential hardware students may need for their capture stations. The type of equipment used will depend on the size of a library's budget, the type of license, and available space. Included with the list are various types of stop-motion formats.

Types of hardware needed with Stop Motion Pro:

- Microsoft LifeCam or Logitech Webcam
- Digital single-lens reflex (DSLR) camera
- Digital still camera
- Video camera
- Tripods
- Computer
- Extension cords
- Firewire cables

Types of stop-motion animation:

- Sand animation
- Claymation
- Cut paper animation
- Action figures
- LEGOS
- Drawing

Throughout the summer programs, students were given different choices for video projects based on the formats above. Hours were spent cutting up old magazines for cut paper animation. Different-sized hole punchers and construction paper proved useful for this format too. Teen volunteers helped create temporary sets and sample videos. In addition, staff created videos inspired by the show *South Park*, and film directors Tim Burton and Terry Gilliam.

Moreover, students were instructed on the use of Stop Motion Pro software. Various tutorials are available on the Stop Motion Pro website that can help novice learners (www.stopmotionpro.com). Depending on the type of license your library purchases, there are many techniques you can introduce in a workshop. These techniques include onion skinning, chroma key, frame painter, looping, and others, and are described on the website.

As students worked on their projects, sample videos were introduced, providing inspiration for their own work. YouTube videos demonstrated the art of stop-motion drawing and the work of Ray Harryhausen. Ray Harryhausen and Tony Dalton's book, *The Art of Ray Harryhausen*, contains artwork and storyboards for Harryhausen's classic stop-motion films (2006). Samples of his work played on a large 60" monitor as teens experimented with clay and sand. Other YouTube examples included time-lapse animation in television commercials and music videos.

In addition to the animation workshops, outreach programs with youth organizations taught students different types of animation. The programs culminated in video projects making use of various media. Two of the most challenging and rewarding programs were with the Girl Scouts. Two groups of Girl Scouts ranging in age from kindergarten to fourth grade visited the library in June. The groups included close to sixty students each on separate days. A programming room was set up to accommodate groups of girls around ten animation stations. Girl Scouts staff members accompanied the groups.

Rather than teaching the young girls the history of animation, youth services staff tried something else entirely. Initially, the large groups were read Michael Hall's (2011) *Perfect Square* much in the manner of a traditional story time. Hall's book is about an ordinary geometric square that morphs into endless possibilities via the reader's imagination. As readers turn the pages, the square changes shapes, morphing into gardens, fountains, and other magical things.

Shortly after, the girls were shown an example of a colored square altered through stop-motion animation. One video transformed the square into a fountain using colored holes from a hole puncher. After a few examples, the girls were instructed in the use of the software and given the opportunity to create their own videos. They started with a 5x5 inch square of colored construction paper and worked at transforming their square to tell a story.

The activities with the Girl Scouts allowed us to take a different approach to teaching animation. Traditional story times converged with digital storytelling and we were able to modify the programs to instruct younger learners. In addition to the stop-motion techniques above, students learned to animate with more innovative formats including light and people.

PIXILATION

Unlike clay or sand, pixilation involves the art of animating people. In *The Animation Book*, Kit Laybourne (1998) compares pixilation to silent movies. As each frame is captured, the actors must reposition themselves for the next shot. When the frames are played back, an illusion of movement is created. The shots occur at irregular intervals, resulting in unnatural movements similar to silent films.

For our pixilation activities we tried a combination of ideas. Students were shown different examples of pixilation such as Norman McLaren's *A Chairy Tale* (1957). One of their favorite examples was from YouTube, entitled *Pixelation HND1*. In the video, a man falls asleep at a bus stop only to awaken in a world full of stop-motion props. The video is shot at an interesting angle with the camera overhead. The man in the video is lying in profile on the grass, yet appears to be standing. The short film consists of three minutes of him dodging bullets, battling Darth Vader, and flying through clouds, among other things.

Pixilation activities took place in the stop-motion workshops and outreach activities with the YMCA. Props were cut from large pieces of cardboard. They could be moved around like cut paper animation, but on a much larger scale. Props included giant hammers, Pac-Man, flying birds, and several Super Mario Brothers objects like mushrooms and tortoise shells. The latter were used to simulate the Nintendo video game in which characters avoid shells, or jump up to hit bricks that reveal stars and fire flowers.

In order to simulate this video game effect, a webcam was attached to the ceiling using USB extensions. This gave us a bird's eye view from which to shoot, in a fashion similar to that of *Pixelation HND1*. The laptop was then connected to a 60" monitor so that teens could see the software interface and play back the video.

In other programs the camera was positioned on a table. It captured frames from a forward perspective. Students explored the illusions of driving and human bowling. To achieve the illusion of bowling, one student would act as the ball and the other students would be the pins and bowler. Simple props like blankets and large cardboard boxes were used in videos where teens explored disappearing and reappearing.

Teenagers enjoy pixilation because they get to work with friends. Social activities work well with this age group and pixilation enables a process of working together. Another activity that involves performing and collaborating with peers is light animation. Light animation is a more complicated process involving a digital single-lens reflex (DSLR) camera, a tripod, and a darkened room. Two programs were held in June 2012 for registered participants in fifth to twelveth grades.

LIGHT ANIMATION

Light animation is a combination of light photography and animation. Animation stills are created through long exposure photography and can be imported into video editing software. In order to understand light animation, it is important to understand the different components of a digital camera as well as the process of photography.

The light animation labs started with a brief overview of classic cameras and photographs. Students held antique cameras collected from flea markets, including an old Kodak Brownie. This provided knowledge of vintage technology similar to the animation toys. Books used to accompany the cameras included Rudolph Hillebrand's (2000) *Photographica: The Fascination with Classic Cameras,* and David Williamson's (2004) *Comprehensive Guide for Camera Collectors.*

In addition, students walked through a timeline highlighting changes in photography, from the camera obscura to photo sharing sites such as Flickr and Facebook. They learned about historical photographs such as daguerreotypes, ambrotypes, and tintypes, noting how the photographs were originally developed on copper, iron, and glass plates. These early photographic processes coincided with discoveries in the history of animation. Both were part of the optical inventions of the nineteenth century. As cel animation developed, it relied heavily on the technologies of modern photography and film.

Following the timeline discussions, teens learned about different camera components including aperture, ISO speed (international organization for standardization), and shutter speeds, understanding that longer shutter speeds create longer exposures, resulting in more light entering the camera. Digital single-lens reflex cameras contain a "bulb" setting on the manual dial that enables photographers to extend the shutter speed indefinitely. In a darkened room one can write or paint using a light source, such as a flashlight, and the camera records the movement of light.

Two excellent videos that explain the process of light animation include a tutorial on YouTube by the Mind Bites group and a short online tutorial called "Making Light Animation" by Corel video editing software. Extended light animation videos can be viewed by searching the groups Graffiti Light Project and Light Animation Studios. They have several examples available online which demonstrate this unique technique.

When composing light photographs for animation, keep it simple and provide examples. One successful example from our programs involved the effect of "zapping" each other with light. Through a sequence of stills, students created the effect of shooting light at friends. While the light videos above require hours of time, teens are pleased with taking home the stills and having acquired the knowledge of something innovative.

MOVING IMAGES: STEM EDUCATION AND ANIMATION

The resources in this article allowed participants to gain multiple perspectives on the history of animation and the science of moving images. Students improved their understanding of animation by having access to different formats and connecting these to science and technology. Basic math and engineering were applied in the zoetrope activity, the construction of animation sets, calculating frames per second, and various other ways.

The history of animation is important to today's students. Multimillion dollar companies like Pixar contribute to popular culture and the media lifestyles of youth. Contemporary animation spans age groups and cultures to include 3D animation, anime, claymation, and other diverse formats. It plays a central role in how kids are growing up and learning to identify with digital media.

When teenagers create with technology, they become producers of digital media, not just consumers. The artifacts they construct demonstrate reflection and meaning beyond traditional types of learning consistent with pencil and paper. The learning that takes place is more relevant to the digital worlds they inhabit. In these worlds, meaning is negotiated between iPads, iPhones, movies, and other forms of digital communication.

Close to 300 hundred students in grades K–12 participated in the animation programs at the EVPL. Sample videos can be accessed by searching "Animation EVPL" on YouTube. Light animation stills are available on the library's Flickr page. Resources discussed in this article can be used to promote STEM education through animation. These resources are intended to promote a critical understanding of animation, from today's history, to infinity . . . and beyond!

WORKS CITED

Harryhausen, Ray, and Tony Dalton. 2006. *The Art of Ray Harryhausen*. New York: Billboard Books.

Hall, Michael. 2011. *Perfect Square*. New York: Greenwillow Books.

Hillebrand, Rudolph. 2000. *Photographica: The Fascination with Classic Cameras*. Atglen, Pennsylvania: Schiffer Publishing.

Hobbs, Renee. 2011. *Digital and Media Literacy: Connecting Culture to Classroom*. California: Corwin Press.

Laybourne, Kit. 1998. *The Animation Book: A Complete Guide to Animated Filmmaking— from Flipbooks to Sound Cartoons to 3-D Animation*. New York: Three Rivers Press.

Merrill, Chris. February 2002. "Integrated Learning: Zoetropes in the Classroom." *The Technology Teacher* 61: 7–12.

Murphy, Mary. 2008. *Beginner's Guide to Animation: Everything You Need to Know to Get Started*. New York: Watson-Guptill.

Pixar Short Films Collection. 2007. Burbank, CA: Buena Vista Home Entertainment.

Price, David A. 2008. *The Pixar Touch: The Making of a Company*. New York: Alfred A. Knopf.

Seckel, Al. 2008. *Optical Illusions: The Science of Visual Perception*. Richmond Hill, Ontario, Canada: Firefly Books.

Solomon, Charles. 1994. *Enchanted Drawings: The History of Animation*. New York: Random House Value Publishing.

Williamson, David. 2004. *Comprehensive Guide for Camera Collectors*. Atglen, Pennsylvania: Schiffer Publishing

SEVEN

How Not to Blow Up the Library

Planning and Facilitating a Homeschool Science Lab in Your Building

Fred Kirchner

Before becoming a librarian, I spent eleven years teaching elementary and middle school students and working in summer camps. I enjoyed designing hands-on science lessons that got kids working and learning together. Kids dug clay out of hillsides using my hatchet. We've measured playground perimeters with homemade yardsticks. I value students' social interactions as much as their acquisition of content area knowledge, knowing that one's professional life is dependent upon being able to collaborate.

While working as teen librarian at a branch of the Dayton Metro Library (DML), I often interact with homeschooling families. With few grade level peers in their families, I wondered how homeschooled students develop the social skills necessary to succeed outside of their seemingly insular world. Since as an educator I valued group learning dynamics, and believed there were homeschooling families out there unable to access these kinds of opportunities, I decided to offer a Homeschool Science Lab (HSL) program to teens at my branch. Programming for community teens must be offered after school, so I thought HSL would make a great afternoon program, as well as provide gathering space for homeschooling families where parents could network or run errands while I taught their students.

GETTING THE WORD OUT

Once I had my manager's approval, some dates (two hours, monthly, on a Thursday afternoon), and an age group (grades 7–12) set, I started publicizing. DML has an art department at the main library, where branches send publicity forms requesting signage. We also publish quarterly inserts of DML programming in the *Dayton Daily News* (the largest newspaper in our service area). Additionally, DML programs appear on our website (www.daytonmetrolibrary.org), via a searchable calendar. DML's website includes a section for homeschooling families, offering website information and other resources. I contacted local homeschooling groups and listservs using the contact information posted in this section. I set up all publicity to have families register in advance as I wanted to know how many people to expect, their ages, and their names.

SETTING UP THE CLASSROOM

All HSL programs take place in our branch's meeting room. I reserve thirty minutes of time on either end of the two hour class for the program set up and take down. Before students arrive, I set up the computer with preloaded websites that I will be using that day, an LCD projector, and arrange tables and chairs. I also gather classroom supplies—pencils, markers, scissors, glue, and papers to hand out. Experiment supplies need to be laid out, but that varies with each lesson. I read over my lesson plan a few times, and head out into the library to gather students. After the dismissal, I take it all down while chatting with parents and kids who are eager to help as well.

FIRST DAY OF SCHOOL!

I started with a lesson that has been popular with students each time I've conducted it. We used paper airplanes, a plastic cup pyramid, rubber bands and paper clips to test the physics law: "force equals mass times acceleration" ($F = M \times A$).

I prefolded about a dozen samples of my favorite model from *The World's Greatest Paper Airplane and Toy Book* (Laux 1987). Called the "Major Arrow," this plane's design allows varying the mass by adding a paper clip to the nose and velocity and/or acceleration by cutting a notch in the nose and using rubber band propulsion. I also created data sheets using the table function in Microsoft Word.

Then we arranged cups into a pyramid, and propelled planes at them, counting cups that were either knocked off the table or displaced after each throw and recording those totals on the data sheets. Each student tried each of the three tests (the unaltered plane, the plane thrown with a paper clip, and the paper-clipped plane shot with a rubber band). We averaged results for each test and proved the law—our afternoon's hypothesis. The heavier and faster the plane was—the more cups it knocked down.

GETTING THE AGE GROUP RIGHT

What I didn't expect were comments I heard from observing parents. They felt the lesson's academic rigor was beneath the students' educational level. And after some reflection I had to agree. The math and the science concepts were too easy for the age group I was trying to target.

That was the first lesson I learned. Somehow, we mostly attracted teens from well-educated families. This may have to do with the proximity of Wright Patterson Air Force Base. Many air force families that my branch serves homeschool their children—perhaps because of the parents' frequent transfers from base to base. Some of these families send their high school students to local universities with modern laboratory equipment. I couldn't compete with that.

Consequently, I adjusted the program focus from grades 7–12 to grades 4–8. Since the switch, I've had better attendance, and the academic rigor dovetails nicely with students' ages and interests. Now the format is well set—we meet once a month, on a Thursday afternoon, for a two-hour class throughout the school year.

FINDING RESOURCES, THEMES, AND EXPERIMENTS

I began teaching science topics in which I was already interested. Each month, I'd skim science reference material and plan a lesson on what caught my fancy. One of my most successful units examined computer history and information science. We constructed a card-stock model of John Napier's (a seventeenth-century English scientist) famous abacus, Napier's Bones, which uses numbered wooden rods and a frame to calculate large products, quotients, and square roots. I found the model for students' projects using a Google image search on Napier's Bones. It worked perfectly, very much like a calculator—long before the digital age.

We also looked at Charles Babbage's Difference and Analytical Engines (nineteenth-century computer predecessors) and early World War II and Cold War era mainframes—like ENIAC, a 1946 machine that weighed twenty-seven tons. We talked about early Internet history, and discussed computer pioneers Admiral Grace Hopper and Vint Cerf. I researched this material and put together minilectures for the students. We finished the computer unit doing rudimentary HTML programming (in WordPad), as they designed prototypes of student web pages.

This method of creating lessons became very time consuming. Then, once when during a magnetism and electricity unit I couldn't get the experiment I planned to work, I realized I needed some curricular support.

AIMS EDUCATION FOUNDATION

The AIMS (Activities Integrating Math & Science) Education Foundation offers teachers and students valuable learning opportunities. They produce over 100 engaging, hands-on activity books for teachers in grades K through 9, in both print and downloadable PDF formats. Their website (www.aimsedu.org) offers free activities and puzzles, and all of their curricular materials and classroom supplies are available for purchase.

AIMS resources contain creative lessons that include student worksheets, step-by-step instructional notes, supply lists, and background material for teachers, thereby providing tools for directed learning and answers to students' questions. AIMS publishes these units of study (called "activity books") as large format paperbacks—sized 8.5" X 11" for ease of reproduction. AIMS books are created and written by teams of teachers and scientists, and the credited author is usually cited as *AIMS Educational Foundation*, although some publications are credited to individual authors.

Many AIMS books also include a DVD/CD-ROM that offers supplementary information. For example, *Gravity Rules* (Cordel 1998), a book I used for a year of HSL programs, covers physics concepts, discussed with a fun, practical focus—as they apply to skydiving. The DVD features lessons from skydivers describing how they steer themselves through the air using hands and feet. A complementary book lesson instructs students on how to make paper skydivers, testing these aerodynamic principles. Using the DVD, students also observe real-time video of an airplane cockpit's instrument panel to determine information about the altitude, wind speed, and climbing rates. This work is then recorded and measured using the book's data sheets.

Last year, I used *Earth Book: Hydrosphere, Geosphere, Atmosphere, and their Interactions* (AIMS 2007), which offered a unique perspective on the earth sciences, teaching that all the "spheres" of the world—the hydrosphere (Earth's water), the biosphere (Earth's living organisms), the atmosphere, and the geosphere (rocks and dirt from core to crust)—are connected and related to each other. Remarkably, this was proved several times throughout the year. One of the students' fathers, a commercial pilot, was kept away from home for almost a week by Hurricane Irene. Another student had relatives living in Japan during the 2011 earthquake and tsunami. In fact, the class constructed models of a coastal fault zone while our student was in Japan visiting family. One night, their hotel was shaken by aftershocks of the original disaster. It was very powerful when our student returned and was able to share these experiences with class-mates.

AIMS units cover every conceivable science topic with lessons children enjoy. The background information is clear and concise. The free activities will challenge young library patrons, and the supplementary classroom supplies for sale on the website are well-designed and child centered.

SUPPLIES FOR THE HOMESCHOOL SCIENCE LAB

Most of the materials I use for classes are common household items: baking soda, vinegar, toothpicks, modeling clay, old 35mm film containers, and yardsticks. The Meijer (local store) across the street from our branch donated a huge bag of empty film containers. All these expenses fit within my yearly program budget. I also have several teacher friends (that I met working on the library bookmobile) who have loaned me classroom materials from their schools—like Unifix cubes (used to approximate a core slice of earth's diameter in one lesson). My goal for summer 2013 is to write a minigrant to my library's Friends of the Library for funding to purchase more equipment—microscopes and balances, for instance.

AUXILIARY MATERIALS AND ACTIVITIES: PAPERCRAFT AND GIANT-SIZE SCIENTIST TRADING CARDS

I've had homeschool classes work on science paper craft models from a website, Creative Park (cp.c-ij.com/en/contents/2024/list_15_1.html), created by the Canon company. While it's a commercial site designed to sell printers and ink cartridges, there are hundreds of paper craft models available as free PDF downloads. The URL supplied above leads to the science section, which includes forty examples of science models ranging from a fault zone to a hydroelectric plant to the Copernican solar system. Print them on card stock and kids will enjoy scientific crafting. (Note: paper crafts can also be projected onto the wall and traced onto poster boards, colored by patrons, and then cut out and glued together—which makes great giant-sized display items for your library!)

I've also had success using what I call "giant-sized scientist trading cards." Early on, during HSL, I asked students to list ten famous athletes, then ten famous singers, then ten famous actors. Then I asked them to list ten famous scientists. Then we discussed: How many of each list were women? Minorities? Why does our culture reward entertainers and athletes more than scientists? The students were surprised by the results. After that I occasionally made giant-sized scientist trading cards for them on the branch copier. I would include an image of a scientist from whatever field we were studying, pairing that with a short biography from the book, *100 Scientists Who Changed the World* (Tiner 2003). Then I'd copy it onto legal-size paper and we would spend a few minutes reading and discussing the scientist's life and work.

COMPUTER/AUDIO-VISUAL RESOURCES USED IN HSL

Most libraries provide a high-speed Internet connection. I've used the Internet (via a laptop) and an LCD projector for most of my classes. Here's some websites and the topics for which they were used:

- Dynamic Periodic Table (www.ptable.com). While teaching chemistry, I found that this was the best online periodic table.
- The Ohio Department of Education's K–8 Science Standards (www.ode.state.oh.us/GD/Templates/Pages/ODE/ODEDetail.aspx?page=3&TopicRelationID=1705&ContentID=126258&Content=134260). I used it as a resource for lesson planning.
- US Geologic Service Education (education.usgs.gov). While studying earth science, we viewed real-time earthquake data and an earthquake glossary, linked to the video that explained relevant concepts.
- The National Library of Medicine's *Turning the Pages Online* (archive.nlm.nih.gov/proj/ttp/v2/books/#!/robert_hooke_micrographia). This is a digitally scanned version of Robert Hooke's *Micrographia*, written and illustrated in the late 1600s. It demonstrates an amazing use of magnification for insect and plant study. It is a compelling model of the importance of careful, structured observation in science. This unique interactive website also includes other astonishing early science books.

PARENT COMMUNICATION AND EVALUATION OF STUDENT WORK

Since we meet once a month, I don't assign homework or grade papers. During each lesson, I move around the room checking comprehension, work completion, and student focus. Students keep a HSL work folder that they share with parents and bring back each month.

In addition to talking to parents, the best way I've found to communicate is through e-mail. Our homeschooling families are scattered around the county, and by keeping all their addresses in a distribution list I can contact everyone at once. I do this monthly to remind folks about the HSL and during summer to market the program. Many parents have forwarded my e-mails on to other homeschool contacts. All parents have been supportive and thankful for this free learning opportunity for their children.

One of the challenges of only meeting once a month, for me, is remembering students' names. Only three of my students live close enough to be familiar faces I regularly see in the library. Each month it was a struggle until I made a game of it. I told the kids that I was struggling with their names (from their giggles I understood that they already knew that) because I didn't get to see them every day. We started keeping tally marks each month when they caught me forgetting a name or when I used a name correctly. At the end of the program year, if they won the "name game" I'd buy them all pizza. The students sometimes had trouble remembering what we studied the month before, but they always knew the score of the name game!

HOMESCHOOL SCIENCE LAB AND DARWIN

I realize that a homeschooling family may have different views on creationism vs. Darwinism; intelligent design vs. evolution. From the very start, I chose to stay away from these potentially divisive ideas. I don't impose any religious views on students or parents. I've never brought up these arguments. It's not my place as a library professional to challenge patrons' religion and child-rearing beliefs.

This year, I'm teaching human anatomy and physiology, using the AIMS book, *From Head to Toe* (AIMS 2010). I told parents in September that we would not be covering the reproductive system (one of the reasons families choose to homeschool is to be able to share this information with their children in their own way). Parents seemed comfortable with that. Judging by the turnout for these classes, they seem comfortable with what's being taught to their children.

KEEPING LIBRARY COWORKERS HAPPY WHILE TEACHING SCIENCE

Science isn't a tidy or neat field of study. When we completed our chemistry unit, the building smelled like vinegar for a month, and we went through a lot of baking soda! (Vinegar plus baking soda produce a classic and safe chemical reaction.) The students' favorite experiment involved creating a mini fire extinguisher by emptying a teabag, refilling it with baking soda, and then dangling the teabag over a half-full water bottle of vinegar. The bottle top has a small hole drilled into it and the threaded lid secures the teabag above the vinegar—until you shake it up! We used these to extinguish a controlled fire we began using untreated steel wool and a nine-volt battery. (Touch battery leads to the steel wool and it "burns" as electricity conducts through the wool.) We did this outside on the library's sidewalk—which helped keep down the stink.

ATTENDANCE AND FUTURE PLANS

The 2012–2013 school year is my fifth year offering Homeschool Science Lab. Because of our meeting room size, I set maximum enrollment at fifteen students. We've averaged over a dozen kids each month for two years. This year, we've added a second HSL section and will serve over twenty-five kids each month. While we only used homeschool e-mail distribution lists for publicity, this second section filled up in one day, and we turned enough students away to potentially fill most of a third class.

In February of 2013, we will be hosting our first Homeschool Science Fair, giving homeschool kids in grades K–12 from around the county a chance to have their science projects judged by community leaders (our library director, for example) and patrons with science backgrounds (we have several retired professors as regular patrons). Because of our science fair's involvement with The Ohio Academy of Science (www.ohiosci.org), a group that runs a state-wide network of science fairs, some of our older science fair winners will advance to a regional science fair at a local university, and perhaps, State Science Day in Columbus.

GETTING STARTED WITH SCIENCE AT YOUR LIBRARY

Maybe you're not sure running a science class is for you or your patrons. Rather than starting out with a monthly class, you might find a few science lessons and have a Science Day. Pick an afternoon and invite your patrons to come play with bubbles. The AIMS website (www.aimsedu. org) offers an activity called Geo-Panes that kids always enjoy! Students create two-dimensional (2D) shapes using modeling clay and toothpicks, tie them to a string, and dip them in a bucket of bubble solution. After a few tries, they start working in three dimensions, constructing cubes, and pyramids, and using clay balls for vertices and toothpicks for edges. Moving from 2D to 3D creates astonishing new bubbles. You could also get bubble ideas from these books:

- *Soap Bubble Magic* by Seymour Simon
- *The Unbelievable Bubble Book* by John Cassidy
- *Tom Noddy's Bubble Magic* by Tom Noddy

Have you considered calling your local science museum—if there is one nearby—and inviting them to lead a science program at your branch? This might be a low-stress way to include science at your library. Once families arrive, it would be easy to talk to parents and gauge their interest in other science-based library programming.

And here's another idea for a science day: paper airplanes! Use duct tape to make a runway on your meeting room carpet. Let kids fold their own planes and compete to see who can get their plane to land on the runway. Use a stopwatch to determine longest flight. Challenge young pilots to fold a plane that can perform a loop. Take a look at your library's paper airplane books and practice some demonstration models to amaze your patrons!

Regardless of how you do science with young patrons, consider many resources in your building and your community. Homeschooling families are eager to find additional learning opportunities for their children in a safe community space, and the library can serve as a classroom for a wide variety of homeschooling families, filling the building with energy and kids while many of your patrons are at work or in school!

WORKS CITED

Aims Educational Foundation. 2007. *Earth Book: Hydrosphere, Geosphere, Atmosphere, and Their Interactions.* Fresno, CA: AIMS Educational Foundation.

AIMS Educational Foundation. 2010. *From Head to Toe.* Fresno, CA: AIMS Educational Foundation.

Cordel, Betty. 1998. *Gravity Rules!* Fresno, CA: AIMS Educational Foundation.

Laux, Keith. 1987. *The World's Greatest Paper Airplane and Toy Book.* Blue Ridge Summit, PA: TAB Books.

Tiner, John Hudson. 2003. *100 Scientists Who Changed the World.* Milwaukee: World Almanac.

EIGHT

Customizing the For-Credit Information Literacy Course for STEM Majors

Rosalia Petralia and Kathy Turner

Societies guide, associations standardize; faculty determine, and librarians collaborate and carry out. Such is certainly the case for Florida Institute of Technology, its Evans Library, and its for-credit information literacy course, Research Sources and Systems.

Many information literacy courses are somewhat general, focused on important standards and skills but geared more loosely to the broad curricula of their institutions (Holder 2010, 1–9). At the other extreme, some universities have specific information literacy courses within the applied, natural, and physical sciences programs. Drawing from these two approaches, Evans Library has designed a one-credit information literacy course, customized for each student's discipline-specific research needs.

At Florida Institute of Technology, one particular event put into play a series of actions that led the instructors of Research Sources and Systems to adopt the practice of carefully tailoring its only credit-bearing information literacy course so that students in each major receive customized instruction. Here's some history that might give you an idea of the path that we took to get to where we are today—certainly not the end of our road, but doing well to meet the high demands and expectations of our university's faculty and students.

In 1978, Florida Institute of Technology's Undergraduate Curriculum Committee approved the addition of a one-credit course, which transitioned to the current Research Sources and Systems (COM 2012) in 1993. Although its early catalog description stated that the students would "learn about library sources most useful in their chosen fields," it relied primarily on two semester-end course requirements, a short paper and an accompanying annotated bibliography to motivate the students to learn to use subject-specific tools. In the late 1980s and early 1990s, Florida Tech's chemistry department began, on occasion, to request to substitute Research Sources and Systems for its Introduction to Chemical Literature, a one-credit 4000-level course required for program accreditation by the American Chemical Society (ACS). Since the chemistry students who enrolled in COM 2012 required knowledge of very specific chemistry reference books, journals, and abstracting services, several librarians committed to providing supplemental materials and assignments. With the approval of the ACS, soon all four chemistry majors were modified to require COM 2012 as a part of their program plans. Not long thereafter, the biological sciences department decided to allow its students to take COM 2012 as a restricted elective. Again COM 2012 instructors developed a special set of supplemental materials and assignments for students in these programs, still maintaining the "general" set for most of the other students who enrolled. These particular curricular events gave COM 2012 both a stable enrollment base and a model upon which to build a customization for all majors. Then the computer science and software engineering departments, which wanted to see an improvement in the quality of sources cited in students' research, added COM 2012 as a requirement for three majors.

Now it was time for the COM 2012 instructors to stop thinking of the chemistry and biological sciences as exceptions with their own set of special helps and assignments. With the addition of the computer science and software engineering students, it was time to customize and specialize the course for all majors and all programs, not just those that required COM 2012. How was it done?

ALIGN LESSONS TO STANDARDS

Most important, the course was and is organized according to the five general Association of College and Research Libraries (ACRL) Information Literacy Competency Standards for Higher Education (Association of College and Research Libraries 2000):

1. The information literate student determines the nature and extent of the information needed.
2. The information literate student accesses needed information effectively and efficiently.
3. The information literate student evaluates information and its sources critically and incorporates selected information into his or her knowledge base and value system.

4. The information literate student, individually or as a member of a group, uses information effectively to accomplish a specific purpose.
5. The information literate student understands many of the economic, legal, and social issues surrounding the use of information and accesses and uses information ethically and legally.

Course planning includes listing the specific ACRL standards covered in each lesson plan, with learning outcomes matched to those standards. Postinstruction assessment of student mastery, as determined by a question-by-question analysis of Standardized Assessment of Information Literacy Skills (SAILS) posttest results, lets us know which standards are taught well and which need strengthening. The ACRL standards give librarians a clear framework for lesson plans, and SAILS results give us a solid idea of where instruction needs to be improved to meet those standards.

FOCUS ON SPECIALIZED RESOURCES

Course components underscore the specialized information sources and specific skills that equip students for their undergraduate coursework, potentially for their graduate work, and possibly for their careers. Although it is challenging and complex, COM 2012 instructors pay close attention to the majors and/or minors of each student. This is the case for both the STEM majors and the multiple non-STEM majors for whom COM 2012 is now required. Florida Tech's quality enhancement plan (QEP), affiliated with its Southern Association of Colleges and Schools accreditation, is to "develop a climate and culture of scholarly inquiry for all undergraduates regardless of major" (Florida Institute of Technology; September 4, 2012). In some Florida Tech colleges, taking COM 2012 was determined to be a necessary part of the preparation for that scholarly inquiry. What follows are some of the lesson particulars that ensure fine-tuned research skills within specific fields, and turn out undergraduate students who are significantly more information literate at semester's end:

- Research topic and portfolio. Each COM 2012 student chooses a fairly narrow research topic within his or her discipline to explore for the semester. No duplicates are allowed within a given section to encourage unique research as well as to provide opportunities for cross-disciplinary awareness. Students are urged to choose a topic that may be part of a project for another current course, a future course, graduate work interests, or a potential career focus. Throughout the semester, topic searches are executed and refined in four databases, one of which is specialized for the field of study.

Ultimately this results in a research portfolio of four bibliographies with between two and twenty high-quality information resources in each. Near the end of the semester, students present posters to share what they have learned about one resource that they have found to be particularly useful for research in their fields.

- Preservation lesson. Course instructors still enlighten students to the basics of preservation and the challenges of ever-changing information formats. The 1986 classic, *Slow Fires: On the Preservation of the Human Record* (American Film Foundation 1987) is required viewing in COM 2012, and many students also view *Into the Future: On the Preservation of Knowledge in the Electronic Age* (American Film Foundation 1997). It is remarkable how many students select a preservation-related subject for their semester's research topic. Course instructors feel particularly fortunate to be able to enlighten all of Florida Tech's computer science, software engineering, and chemistry undergraduates, the very population who can have a positive influence and may be able to make improvements in safeguarding precious information, about the importance of preserving and protecting information across time and in consideration of technological changes.

- Research guides. Even before the Evans Library implemented web-based, discipline-specific research guides (LibGuides) in 2010, home-grown research guides were used to orient faculty and students to essential resources, services, and strategies within their fields of study. Now, each academic department has a discipline-specific guide affiliated with it. All subject guides include tabs that collect reference sources, articles and databases, books and e-books, and information about citing sources. They also include resources that are very specific for each department/major. Some examples are the *Computer Sciences Research Guide*, which includes the Association of Computing Machinery (ACM) news feed, and the *Chemistry Research Guide*, which features tips and tutorials for using Sci-Finder, the American Chemical Society's powerful research database that allows searching for chemical substances, reactions, patents, and journal references.

- Specialized reference resources. During the reference sources lesson, students are introduced to general reference sources, both print and electronic, that are broad based, yet relate to their majors. For example, the *Encyclopedia of Associations* and *Access Science* can be used in specific ways for all majors. The students are required to review the list of subject-specific references that is available in the research guide, choosing three print and three online to explore in depth. Each student then selects one print and one online reference source, presumably the most pertinent to their research topic among the specialized reference sources, to evaluate.

- Specialized databases. During the specialized database lesson in the course, each student participates in a breakout session with his or her library liaison. Called the "information advocates" at the Evans Library, these subject specialists introduce the students to the specific databases essential in their fields of study. Affiliated helps are also introduced. The assignment for that lesson requires the students to detail the scope (subject coverage, date coverage, types of resources indexed, and type of information provided) and search strategies (use of help, Boolean logic, nesting, truncation, and controlled vocabulary) of the specialized database. Students are also required to design and refine a search that produce between two and twenty high-quality results that pertain to the research topic.
- Relationship with an information advocate. After the specialized-database lesson, each student has been introduced to the library liaison for his or her major. Often, this results in a long-lasting relationship that develops between the student and the information advocate. Students feel comfortable contacting these librarians about specific questions, for follow-up consultations, and for research assistance for the duration of their undergraduate work and often in subsequent graduate work.
- Poster presentation. Near the semester's end, students choose one particular excellent resource from among the many high-quality resources they've discovered in the course of doing research. That resource is then evaluated (using a "who, why, when" questionnaire) and presented in a poster session that details the scope and academic applications of the tool. Students are given detailed guidelines and a rubric, which is used in the assessment of their poster presentation. This noisy and meaningful activity also serves as worthwhile preparation for poster sessions at professional conferences.
- Standardized Assessment of Information Literacy Skills (SAILS) data. Semester after semester, students' pre- and posttest SAILS scores are analyzed for several purposes. Individual student improvement is measured and then serves as an assessment for one of the campus' student learning outcomes. Mastery of the course and lesson objectives is evaluated and re-evaluated. Preliminary data suggests that the STEM majors improve an average of 4.9 points on their information literacy posttest scores, as opposed to a 3.7 point improvement in students overall. Therefore STEM majors leave COM 2012 better equipped for the high-level research required in their fields. Future analysis will be able to answer research questions related to other specific student populations even in relationship to specific SAILS questions.

EMPHASIZE ACTIVE LEARNING

COM 2012 instructors stress the importance of hands-on learning by designing classroom activities that require students to come up with results or solutions and to visit special library and campus resources that round out what they've learned from lecture or course materials. Here are some examples of specific lesson components that engage students during class:

- Students introduce themselves to guest lecturers and their fellow classmates by telling about a major-related topic in which they are interested. The topic title should begin with either the first letter of their first name or the first letter of their last name. This breaks the ice with guest speakers, requires students to think about possible research topics for the course, and allows them to get to know each other better. This leads to higher interactivity and a greater likelihood that two students will pair up to present a common high-quality information resource during the poster session.
- Students visit four different guest presenters during the preservation lesson. (1) they learn about the detrimental use of sticky notes, paper clips, and such to mark their place in a book and choose from among a wide assortment of bookmarks; (2) they enjoy a walk down technology memory lane as they are shown many examples of data storage media at a digital transitions display; (3) they peruse a 1561 edition of Stow's "Chaucer," being able to see first-hand how well the paper has survived; and (4) they watch a librarian use alkaline tapes, glue, and other preservation supplies and equipment to extend the life of library materials.
- For each section, COM 2012 instructors devote an entire class period to teaching students about controlled vocabulary in general and about the Library of Congress subject headings (LCSH) specifically, and to having the students select their semester research focus. The value of this activity is high, as students see evidence that standardized terminology can actually help them find resources of interest. After the brief presentation on LCSH, students queue up to meet with one of their instructors, transitioning from a vague topic that has come to mind all the way to identifying LCSH terms and their broader, related, and narrower counterparts. As each student settles on a topic, he or she logs it on a white board, so that others will not choose the same subject. This visual representation also increases the likelihood that two or more students may decide to partner on an excellent poster resource.
- Students begin each of the four class sessions by applying five basic search strategies to a collection of "data elements." Hard candies are used in place of these elements to identify results from specific

search strings. For example, a student will review the collection of data elements (Werther's, Jolly Ranchers, mints, strawberries, and such) to determine which ones meet the requirements for this search:*cand* AND (red OR yellow) AND circ**

- Another student will grade the answer set. Throughout the semester, search strings use Boolean operators, truncation, nesting, and controlled vocabulary, giving students weekly review of these basic search strategies. Needless to say, students willingly retrieve data elements for their own enjoyment as well.

- Both course instructors and guest lecturers frequently invite students to do the keyboarding, at the librarian's direction, during computerized demonstrations. It is gratifying to see the level of engagement climb once the students take the reins.

- During the general reference lesson and the government information lesson, students are assigned resources about which they present basic facts to their classmates. During the specialized reference lesson, students physically go to the print reference collection to examine these subject-specific books and use available computers to go to online specialized reference sources. COM 2012 instructors and guest lecturers see evidence that this type of delivery makes these resource types much more concrete and practical to the students.

- Last, but not least, is the SAILS pretest and posttest. Taking this online test keeps the students occupied for the entire examination period; receiving their score on-the-spot gives them much-appreciated feedback.

COM 2012 instructors and students alike enjoy our highly interactive and energetic classroom environment where we encourage discussion, academic argument, and, of course, an atmosphere of fun and engagement as part of our courses.

Is it necessary to design information literacy courses for STEM majors from scratch? Certainly not! Many libraries already include specialized components for their STEM majors, and others already have a flexible course design that allows for a more intentional focus on STEM-specific research instruction. Yet even librarians designing new information literacy courses with STEM majors in mind need not feel overwhelmed. Our own experience with COM 2012 is that the ACRL Information Literacy Competency Standards for Higher Education exist to provide a solid framework for lessons, STEM program curricula give direction to students' research objectives within the library course, and students' own interests drive their in-class engagement. Add to these basics a willingness to develop and maintain relationships with STEM program faculty, library liaisons, and even former students, and you begin to realize the many resources already at hand! Knowing the curriculum requirements for STEM programs allows librarians to lead their own instruction in helpful directions. Library liaisons share their extensive knowledge of the resources that are most helpful to STEM students with the class and instructors. Former COM 2012 students are encouraged to accept work study or college roll positions within the instruction department, not only for their familiarity with the material that they will be grading, but also to offer their feedback on the usefulness and pertinence of the course to their own fields. At Evans Library, we value the wealth of knowledge that faculty and students represent, and readily accept contributions and feedback to improve our course for everyone, including our STEM students.

Is it ambitious and effective to make it a priority to customize the for-credit information literacy course for STEM students? The Evans Library faculty librarians think it is. The feedback from departmental faculty is very favorable. Course evaluations and follow-up correspondence are very positive. Is there tremendous potential for measuring the information literacy of the students in new and beneficial ways? COM 2012 instructors believe they have just begun to use statistical tools to understand better the value and customizing opportunities of the course for STEM and other majors. Careful consideration of STEM program requirements and the resources—online, offline, in-person—that best prepare students for their current and future research impacts library-taught information literacy courses in promising ways. As for Evans Library, we will continue on our path toward increased information literacy for Florida Tech's students, taking advantage of the specialized resources and knowledge most pertinent to each.

WORKS CITED

Association of College and Research Libraries. *Information Literacy Competency Standards for Higher Education.* Chicago: Association of College and Research Libraries, 2000. http://www.ala.org/acrl/sites/ala.org.acrl/files/content/standards/standards.pdf

Florida Institute of Technology. "Key Features," *Florida Tech Quality Enhancement Plan.* Accessed September 4, 2012. http://www.fit.edu/qep/key_features.php.

Holder, Sara. "History and Evolution of Credit IL Courses in Higher Education." In *Best Practices for Credit-Bearing Information Literacy Courses,* edited by Christopher V. Hollister, 1–9. Chicago: Association of College and Research Libraries, 2010.

III

Information Literacy and Educational Support

NINE

Kid-ventions with the US Patent Library

Barbara J. Hampton

Where will we find the innovators, inventors, and creative designers of tomorrow? They are in our classrooms today! Kids and young adults aren't just dreaming about inventions. They are creating marketable products; some having earned substantial scholarships and profits. Yet K–12 teachers who value engineering and technology education often have little access to supporting content. This chapter shows how school and public librarians can engage inventive young minds using actual patents (especially ones by children) in the US Patent and Trademark Office databases. When students see these STEM skills in use, they realize, "I can do that!"

GATHERING ACTIVITIES

Plant the seeds of engineering (the "silent E" in STEM) for your program. Create a "kid-vention gallery" of actual patent drawings for a virtual field trip with a challenge activity to engage users before your program begins. I've selected some patented kid-ventions that are engaging and readily understood (See primary sources at the end of the chapter).

Possible activities include:

- "Name that Invention": have participants match displayed patent drawings to captions with legal title of invention, patent number, name and residence of inventor, and date granted.

- "What's Your IQ (Invention Quotient)?": offer a kid-vention factoid quiz.
- "Patent Art Puzzles": prepare several patent drawing puzzles by gluing drawings to poster board, cutting them into jigsaw pieces and having kids reconstruct them.
- "Kid-vention Scavenger Hunt": offer clues for students to find special patents.

Microprizes (pencil, eraser, ruler, inventor's composition notebook) could be awarded to participants.

INVENTION STORIES AND ROLE MODELS (15 MIN.)

Begin with the drama of invention. Children often view engineers as laborers who use tools rather than solve creative problems (Capobianco et al. 2011). Inventors start with imagination, then use the engineering design process to identify constraints, develop, test, and refine solutions. Inventive heroes in popular films and children's literature are a good introduction to the skills and process. Present an excerpt from an age-appropriate book or video to illustrate inventive thinking, such as:

- *Apollo 13* (2005; 1:20:40–1:21:47, 1:27:45–1:33:41): astronauts battle accumulating carbon dioxide levels (recognizing the problem); engineers race against the clock to jerry-rig a filter (working within constraints of time and materials).
- *The Great Serum Race: Blazing the Iditarod Trail* (Miller 2002): Delivery of critical medicine for a diphtheria epidemic despite weather, distance, and time.
- *Hatchet* (Paulsen 2007): After a plane crash, a thirteen-year-old boy survives in the wilderness with a hatchet and little else.
- *The Sign of the Beaver* (Speare 1997): A thirteen-year-old boy alone in the colonial wilderness survives despite limited resources.
- *A Big Ball of String* (Holland 1993): A sick child uses a string to operate everything in his room — all without leaving his bed!
- *Robots* (2005): A young inventor dreams of making the world a better place.
- *Flash of Genius* (2009): The persevering inventor of the intermittent windshield wiper battles against Ford Motor Company's theft of his idea.
- *Percy Julian: Forgotten Genius* (2007): An African-American chemist facing discrimination discovers a method for synthesizing and mass-producing cortisone.

Next, share the story of the children behind the kid-ventions. Sources of brief biographies include Caney (1985), Casey (2005), Erlbach (1997), Lemelson-MIT Program (2012), Sleet (2000), and Tucker (1995). Search magazine databases and the Internet ("inventions by children") for additional articles and videos about kid-ventions. Participants can discuss the inspirations, constraints, and design evolutions of these inventors.

HANDS-ON INVENTION (20 MIN.)

Students better understand engineering design by exploring, using, constructing, or deconstructing an inventive product. Depending on available time, space, tools, and budget, select an active participation period in your program that is appropriate to the participants' age and experience:

- Assemble a kid-vention laboratory with products corresponding to the patents (Makin' Bacon, Wristies, MagnaCard Magnetic Locker Wallpaper, crayon holder); give students a chance to examine and/ or deconstruct. (If no actual products are available, provide photographs of products from websites.)
- Create a brainstorming laboratory using an Odyssey of the Mind spontaneous problem (Micklus and Micklus 2000; 2003; 2007).
- Conduct product testing by playing with a "next generation" toy, such as KanJam, Frisbee Mini-Golf (outdoors), or a domino race game (indoors).
- Assemble a broken gadget laboratory (mixer, wind-up alarm clock, film camera, tape recorder, CD player, telephone, keyboard, computer mouse, etc.); deconstruct, study, salvage parts (Sobey 2011).
- Explore digital technology with LEGO, MaKey MaKey keyboard invention kit, mobile app development, and so forth (for tech savvy students).

End this activity with a brief discussion of observations and questions that arose in their "laboratory."

KID'S-EYE VIEW OF PATENTS (20 MIN.)

Students may be surprised to learn that they can look at official government patent records right from their computers. Ignore the legalese; you won't be doing a legal analysis. Teachers and students will be looking at the construction, features, and operation of the invention. Provide copies of the primary source list (at the end of this chapter). Model search tools using one of these techniques that is age-appropriate, and then allow participants to explore the patent databases.

Kid-Friendly Simple Patent Number Search.

The kid-vention patent numbers in the primary sources list provide students a simple, sure-fire way to locate interesting patents before they've learned the more advanced searching tools. These patents are short, with many line drawings of the invention.

From Google Patents (simple and familiar look):

1. Enter the patent number (commas optional) in the search box and click "Search."
2. Save or print the patent document using the "Download PDF" link near the top of the page.

From the US Patent and Trademark Office Database (includes more advanced options):

1. Before the program, install a TIFF viewer (browser search "USPTO Plugins TIFF"). Internet Explorer, Netscape, and pre-Safari Apple browsers have been tested to work with these free TIFF viewers. See additional information on the USPTO TIFF page.
2. Select "Patent Number" search in the USPTO Patent Full-Text and Image Database ("USPTO patent number search").
3. Enter the patent number from the table (commas optional) in the "Query" box and click "Search."
4. Click "Images" on the summary page to view full patent.

Students can find more patent numbers for familiar inventions at the National Inventors Hall of Fame website, including: Flexible Flyer sled, ballpoint pen, gas mask, three-way traffic signal, Phillips-head screw, and Zamboni ice-rink resurfacer. Remember when Super Soakers replaced water pistols? ("History of the Super Soaker" 2012). Using the patent number search, they can see these original designs.

Looking at Frisbees and Mouses: Intermediate Searching for Related Inventions

Each new patent discloses the numbers of existing related inventions ("prior art"). The Google Patent Search results also display a list ("Referenced By") of later related inventions, or search the "referenced by" field in the USPTO Full-Text Database Quick Search. A trending outdoor game, KanJam was patented in 1995 (Sciandra and Swisher 1995). Its ancestral inventions included the "Aerial Disk" (Robes 1955) and the "Flying Toy," (Morrison 1957). Brand names aren't used in patents, but your students will quickly recognize the Frisbee, which is also known as Dartmouth Disk, Space Saucer, and Pluto Platter (Davant 1995). Show students how to use the Google Patent Search results for the original "Aerial Disk" patent to link to the many subsequent inventions it inspired.

You can see inventions grouped by subject. Students looking at the drawings for Engelbart's "X-Y Position Indicator for a Display System" will recognize the original computer mouse. Its current U.S. classification (Class 345/Subclass164), leads to other computer interface devices. Under

"Quick Search" ("USPTO Full-Text Database"), select the field "Current US Classification" and enter the class/subclass in the search box. Another example: "Makin' Bacon" (Fleck and Fleck 1996, see figure 3) shows U.S. Cl. 219/732; this leads to 250 microwave cooking-related inventions.

Advanced Searching Using USPTO Classifications

The alphabetical classification index (browser search "Index to the USPC") links terms to related classification numbers. Some terms that students could explore include: game, horse, horseshoe, dog, dolls, bicycle, tent, chairs, and condiment. The class "music" has many interesting subclasses, including mouse guards, guitars, toy, and so forth.

Students should preplan a search, developing many possible synonyms for the purpose, construction, and use of the invention. Consider the examples of the Frisbee. One was a "disk," one was a "toy," and one was a "disc." Remember, patent filings do not use "brand names" and may use old-fashioned terminology; patent documents related to "rocking horses" might use "hobby horse." Next, list the specific features, components, and operation of the invention, such as "simulated animal sounds."

Continue exploring the patent databases with the official (browser search "USPTO Full-Text Database") and unofficial (browser search "Google advanced patent") search tools. The USPTO provides patent search strategy tips in a four-page guide (browser search "USPTO 7 step") and an online tutorial (browser search "USPTO conducting patent search"). Refer to a library research guide for further examples (browser search "Patent LibGuide Sacred Heart"). *One caution:* Keyword searching of the full text of a patent produces overwhelming and confusing results for nonexperts; guide students to the faceted search tools for a better experience.

STARTING AN INVENTOR'S NOTEBOOK (10 MIN.)

Close your program by giving students the opportunity to begin a personal "idea book" (to jot down rough ideas whenever they occur) and "inventor's notebook" (to make a complete record of the development of an invention) (Caney 1985,Grissom 2008). Tell them to (confidentially) brainstorm problems to solve, areas of interest, or design concepts and to date their notes. Creating these records protects the inventor's legal rights and develops "design thinking" skills and habits of mind.

Not every invention qualifies for the legal protection of a patent; not every inventor chooses to apply for a patent; not every patent-holder actively enforces patent rights or offers the item for sale; not every patented invention will be a commercial success. A lesson plan, "Patent It Fast!"

gives young kids a quick introduction to the invention process and documentation (2002).

STRATEGIES FOR SUCCESS

Select target audiences based on ages, reading levels, and STEM-specific education. Identify classroom and extracurricular connections and resources available. Build interest in your program by coordinating with student events (invention convention, science and engineering fairs, Odyssey of the Mind, *FIRST*, etc.) and annual engineering and inventing celebrations, such as National Engineering Week (February), Introduce a Girl to Engineering Day (February), National Inventors Month (May); and National Inventors Hall of Fame Induction (May). Identify local inventors and competitors.

Ask patent experts for handouts, advice, and possibly a guest appearance. Nearly every state has a Patent and Trademark Resource Center (PTRC) (browser search "PTRC location"), with librarians familiar with patent searching tools. Contact local intellectual property law associations (browser search "US IP law associations") to request a speaker who connects with kids.

Your budget for this program can range from minimal costs for printing Internet images to a few hundred dollars for hands-on materials. For deconstruction activities, collect donated worn-out toasters, mixers, computer keyboards and towers, and so forth, and some basic tools. Collaborate with your school's technology teacher to use tools and electronics, if possible. Seek donations from local businesses or maker groups for the cost of advanced electronic components such as MaKey MaKey. Participants can bring their own inventor's notebook. Bound composition books with grid-lined paper work well.

Students need generous table space to explore invention records, deconstruct gadgets, and build their own models. Choose an area with ample Internet connections and electrical outlets. Use a multimedia projector to demonstrate key points about the PTRC. Consider safety and ease of clean-up issues based on the specific activities you've selected. Some optional activities require an outdoor play or test space.

MARKETING

Build interest in your program by marketing directly to families, schools, community programs, and businesses. Include youth groups such as Girl Scouts, Boy Scouts, and 4-H that have design and inventing activity programs. Synergize with "makers" groups that have formed in many areas. Ask local stores selling tools, parts, supplies, computer programs, and books that designer-builders use to post your event flyer and perhaps offer a discount coupon to your participants. Prepare press releases according to your library's publicity plan. With pathfinders for the students, parent groups, educators, and community members, your library becomes a hub for inventing and patenting information.

GOALS, OBJECTIVES, AND EVALUATION

Teaching about inventions and patents supports an integrated curriculum, enriches cultural knowledge, and demonstrates respect for intellectual property. A virtual visit to the patent library shows them the fun, excitement, challenge, and rewards of STEM as they see innovation at work (and play)!

"[M]astering tools and working with one's hands is receding in America as a hobby, as a valued skill, as a cultural influence that shaped thinking and behavior" (Uchitelle 2012). Tinkering, a crucial component of engineering and technology education, gives students experience with engineering "design process" and "habits of mind." Today, while schools have reduced the "making" shop classes, libraries have created "makerspaces." Kids can join the "maker" movement, tinkering with tools, hardware, and programming (browser search "makerspace")" inspired by magazines (*Make: Technology on Your Time*) and books. The Arduino and MaKey MaKey digital interface and invention kits are inexpensive (less than $50) "maker" tools. These may be a millennial student's first exposure to creating technology.

The primary goal of this program is to help children and young adults see themselves as capable of developing original and useful products as inventors and engineers and to motivate them to master the foundational STEM skills for this work and for higher education. In addition, collaboration with families, educators, and community groups will demonstrate the value that librarians can bring to STEM education and text next generation of inventors. Progress toward these goals will be indicated by

- Ability of participants to search and access patent records by number and classification code
- Ability of participants to interpret patent drawings and compare to final product
- Increase in number of users who are interested in and/or confident that they can become developers of useful new products
- Increase in students participating in voluntary inventing, engineering, and maker activities (curricular and extracurricular)
- Increase in collaboration by educators with librarians to develop resources for STEM lesson plans
- Increase in library USPTO reference transactions by community members

Indicators will be measured by pre- and postactivity library statistics, pre- and postactivity participant self-evaluations (conforming to school and library testing and human research protocols), and school and community group reports of participation in voluntary inventing, engineering, and maker activities (curricular and extracurricular).

After reviewing the outcomes demonstrated by these indicators, the librarian should report results to educators and community groups as well as library staff with recommendations for future programs, resources, support, and collaboration. Build a "makerspace" and they will come. As information specialists, librarians are uniquely qualified to support K–12 engineering curriculum standards, testing, and pedagogy using the patent library.

WORKS CITED

Primary Sources (Patents)

Bomkamp, Katherine Emily. Pain Reducing and Eliminating Prosthesis Socket Device, U.S. Patent 8,192,502, filed Feb. 7, 2010, and issued June 5, 2012.

Buckel, Sarah. 2009. Magnetic Wallpaper. U.S. Patent Application 20090110948.

Dittman, Sydney C. 1993. Aid for Grasping Round Knobs. U.S. Patent 5,231,733, filed Apr. 14, 1992, and issued Aug. 3, 1993.

Engelbart, D. C. 1970. X-Y Position Indicator for a Display System. U.S. Patent 3,541,541, filed June 21, 1967, and issued Nov. 17, 1970.

Fleck, Jonathan E. and Abigail M. Fleck. 1996. Microwave Cooking Vessel with Removable Food Supports. U.S. Patent 5,552,585, filed Oct. 6, 1994, and issued Sept. 3, 1996.

Goldstein, Cassidy. 2002. Device for Holding a Writing Instrument. U.S. Patent 6,402,407, filed June 29, 2000, and issued June 11, 2002.

Gregory, minor, Kathryn and Susan B. Gregory. 1999. Article of Thermal Clothing for Covering the Underlying Area at the Gap between a Coat Sleeve and a Glove. U.S. Patent 5,864,886, filed June 24, 1996, and issued Feb. 2, 1999.

Ishak, Alec Andrew. 2010. Footwear with Deployable Crampons. U.S. Patent 7,832,121, filed Mar. 8, 2007, and issued Nov. 16, 2010.

Krasik-Geiger, Ariel and Michael Krasi. 2003a. Calibrated Angle and Depth Scissors. U.S. Patent 6,513,247, filed May 4, 1998, and issued Feb. 4, 2003.

Krasik-Geiger, Ariel and Michael Krasik. 2003b. Calibrated Angle and Depth Scissors. U.S. Patent 6,647,842, filed Dec. 17, 2002, and issued Nov. 18, 2003.

Macocha, Chandler Matthew. 2008. Pivoting Wheelchair Backpack Holder. U.S. Patent 7,344,055, filed May 12, 2004, and issued Mar. 18, 2008.

Meggitt, Austin Stephen. 2000. Article Carrying Device for Attachment to a Bicycle for Carrying Baseball Bats, Gloves and Other Sports Equipment or Objects. U.S. Patent 6,029,874, filed Oct. 20, 1998, and issued Feb. 29, 2000.

Low, Elizabeth S. 1994. Pliable Paperweight and Article Holder. U.S. Patent 5,322,718, filed May 24, 1993, and issued June 21, 1994.

Low, Jeanie S. 1992. Folding Step for Cabinet Doors. U.S. Patent 5,094,515, filed Sept. 26, 1990, and issued Mar. 10, 1992.

Morrison, Walter Frederick. 1957. Flying Toy. U.S. Patent D183,626, filed Jul. 22, 1957, and issued Sept. 30, 1958.

Patch, Robert W. 1963. Toy Truck. U.S. Patent 3,091,888, filed June 11, 1962, and issued June 4, 1963.

Reinhart, Robert R. 1999. Thigh Pack. U.S. Patent D417,072, filed Nov. 25, 1998, and issued Nov. 30, 1999.

Robes, Ernest C. 1955. Aerial Disk. U.S. Patent 2,822,176 filed Sept. 16, 1955, and issued Feb. 4, 1958.

Schroeder, Becky J. 1974. Luminescent Backing Sheet for Writing in the Dark. U.S. Patent 3,832,556, filed Dec. 26, 1973, and issued Aug. 27, 1974.

———. 1975. Luminescent Backing Sheet for Writing in the Dark. U.S. Patent 3,879,611, filed Aug. 19, 1974, and issued Apr. 22, 1975.

Sciandra, Charles C. and Paul L. Swisher. 1995. Apparatus and a Method of Play for a Disc Tossing Game. U.S. Patent 5,382,028, filed Nov. 2, 1993, issued Jan. 17, 1995.

Stachowski, Ritchie C. 1999. Device for Talking Underwater. U.S. Patent 5,877,460, filed Sept. 16, 1997, and issued Mar. 2, 1999.

Whale, Spencer R. 2008. Toy Vehicle Adapted for Medical Use. U.S. Patent 7,374,228, filed Jan. 6, 2005, and issued May 20, 2008.

Secondary Sources

Apollo 13. 2005. Directed by Ron Howard. Universal City, CA: Universal. DVD.

Capobianco, Brenda M., Heidi Diefes-Dux, Irene Mena, and Jessica Weller. 2011. "What Is an Engineer? Implications of Elementary School Student Conceptions for Engineering Education." *Journal of Engineering Education*, 100(2): 304–28.

Caney, Steven. 1985. *Steven Caney's Invention Book*. New York: Workman Publishing.

Casey, Susan. 2005. *Kids & Inventing! A Handbook for Young Inventors*. Hoboken, NJ: John Wiley/Jossey-Bass.

Davant, Charles. 1995. "Is Dartmouth the Home of the Frisbee?" *The Dartmouth*, Oct. 13, 1995.

Erlbach, Arlene. 1997. *The Kids' Invention Book*. New York: Scholastic.

Flash of Genius. 2009. Directed by Marc Abraham. Universal City, CA: Universal Studios Home Entertainment. DVD.

Grissom, Fred E. 2008. *Inventor's Notebook: A "Patent It Yourself" Companion*. 5th ed. Berkeley, CA: Nolo.

"History of the Super Soaker." 2012. iSoaker.com, http://www.isoaker.com/Info/history_supersoaker.html.

Holland, Marion. 1993. *A Big Ball of String*. New York: Beginner Books.

Lemelson-MIT Program. 2012. "Inventor of the Week Archive" Invention Dimension. Lemelson-MIT Program, accessed Oct. 1. http://web.mit.edu/invent/i-archive.html.

Micklus, C. Samuel, and Samuel W. Micklus. 2000. *Applying Your Creativity: Odyssey of the Mind Long-Term and Spontaneous Problems*. Gloucester City, NJ: Creative Competitions.

———. 2003. *Creative Interaction: Odyssey of the Mind Long-Term and Spontaneous Problems*. Gloucester City, NJ: Creative Competitions, Inc.

———. 2007. *Lots of Problems: Many Solutions*. Gloucester City, NJ: Creative Competitions, Inc.

Miller, Debbie S. 2002. *The Great Serum Race: Blazing the Iditarod Trail*. New York: Walker.

"Patent it Fast!" 2002. *Technology and Children*, 6(4): 13.

Paulsen, Gary. 2007. *Hatchet*. New York: Simon & Schuster.

Percy Julian: Forgotten Genius. 2007. Directed by Llewellyn M. Smith. Boston: WGBH Video. DVD.

Robots. 2005. Directed by Carlos Saldanha and Chris Wedge. Beverly Hills, CA: 20th Century Fox Home Entertainment, 2005. DVD.

Sobey, Ed. 2011. Unscrewed: Salvage and Reuse Motors, Gears, Switches, and More from Your Old Electronics. Chicago: Chicago Review Press.

Sleet, Enzo. 2000. *Awesome Inventions by Kids Like You! Move Over, Edison; Kids Can Invent, Too!* Chicago: Kidsbooks.

Speare, Elizabeth George. 1997. *The Sign of the Beaver*. New York: Dell Publishing.

Tucker, Tom. 1995. *Brainstorm! The Stories of Twenty American Kid Inventors*. New York:
    Farrar, Straus and Giroux.
Uchitelle, Louis. 2012. "A Nation That's Losing Its Toolbox." *New York Times*, July 21,
    2012, BU1.

TEN

A Math Emporium Project

Nastasha Johnson and Tiffany B. Russell

Since its advent in the late 1990s, there has been an increase in adoption of the Math Emporium, a model of mathematical education in which the common lecture is forgone in favor of an information technology model. Based on research, the Math Emporium model is successful for students less prepared for college and for students from underserved demographics. It has also been identified as the solution to the dismal performance in basic math in two- and four-year institutions. A guiding principle of why the emporium model works in mathematics is simple: "Students learn math by doing math, not by listening to someone talk about doing math" (Twigg 2011, 26). Interactive computer software, personalized on-demand assistance, and mandatory student participation are the key elements of success.

The F. D. Bluford Library and the Mathematics Department on the campus of North Carolina Agricultural and Technical State University (NC A&T) collaborated on the university strategic plan to improve student outcomes. Together, they planned, located funding for, and established a multisite Math Emporium as an avenue to profoundly have an impact on the success of students. In this chapter, we describe the considerations and lessons learned from engaging in this project as well as ways to navigate the diplomatic waters of inter-departmental collaboration.

BACKGROUND

The Math Emporium is a nationally recognized instructional model that was originated at Virginia Polytechnic Institute and State University (Virginia Tech) in 1998. The first model was homegrown, with software designed by the staff and faculty of the university. What distinguished this space was the ingenuity of the delivery and functionality. The Virginia Tech model is one of the earliest examples of a blended learning space. Human teaching and digital adaptability are blended to create a flexible learning environment. This online math program is a self-paced, module-based, digital learning environment where students determine the speed with which they learn and test on the course material. The environment, however, is not virtual. Faculty and student assistants are available to tutor and help students in a computer lab space. The technique is called "assistance on demand." Since its inception, the Math Emporium design has extended to community colleges and universities across the United States. Our model here at NC A&T is the first in the state of North Carolina. We hope that it will serve as a model to the other sixteen universities in our system.

GOALS AND OBJECTIVES

As mentioned before, one of the chief goals of the project is to improve success in foundational math courses for non-STEM majors. Traditionally the courses were often repeated by students, and there was a high incidence of low and failing grades. Therefore, the university was interested in improving statistics, but also in solidifying the math skills of the students as they matriculated.

Another goal of the project was for the library to create a tangible, measurable partnership with an academic department. We desired to be more integrated into core curriculum of the university's students and faculty, and not just in the traditional supporting role. Our viability could be enhanced by stronger collaboration which was encouraged by the university and administration.

PLAN

The initial plan of the Math Emporium partnership was to create a single space that would host several Math Emporium class sections. The initial site was an underutilized space in the library. However, shortly after we received the grant and analyzed the logistics, we realized that the space was too small. The pilot class sizes were supposed to have thirty-five students, with fifteen sections of each course. The library space, even with retrofitted furnishings and technology, could only hold twenty-four students. Another lab space on campus had to be selected.

In addition to the space allocation, the plan was to test the online virtual environment using less expensive thin-client computers, which would save energy and allow updates via remote access.

BUDGET

NC A&T was awarded $87,000 and charged with piloting the Math Emporium program within twelve calendar months. According to the original proposal, an underutilized space in the lower level of the library would house the pilot Math Emporium. The funding was the result of federal performance-enhancing project grants received by the general administration of the UNC system.

Due to space limitation on the lower level of the library, we selected another location as the main Math Emporium site. The library still remained vital to the project as the newly designated proctoring location. The granting agency approved the reallocation of the funds for the new space. Additionally, the granting agency allowed us to exchange funding sources so that the academic space to be retrofitted first would use the funds that expire sooner. The latter was necessary in the best interests of the project timeline.

LAYOUT

In the initial planning stages the library team wanted to have round- and/ or trapezoid-shaped tables, but with vendor issues, spacing limitations, and short turnaround time, designing and using those tables proved to be unrealistic. After the vendors measured and evaluated the room, we realized that only twenty-four stations would work with the room's space limitations. The final vendor developed a sketch to accommodate the needs and limitations of the space. The vendor told us that round and trapezoid tables do not meet our expectations for clean, hidden wire management nor quick delivery, as they would likely require customization. Since this was our second vendor, the customization was out of the question if we wanted to implement the project on time.

IMPLEMENTATION

A team of the library faculty and staff was formed to begin the execution process for the project. The acquisitions librarian and the math subject librarian were both involved in the overall execution of the project. Over several months the team made decisions about material and equipment needs for the space. The day-to-day communications with vendors and the university facilities group were handled by the library project manager. Complications in the purchasing process, challenges with vendors, infrastructure age, and technological limitations caused the completion of the project to be delayed.

Fast forward eight months, the room renovations are wrapping up, the thin clients are in place, and the new 3D SMART Board is screaming for someone to play with it. Unfortunately, since there was no additional funding for staffing, it presented another challenge. Six math faculty members have signed on for the pilot, but there were no undergraduate or graduate student assistants in place to work in the new learning space. Finally, another department graciously agreed to fund teaching assistants. They were hired on such short notice that the equipment and process training had to be done on site. Also, because of IT infrastructural challenges and resource management, the library location could not receive technical support until the middle of the semester. As a temporary solution, a small classroom was set up in a smaller alternate location with existing computers and the available proctors.

Our next obstacle was the issue of web access. The online learning environment used for this pilot was largely designed and hosted by a popular textbook publisher. Therefore, students and faculty needed to log into the publisher's site for access to the course materials and videos. The videos and media used in the class required add-ons and scripts that had to be installed and tested ahead of time, browser by browser, computer by computer. However, the library faculty and staff were not given access to the online modules to activate and install plug-ins, players, and control software, so they were unable to test materials and exam modules to ensure their viability. Although library staffers were not teachers, they needed access at the teacher and student level in order to check the connectivity and reliability of the sites and media needed. A temporary thirty-day account was eventually created by the publisher, which allowed for the computers to be tested. We are still negotiating this issue and will need to resolve it permanently before the full implementation.

The day-to-day logistics rest solely on the staff and faculty of the library. The proctors arrive at the library to perform their assigned duties but the library is responsible for any hiccups along the way. The library has agreed to provide the paper and pencils for the student proctors, which means that these materials need to be purchased, stocked, and stored with consistent maintenance. Procedures for securing locker keys and SMART Board pens, allowing proctors to enter the testing location and so on, have to be implemented. Although these are not time-consuming duties, they still require staff time. Other library staff and faculty not involved in the project have to be flexible to allow their colleagues time to handle necessary tasks.

Of all of the details associated with the project, the day-to-day logistics were both the easiest and the most stressful. The other duties of the staff involved in this project were secondary to the success of this single project, which could affect all other meeting times and reference desk schedules. Figuring out where the library's responsibilities began, ended, and changed was always at the forefront. Turbulence is inevitable in any pilot project and glitches had to be fixed as the project matured.

CHALLENGES/HOW TO NAVIGATE/HINDSIGHT

1. Partnering with others:

How to Navigate

When considering a partnership with another unit or entity, study all of the possibilities, including alternative plans. In our case, even though everyone wanted the project to be successful it was clear that the library part of the project was not sufficiently outlined. We realized during the process that the library needed to take complete ownership of the project in order for us to succeed.

Hindsight

The library was excited to partner on this new collaborative endeavor with another department. However, there were instances in which we should have taken more ownership of the project. The library team realized that they needed to be at least as professionally astute as if we were sole owners of the project. Being a rookie to multidepartmental ventures made us prone to missteps, but over time we gathered our footing. This collaboration gave us the opportunity to learn.

2. Managing Money:

How to Navigate

Know the rules for the type of funding used for your project. We were extremely fortunate that our granting agency was just as dedicated to seeing the project succeed as we were, and allowed for us to make changes as needed. It is important to know what is allowed and what is not before committing to spend grant money on a project so significant to student success. Figuring out how to manage money that does not have one official owner is an uncharted territory without a beginner's guide. Keys to making this situation work to your best interest include asking questions, processing orders as early as possible, learning the purchasing processes, keeping track of procedural changes, staying in contact with vendors, and forming relationships with vendors and other project managers to avoid miscommunication when issues arise.

Hindsight

In hindsight, it would have been best if the library was able to have complete control over the money allocated for the project. Our spending would have been more efficient and our planning process would have been more concise and complete.

3. Vendor Selection:

How to Navigate

Choose your own vendors: Though this was a collaborative venture with another academic unit, because there was no mandate on the furnishings and technology, being "in charge" of our vendors was paramount to our success. Once we had our big hiccup with the first furniture vendor, we saw that we needed to take control of our part of the project. No one knows the library space as well as librarians. As our library project team had to learn a lot about space planning, technology infrastructures, and material composites in a very short time, it proved to be in our best interest to maintain control.

Hindsight

Looking back, awkward issues could have been avoided if the library had done more research on the intended vendors. Being new to completing a project of this size and scope was a disadvantage.

4. Tackling the Unknown

How to Navigate

Ask the hard questions so you can handle whatever unknowns arise. For example, we had to seek answers from vendors about the data-wire management of the library space. It was this question that led us to cancelling an order and securing another vendor, but it ultimately saved the project.

Hindsight

Dedicating a library space to a nonlibrary function is a hard call. On one hand, it seems like a natural extension of our services, meeting our students and faculty in the place of need. The library is a high-traffic space; it is open longer hours than academic buildings, and benefits from having more students come to us. We are a student destination and we want to engage even more students. Knowing the detailed limitations and advantages of the space is essential to the planning. It would have been advantageous to recognize the networking issues that existed before the project began. The room repurposed for the Math Emporium proctoring location is in the lower level of the library and had serious networking issues that limited the technical capabilities of the space. But now that we know, it is productive to document how the limitations of the space hindered the possibilities of the project. This knowledge could be used in the future to explain how our outdated space limits the manner in which we serve our constituents. In the long run, these reports could lead to more funding. In the current economic climate, having fact-based evidence is the best method to accumulate funding.

5. Planning Process:

How to Navigate

Plan, plan, plan, and then plan again. Navigating through a flawed planning process will be the most challenging part of the entire venture. Not knowing which way you are going day to day can destroy a project. No matter what the space looks like, no matter what state-of-the-art equipment and software you have, the planning phase can make or break your venture.

Hindsight

During the planning process you may encounter problems that will need to be solved on the fly with no time for forethought. This process has taught all those involved that plans will eventually change causing numerous stressful situations, so you need to plan for every eventuality, always have a plan B, and remember that the ultimate goal is to serve the students. With careful planning, implementation can be the easiest part of the process.

EVALUATION

Our own personal evaluation has two layers. First we believe we thought outside of the box. It is not often in the career of a librarian that you get to create things this big. Because of the fresh ideas presented and discovered by our library team, we were able to create a collaborative student and faculty space unlike any other in our building, and unlike any other on our campus. Sometimes libraries can be predictable and dull, but our space is unexpected, bright, and engaging. We made some tough choices, but we are proud of the decisions that we made because they are our own.

Second, we realize and recognize our missteps. There are things that we learned that will help us in future projects. Embarking on this venture made us exchange valuable meeting and instruction space for a less flexible computer lab space, but our commitment to collaborate and extend our services to the larger university community has definitely been demonstrated.

Formally, there are three evaluations in place for the first semester of the project. There is the standard university-wide end-of-course evaluation, a technology survey, and a customized survey for the developmental math students. The surveys are still being analyzed; however, a major change is already in place for the next phase of the pilot. Three additional servers will be prepared to stabilize the technology infrastructure, and a detailed pacing guide will be in place to help guide the students and faculty through the semester.

RECOMMENDATIONS

It is our recommendation that when embarking on a Math Emporium pilot/project, you need to remember the following keys to success:

- **Don't blame yourself.** The pilot is a test of the real thing. The pilot is supposed to be full of kinks and headaches, and all of the other unpredictable things that can cause havoc. But the purpose of the pilot is to iron out the kinks before the entire world sees them.
- **Listen.** It is important to listen to all of the different scenarios before making a decision. Once a project goes live, you do not want a lot of surprises. It is important to listen to what other staff are facing with their portion of the project, because it will likely affect you.
- **Plan before you act.** Some of the most frustrating parts of the pilot were the unexpected issues that we should have known about. The campus project team was so focused on the space planning that we lost sight of the technology planning (two more servers) and staff planning (assistants and proctors).
- **Plan your team wisely.** There should have been a logistics/administrative "expert" on the university team whose main purpose was to think of the real-world issues such as networks and staffing, and not just furniture and space. Be sure to have a well-rounded, well-informed team that will keep sight of all of the angles and components needed for the success of the project.

SUSTAINABILITY OF THE PROJECT

There were several hard lessons learned during the pilot. Ultimately we learned how much work is required to move a collaborative project forward. It takes tenacity, know-how, and willingness to learn. There were some unpredictable moments and questions that we were not prepared for, but learned a great deal from. Because of them, the library is more engaged and invested in the larger success of the university, and in a way that is very different from traditional research support. We learned about performance funding and the details of retrofitting government buildings. We learned about the vendor access and expectations. We also met some great partners and established lasting relationships with people outside of our building.

Will the project last? It is hard to say while we are still in the pilot phase. Issues with staffing and technology infrastructure would have to be handled successfully for the project to reach its full potential. Each of those issues would have to be stabilized before the project could become a cornerstone of developmental math on campus. Additionally, it is hard to predict whether students will succeed in the long term because of their involvement in the Math Emporium model. Data will be collected and analyzed before any permanent decisions can be made. Student success will determine the real sustainability of the project.

CONCLUSION

The future of the Math Emporium at our university library is still uncertain; the pilot phase is still underway. We are assessing the viability and efficacy of the project on our campus. We are also assessing the value of the proctoring location in the library. The library project team has learned a lot about the university community and hopes to partner with more academic units in the future. We are committed to helping our students succeed and collaborating can be a way to help them do it. We hope that more libraries will consider partnering with academic units, like math and engineering, to meet the students and faculty at their points of need.

WORK CITED

Twigg, Carol. "The Math Emporium: Higher Education's Silver Bullet," *Change,* 43(2011): 25–34

ELEVEN

The School Librarian Role in the *FIRST* LEGO League Team Project

Karla Steege Krueger

THE PROJECT

"Identify and learn about a problem": these six simple words comprise the first step for *FIRST* LEGO League (FLL) teams and should signal school librarians to seek out an FLL team in their schools or communities (firstlegoleague.org SENIOR SOLUTIONS Challenge, The Project). Step two states, "Create an Innovative Solution to the Problem You Identify." Although objectives for students to analyze and solve problems are common in school curricula, this often implies solving of mathematical or practical problems, rather than those that require information research. The FLL Project is different; students use multiple sources to research a thematic engineering topic, identify a specific problem and develop an innovative solution, either by creating something that doesn't exist or building upon something that does. This requires research and intense skills in digital literacy and digital inquiry for individuals and the team. Further, the project requires self-directed learning with minimal guidance from coaches.

Although the project might not be the primary draw for students ages 9–14 when they express interest in the school FLL team, it is equally as important as building and programming an autonomous robot. There are three parts to the annual FLL Challenge: the Robot Game (programming an autonomous robot to score points on a themed playing field); the Project (developing a solution to a problem they have identified); all guided by the FLL Core Values (teamwork, friendly competition, and independent initiative with guidance from coaches). Whereas previous articles have detailed robot competition technical selections (Habib 2012; Johnson and Londt 2010), the focus of this article is the FLL Project. The purpose of this chapter is to suggest contributions of school librarians in guiding students' digital literacy skills and inquiry research process, while promoting independent learning through the FLL Project.

SCHOOL LIBRARIAN OPPORTUNITIES

School librarians have a great deal to contribute to the overall mission of FLL. FLL is a partnership between *FIRST* (Foundation for Inspiration and Recognition of Science and Technology) and the LEGO Group. FLL has created a powerful program that helps young people discover the fun in science and technology and gain valuable employment and life skills. The founders seek to inspire teams through this process: "research, build, and experiment, and by doing so, they live the entire process of creating ideas, solving problems, and overcoming obstacles while gaining confidence in their abilities to positively use technology" (firstlegoleague.org, Mission).

Specifically, the FLL Project is an ideal design for team and school librarian collaboration because librarians are experts in helping students develop digital literacy skills and they specialize in fostering self-directed learner inquiry. Labeled by FLL as the "Challenge," the title is fitting for a scenario in which students will undertake inquiry research (many for the first time) of science- or engineering-related topics during an intense eight-week period. Further, students emerging from elementary classrooms where collaborative library research instruction and in-depth guided research practice are not the norm often struggle with understanding of the task, motivation about research, and research achievement. For many school librarians, this presents an opportunity to share these much-needed skills and creates an exciting experience for students in schools tied to standards and guidelines that rarely allow enough time in the regular curriculum for in-depth, student-led research.

Most important, even if a school does not currently send a team to an FLL regional competition, it does not preclude classroom teachers and school librarians from participating with students in these activities. FLL in its entirety may be used in a classroom setting, or even simply the Project could be a class activity with upper elementary or middle school students.

CLASSROOM APPLICATION FOR A MIDDLE SCHOOL LIBRARY/ TECHNOLOGY CLASS

School librarians who teach a middle school library or technology class might want to consider using the Project as a classroom, semester-long digital literacy and technology-based activity. The activities are appropriate for this class because students will use a range of technology systems to conduct research; students may use Web 2.0 tools, such as a wiki, Diigo, or GoogleSites, for group informational exchange; students research innovative technological solutions to an identified problem; and finally, students create presentations using technology tools. The glue that holds all these steps together, however, is the essential digital literacy and digital inquiry skills integration of the school librarian.

In the spirit of collaboration, the school librarian who embarks on this project may want to also involve the science teacher. Perhaps the science teacher would have students turn in their written presentation script in multiple drafts to verify accuracy of science content understanding. Likewise, a school librarian could suggest the activity to a middle school science teacher for the science and technology curriculum.

This chapter contains strategies for school librarians who may be team coaches or mentors, teachers who use an FLL Project in a class, or collaborators with other teachers. Regardless of the scenario, this chapter emphasizes the instrumental nature of the school librarian working with middle-grade students in this context to foster digital literacy skills, use of the inquiry research process, and independent inquiry learning.

SHARING, CELEBRATIONS, AND PUBLIC RELATIONS OPPORTUNITIES IN THE LIBRARY

For the Project presentation component, friendly competitions may be arranged in the classroom or library, or alternately, may be structured as noncompetitive sharing sessions. Since team projects are presented to an audience, this may even be the activity a school librarian could rally around and hold annually in the library, for example, during parent-teacher conference night so that parents, families, and the community could come in to watch team presentations.

A theme for a family night to showcase Project research could be derived from the FLL concept that this is a "Sport for the Mind" (firstlegoleague.org, Marketing Tools). Research is an exercise for the mind, and it requires practice to develop the muscle needed to work through this rigorous project.

INFORMATION LITERACY SKILLS: AMERICAN ASSOCIATION OF SCHOOL LIBRARIANS (AASL) STANDARDS FOR THE TWENTY-FIRST CENTURY LEARNER

Fortunately, the FLL judging criteria recognize research rigor for the Project, much in the same way the AASL (2007) identifies research standards for students. Table 11.1 shows connections between the FLL Project judging criteria and the AASL student standards. This confirms that those items that are held up as FLL judging expectations are also instructional standards for information literacy.

STRIPLING'S DIGITAL LITERACY AND DIGITAL INQUIRY AND FLL CONNECTION

Stripling (2010) defines digital literacy and digital inquiry. Digital literacy is defined as skills that include "more than the ability to read and write. Students must be able to gather information from any format and, more importantly, make sense of that information, use it, and communicate it to others" (Stripling 2010, 16). Digital inquiry is the active research process that helps students learn digital literacy skills: "connecting ideas to personal interests and a desire to know, asking questions that probe beyond simple fact gathering, investigating answers from multiple perspectives, constructing new understandings, expressing new ideas . . . , and reflecting on both the process and product" (Stripling 2010, 16). Digital literacy is by nature a combination of subtle skills gained through practice.

The six phases below are based on Stripling's Model of Inquiry. For each phase, I have selected one or two skill areas that are applicable to the FLL research problem. The explanations of these skills may make digital literacy and the inquiry process more transparent. Each of the phases of research includes a how-to tip for a student inquiry activity to facilitate that skill.

Stripling Phase #1 Connect

Stripling Digital Literacy Skill: Contextualization and Focus

Contextualization means students find a topic background and context; for example, through an online encyclopedia. This helps them identify prominent terms, dates, and people associated with it, and they use this overview to construct a schema to guide their research. Focus means the introduction of "central themes and big ideas" to help students "maintain focus as they encounter an overabundance of information" (Stripling 2010, 17).

Table 11.1 First Lego League Project Judging Criteria and AASL Student Standards

First Lego League Project Judging Criteria	AASL Standards for the 21 st Century Learner
Problem Identification: Clear definition of the problem being studied	**1.1.3** Develop and refine a range of questions to frame the search for new understanding.
Sources of Information: Types (e.g., books, magazines, websites, reports and other resources) and number of quality sources cited, including professionals in the field	**1.1.4** Find, evaluate, and select appropriate sources to answer questions. **2.2.1** Demonstrate flexibility in the use of resources by adapting information strategies to each specific resource and by seeking additional resources when clear conclusions cannot be drawn.
Problem Analysis: Depth to which the problem was studied and analyzed by the team	**1.2.1** Display initiative and engagement by posing questions and investigating the answers beyond the collection of superficial facts. **1.3.2** Seek divergent perspectives during information gathering and assessment.
Review Existing Solutions: Extent to which existing solutions were analyzed by the team, including an effort to verify the originality of the team's solution	**2.1.1** Continue an inquiry-based research process by applying critical-thinking skills (analysis, synthesis, evaluation, organization) to information and knowledge in order to construct new understandings, draw conclusions, and create new knowledge.
Team Solution: Clear explanation of the proposed solution	**2.1.2** Organize knowledge so that it is useful. **2.1.3** Use strategies to draw conclusions from information and apply knowledge to curricular areas, real-world situations, and further investigations.
Innovation: Solving the problem in a completely new way	**2.1.5** Collaborate with others to exchange ideas, develop new understandings, make decisions and solve problems.
Implementation: Consideration of factors for implementation (cost, ease of manufacturing, etc.)	**2.2.2** Use both divergent and convergent thinking to formulate alternative conclusions and test them against the evidence. **2.3.1** Connect understanding to the real world.
Sharing: Shared their project before the tournament with others who might benefit from the team's efforts	**2.1.6** Use the writing process, media, and visual literacy, and technology skills to create products that express new understandings. **3.1.3** Use writing and speaking skills to communicate new understandings effectively.

Student Inquiry Activity   Give students an initial topic for practice (i.e., presbycusis, a health issue of age-related hearing loss affecting senior citizens). Direct students to read about the topic from three given sources chosen to provide background and context for the topic: Britannica Online, National Institutes of Health, and the American Speech-Language-Hearing Association. Complete the activity, "Using Background Information to Brainstorm Ideas," adapted from the New York City information skills benchmarks for fifth grade (New York City Department of Education 2010). The rationale for giving students the initial three sources is to provide a common background for group discussions and keywords for accessing more specific articles online.

Stripling Phase #2 Wonder

Stripling Digital Literacy Skill: Questioning

"Scaffold the generation of students' questions by providing provocative and diverse sources as well as teaching students to question the text" (Stripling 2010, 18).

Student Inquiry Activity   Complete the activity, "Writing Questions that Lead to Investigations," adapted from the New York City Information Skills Benchmarks for fifth grade (New York City Department of Education 2010). This activity asks students to write out questions about their topic that interest them. Prompts help them to rewrite and improve their questions several times: "Will there be facts as well as opinions about this topic?" Give examples. "Do the questions go beyond a yes/no answer?" How? "Are the questions complex enough to require information beyond a few simple facts?" How? "Do the questions lead to investigating multiple points of view?" How? Finally, students revise their questions to make them even more interesting and complex.

Stripling Phase #3 Investigate

Stripling Digital Literacy Skill: Sourcing

Sourcing is "determining the authority of sources." The criteria for evaluating sources include items such as "authority, purpose, currency, credibility, and perspective" (Stripling 2010, 18).

Student Inquiry Activity   Once students select a variety of useful sources for their topic, figure 11.1, Evaluating ABCD (authority, bias, coverage, date), may be completed for each of the students' selected sources. As students complete the questions, they discuss each source, analyze diverse perspectives, and potentially eliminate sources and identify gaps.

Stripling Phase #4 Construct

Stripling Digital Literacy Skill: Synthesis

"Students need to be able to synthesize large amounts of specific bits of information and ideas and weave them into a meaningful whole of substantiated opinions, valid conclusions, and conceptual understand-

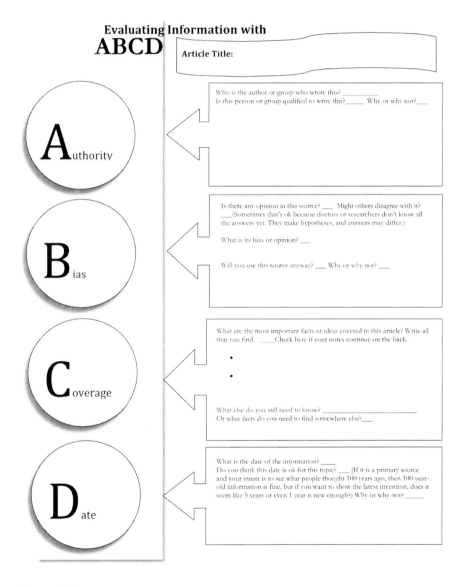

Figure 11.1.

ing. Specific strategies must be taught, such as determining the importance of ideas, identifying main ideas and supporting evidence, combining ideas to develop robust arguments, and interpreting ideas in relation to similar and contrasting information" (Stripling 2010, 19).

Student Inquiry Activity   Complete the activity, "Notetaking by Question," adapted from the New York City information skills benchmarks for fifth grade (New York City Department of Education 2010). Students take notes on a chart specific to each of three questions they are asking. Notes include listing important information, paraphrasing it in their own words, and identifying key words.

Stripling Phase #5 Express

Stripling Digital Literacy Skill: Shared Learning

"Students must be taught the skills of collaboration to build shared understandings with their peers" (Stripling 2010, 19).

Student Inquiry Activity   Table 11.2 shows a structured discussion activity that may be used with a small group of students to ensure that all group members have a chance to talk. "No Talk, All Talk, Any Talk" activity rules are adapted from Stephen Brookfield's (2012) "Circle of Voices" activity.

Stripling Phase #6 Reflect

Stripling Digital Literacy Skill: Metacognition and Self-Assessment

This stage is for students to reflect back upon the research process and the product of their learning (Stripling 2010).

Student Inquiry Activity   Complete the activity, "Strengths and Goals," adapted from the New York City information skills benchmarks for fifth grade (New York City Department of Education 2010). Students list three things they did well and why, and three things that could have been better and why.

CONCLUSION

One FLL middle school student who has experienced a recent breakthrough in understanding the research process, as a result of librarian-led, digital inquiry activities, expressed his perspective about the subtle ways completing the research packet from the school librarian may have helped: "It's kind of more like advice. You read the questions over and over. Have someone else read it. When you have someone with a different voice read it, it sounds different. You say, 'Oh, now I get it.' It's like you need another tone." Finally, asked specifically how a school librarian

Table 11.2 No Talk, All Talk, Any Talk

Questions (replace with new questions each meeting):

1. What have you learned so far about seniors that you didn't know before?

2. What is an important problem seniors have to deal with?

3. What is one way we could help solve a problem seniors have to deal with?

Activity: No Talk, All Talk, Any Talk

Rules:

1. No talk. For 2 minutes; let people think quietly or jot down ideas

2. All talk. For 1 min. each, 1 at a time, uninterrupted by others, go around circle, in order.

3. Any talk. For 1 min each, must respond to what someone else said–may agree, disagree, or ask a question.

Examples: "I like that idea because . . ." or "That's good thinking, but I'm not sure if that idea would work because . . ." or "What do you think would happen if we . . ."

could help the research process elicited a response about research activities that may take place in the physical space of the library, the student said, "Go to the library. Most school libraries have computers. They [librarians] are good researchers. It's why they have that job. They like to help people find things. You ask the school librarian where would be a book I could find on this? Teachers could also help. Tell them I have this thing, and I'm not sure I understand the question."

Interestingly, although none of the school librarian-led inquiry activities took place physically in the school library, the student connected thoughts about library research to the physical space. School library standards have distinguished between the basic ability to physically locate information sources and the more rigorous ability to access information intellectually (American Association of School Librarians 2007; American Association of School Librarians and Association for Educational Communications and Technology 1998). The rigor of intellectual access has increased as users are required to become their own quality control experts in the world of Internet self-publishing and commercialization. Interestingly common public perception is that physical access to information is easier with online sources, and little attention has been directed to the increased demands of intellectual access (Krueger 2009). While intellectual access remains the more challenging aspect of the research process, much like in athletics, the training needed to improve requires a highly skilled coach and often takes place behind the scenes. Given that much of students' current access to resources is digital, the school librarians' role in teaching about intellectual access has dramatically increased (Stripling 2010). The FLL research activity provides an exciting context for the school librarians to connect with students involved in online research and to enhance the library online presence in the virtual space of the school web pages to serve this need.

In conclusion, school librarians are essential to FLL teams who engage in the research process for several reasons. School librarians help students connect with initial background sources, wonder about the variety and conflicting information, find and use information for a problem-solving purpose, identify the best quality and variety of sources, interpret information for their purpose, and communicate their findings. FLL provides a list of websites, however, school librarians are also able to tap into local or regionally provided print and databases available to students in their schools. School librarians also help students navigate through complex information, multiple sources and authority levels, and biases while motivating students and supporting them through this process. This is especially important for students of the middle school age group who may be experiencing this level of research for the first time.

WORKS CITED

American Association of School Librarians. 2007. "Standards for 21st-Century Learners." Last modified 2007. Accessed October 2, 2012. http://www.ala.org/aasl/sites/ala.org.aasl/files/content/guidelinesandstandards/learningstandards/AASL_Learning_Standards_2007.pdf

American Association of School Librarians and Association for Educational Communications and Technology. 1998. *Information Power: Building Partnerships for Learning.* Chicago: American Library Association.

Brookfield, Stephen. 2012. "Circle of Voices." In "Teaching Critical Thinking Across the Disciplines" PowerPoint. In "Workshop Materials." *Dr. Stephen D. Brookfield.* Accessed October 15, 2012. http://www.stephenbrookfield.com/Dr._Stephen_D._Brookfield/Workshop_Materials.html

FIRST LEGO League. 2012a. "2012 Senior Solutions Challenge." *First Lego League.* Accessed October 2, 2012. http://www.firstlegoleague.org/challenge/2012seniorsolutions

FIRST LEGO League. 2012b. "FLL Marketing Tools." *First Lego League.* Accessed October 2, 2012. http://www.usfirst.org/roboticsprograms/marketing-tools/fll

FIRST LEGO League. 2012c. "Support Our Mission." *First Lego League.* Accessed October 2, 2012. http://www.firstlegoleague.org/mission/support

Habib, Maria A. 2012. "Robotics Competitions: An Overview of *FIRST* Events and VEX Competitions." *Journal of Extension,* 50(3): Article Number 3IAW3. Accessed October 2, 2012. http://www.joe.org/joe/2012june/pdf/JOE_v50_3iw3.pdf

Johnson, Richard T., and Susan E. Londt. 2010. "Robotics Competitions: The Choice Is Up to You!" Tech Directions, 69(6): 16–20.

Krueger, Karla S. 2009. "A Case Study of a Rural Iowa School Preparing to Meet New State Guidelines for School Libraries." *School Library Media Research,* 12. Last modified 2009. Accessed October 2, 2012. http://www.ala.org/aasl/aaslpubsandjournals/slmrb/slmrcontents/volume12/krueger

New York City Department of Education/Office of Library Services, New York City School Library System. 2010. "Information Fluency Continuum: Benchmark Skills for Grades K–12 Assessments." Last modified 2010. Accessed October 2, 2012. http://schools.nyc.gov/NR/rdonlyres/27A1E84E-65EB-4A54-80DF-51E28D34BF4F/0/InformationFluencyContinuum.pdf

Stripling, Barbara. 2010. "Teaching Students to Think in the Digital Environment: Digital Literacy and Digital Inquiry." *School Library Monthly,* 26(8): 16–19.

TWELVE

STEM Library Services for High School Students Enrolled as University Students: STEMming From Scratch

Janna Mattson and Heather Groves Hannan

The United States' competitiveness and individual success has increasingly been tied to the emphasis placed on STEM (science, technology, engineering, and math) education. Dual-enrolled George Mason University students who are also high school students in Virginia Governor's School @ Innovation Park are a growing contingent of students who are immersed in STEM learning and research. Their experience differs from other STEM programming in that their learning environment partners with a four-year collegiate institution. These gifted high school juniors and seniors excelling in STEM with a focus on earth sustainability are held to the same conduct codes as traditional college freshmen.

The authors will share practical matters concerning the development of the George Mason University Mercer Library's response to this new program as well as addressing communication, materials requests, and collection development with STEM faculty. Emphasis is placed on clear communication with parents and students as well as communication among library staff. Finally, the authors will give examples of STEM assignment-based library instruction as well as STEM resource suggestions.

PRACTICAL MATTERS

In 2006, there were eighteen Governor's Schools in the state of Virginia: from Abingdon to Lynchburg to Norfolk and up to Warrenton, Virginia. Schools were academic-year, summer-residential, and summer-regional. Up to that point, none of the schools were associated with a four-year institution though several were partnered with various community colleges in their area. In February 2007, Michael I. Otaigbe, Ph.D., Coles District Prince William County School Board Member, thought of by many as the "father of the Governor's School" on George Mason University's Prince William campus, made a request to the Prince William County Public Schools to explore the possibility of a regional academic year Governor's School (Carmichael 2012). By September 2010, all of the necessary approvals, curriculum development, and student applications were finished and the first class of high school juniors started their coursework in a STEM program focused on earth sustainability in the Governor's School @ Innovation Park on George Mason University's Prince William Campus, Manassas, Virginia. Integrating support for the Governor's School into the workflow of Mercer Library, George Mason University Library's Prince William campus facility, required a review of current liaison librarian assignments:

> Serving as the Libraries' primary contacts for specific academic departments and some administrative units, liaisons are responsible for providing a variety of library services, programs, and outreach to the University community. The essence of the role played by a liaison is to foster two-way communication between the Library and the university's academic programs on all campuses. Liaisons serve specific subject needs on their "home" campus, though in some cases the liaison may serve an entire academic program. As academic programs grow or shift, adjustments in liaison assignments may be made to assure that the local library reflects and supports the current local campus environment" (George Mason University Libraries Library Advisory Team 2005).

Given the Governor's School's underlying educational focus, the head of Mercer Library decided the social sciences liaison librarian on the Mercer Library team would assume responsibility to the program. She was to be supported on an as-needed basis by other subject-area liaison librarians to meet the science-related curriculum focus. Blending expertise to meet a program's needs has been the rule of thumb for George Mason University Libraries' support.

Other changes to workflow came later. After the Governor's School had been on campus for one academic year, it was apparent that Mercer Library needed to adjust its hours of operation. Patron head-count data collected hourly by circulation personnel showed that Mercer Library needed to be open earlier than historically was necessary for traditional college students, faculty, and staff. Furthermore, when the Governor's School opened on Mason's Prince William campus, Mercer Library staff consisted of one library manager, two liaison librarians, five paraprofessionals, one graduate research assistant, and various part-time wage employees. Because of the growth of Mason's Prince William campus due to the Governor's School and a new medical education program as well as the rapid growth of Mason's recreation, health, and tourism department (also based on Mason's Prince William Campus), the head of Mercer Library submitted paperwork requesting the addition of a team member to the library. With the approval of the new team member all the employee work profiles were reviewed, adjusted, and aligned to meet the growing service needs from access services to reference assistance to instruction support. It was also clear that cross-training provided to Mercer Library team members would need to be reviewed, revised, and enhanced to maintain a satisfactory level of customer service.

In addition to customer service training, library staff was trained by university departments outside of library services. Traditional college students expect that certain university services will be made available to them. Services such as copyright guidance or assistive technology were not readily expected by the Governor's School students, but staff training in these areas gave library staff the knowledge base they needed to be prepared for the growing needs of the Mercer Library users, Governor's School students included. Mercer Library opened these instructional sessions to the Mason community as part of library research instruction as well as offered drop-in opportunities for those students needing additional help with understanding both what was expected concerning copyright adherence and what was offered through assistive services for students with physical or visual challenges.

COMMUNICATION WITH STEM FACULTY

Regular and good communication with STEM faculty is essential to meeting the needs of both STEM faculty and students. STEM faculty at Mason come from a wide variety of past work experiences so nothing was assumed in terms of their academic library experience. For example, faculty needed to be informed about the procedure for requesting library materials so that expectations could be managed as to how quickly items would be available for use. Given that Mason Libraries is a distributed system with five libraries that meet the needs of 30,000+ users, getting requests in as early as possible is important. At the beginning of the Governor's School program, this was not always possible as faculty members were being hired through the end of August just before the school year began in September. It was useful to let faculty know that while rush orders were certainly acceptable, the materials cost a premium, which made funds less available for future library materials purchases. Reminders of library materials purchase procedures are sent at the end of the school year before faculty leave for the summer.

Another benefit of the partnership with Mason to the STEM students and faculty is that the library collection was already rich in STEM materials before the program came to Mason. STEM faculty members are most interested in supplementing student learning with journal articles and appropriate web resources. Mason's database subscriptions are more than adequate to meet the student and faculty research needs. A quick orientation of where to find the databases on Mason Libraries' webpage was all that the faculty (though not the students) needed. Any print and media collection development is completely driven by faculty. Examples of materials purchased are AP Exam study guides and educational science films for faculty.

In addition to familiarizing faculty with library procedures and databases, it is important to introduce them to library support staff and other library services. The aforementioned AP Exam study guides were placed on reserve, so faculty members were introduced to Mercer Library's Reserves Coordinator. Faculty members also need to know whom to point their students to should any circulation issues arise. Introductions were made either in person or through e-mail.

STEM Director Karen Dalfrey indicated that she wanted students to learn how to use Zotero (search "Zotero" in your web browser), a free research and bibliographic management tool developed at Mason, during preliminary meetings with the librarian. The librarian planned a hands-on workshop for the students for mid-September; however, there was one minor roadblock in regards to the technology needed for the students to use Zotero. Zotero is a Firefox extension, but the students were only allowed to use Internet Explorer on the laptops their base high schools provided to them. Unfortunately, this discovery was not made until the day of the workshop, but a statement provided by the librarian for the STEM Director to forward to the students' respective IT departments sufficed to allow the students to be able to download Firefox onto their laptops. It is important to remember that while the high school students are expected to work at the academic level of traditional university students, they do not necessarily have the same autonomy over their technology choices that regular university students have. It is necessary to be an advocate for their learning, above all, whenever possible.

COMMUNICATION WITH PARENTS AND STUDENTS

Joining a university community as a high school junior or senior may expose a young person to content that might be deemed unfitting if a clear context is not shared. During an orientation coordinated by the

Governor's School administration the library presented an informational reality to the parents of the STEM students. Unlike the public school system, there are no filters or restrictions placed on the resources provided for use at the collegiate level. Students may view or check out materials they choose necessary for their coursework. Given the strong science focus of the Prince William campus, which includes several medical-related programs of study and research, some materials in the Mercer Library collection contain graphic, explicit, and detailed content both in print as well as viewable via electronic means. Parents needed to understand that not only would their STEM students have access to materials from within the Mason libraries system, but they would also have the ability to request materials from almost anywhere via the document delivery services offered as a standard service through the Mason libraries system. Furthermore, the STEM students would be charged the same fines and fees should materials not be returned in a timely manner or not returned in an acceptable condition.

The students also received their own information session. The school districts in which the STEM students are enrolled begin school after Labor Day, but George Mason University begins classes the week earlier. Dual enrolled high school students are required to be on campus and hold class at that time. STEM faculty took this opportunity to orient students to the program and to the campus in what they called "Boot Camp Week." The year the Governor's School began included a general library orientation that had three components, a general library information session (library 101), a library tour, and an opportunity for the students to link their identification cards to the Mason libraries circulation system.

The general library information session, library 101, included very basic and practical information including operational hours of Mercer Library, the students' "home-base library," the names and locations of the five Mason libraries, and general circulation policies. The facilitators also pointed students in the right direction to find the resources they needed for their assignments. While these are very general details that have little to do with STEM learning, it is important to remember that these students are being put into an adult learning environment while they are still minors. There is a definite shift in the way students need to use the library and access materials. It is necessary to make students aware that the university library is a different environment from their high school library. Library items were not necessarily right at their fingertips given the distributed nature of George Mason University. Learning to plan ahead when doing research is a particular lesson that was reinforced not only in library 101, but in assignment-specific library instruction workshops, which will be discussed later in this chapter.

While the expectation is that these high school students utilize the library as university students, this does not mean that their age was not considered when planning library 101 sessions. The presentation included several pop quizzes, which gave the students opportunities to win small prizes (in this case, candy bars). This brought an element of fun to a potentially dry presentation. The students enjoyed the friendly competition and were more apt to listen to the presentation.

Finally, a large academic library system can be overwhelming for the average college freshman and it is potentially even more so for a sixteen-year-old high school student. After library 101, the students were broken up into small groups, given a quick library tour, and then given the opportunity to have their university identification cards linked to the library circulation system. While this is not typical of the way library instruction occurs for a regular undergraduate student at Mercer Library, the STEM students' age and relative inexperience were taken into consideration when making this decision.

ASSIGNMENT-BASED LIBRARY INSTRUCTION

It is crucial to make library resource instruction as practical and relevant to the student as possible. It is not necessary to repeat basic library information (hours, circulation policies, etc.) during each interaction with students. Instead, "teaching students the tools of information literacy and how to use them over time via step-wise exposure to research skills" will be much more effective for most students, particularly those new to academic library research (Scarmozzino 2010, 317). While it is the librarian's job to teach the students how to choose appropriate resources and how to use them, it is ultimately the students' job to choose appropriate information for their topics, making them the subject matter experts. When developing library research workshops, do not be afraid to ask for help from other librarians who may have more experience in STEM resources. The librarian who worked with high school students relied on the expertise of subject specialist colleagues, including the life sciences, chemistry, and engineering librarians, to choose appropriate resources for the Governor's School students. However, if other librarians are not available for assistance, the National Science Digital Library (search "NSDL" in your browser) is a great place to start.

The librarian has had multiple opportunities to work with the Governor's School students using the assignment-specific approach. For example, a group of students had an assignment that involved phage biology research. To conduct their research, they learned how to use MEDLINE database. Another group of students had to complete a rather extensive taxonomy project. For this project they needed to find multiple images of various organisms and write scientific description about those organisms. This was a great opportunity to teach the students about finding sound information on the Internet and using the Mason libraries' catalog to find books, both electronic and print, about scientific description. Finally, when another group of students were challenged to design their own rockets, the librarian compiled a short list of relevant journal articles, along with a live demonstration of how to look up journal articles through the Mason libraries' website. The librarian also worked with the students to find pertinent information on the NASA website (search "NASA" and "higher education" in your web browser). All of these resources are posted on an online information guide the librarian created specifically for the Governor's School, which will be discussed later in this chapter.

COMMUNICATION AMONG LIBRARY STAFF MEMBERS

Clear communication with one's work colleagues is necessary to provide effective library services. Continuous communication is vital both in the planning process and after student instruction has occurred. During the planning process, the librarian assigned to the Governor's School gave other library staff an opportunity to provide input as to what information should be included in library 101. Circulation staff members have invaluable insight on library user behavior, particularly common mistakes new users make. It is wise to use that insight when planning an orientation for a new student population.

Communication, formal (staff meetings) and informal (quick informational e-mails), should be encouraged as the academic year progresses. For example, early in the academic year during the first year of the Governor's School, students needed to print something in the library for their class. Like most universities, Mason uses a pay-for-print system connected to student ID cards/student accounts, but many of the students had no funds available on their cards and no way to add money to their accounts at that exact moment. Circulation staff assisted students by allowing them to print behind the circulation desk free of charge. Staff communicated that incident to the liaison librarian, who then alerted the Governor's School director. Clearly, this was a communication deficiency that was noted and would be addressed for future student orientations.

Making library staff members aware of any student assignments, projects, and general information needs is also incredibly useful. This is particularly important since Governor's School hours did not always coincide with the liaison librarian's hours. Once the librarian had the opportunity to learn more about the STEM curriculum, information was communicated back to library staff. In addition, the librarian created an online information guide especially for the Governor's School students to include assignment-specific resource recommendations whenever possible (search "Governor's School" and "infoguide" and "George Mason University" in your web browser). The librarian trained all library staff members to utilize the Governor's School @ Information Park Infoguide to assist students in the librarian's absence.

Communication and collaboration are the key elements in developing and delivering library services to STEM students and faculty. These two factors are especially important in helping meet the needs of a new STEM program like the Governor's School @ Innovation Park. As the demand for STEM education increases in the United States educational system, academic librarians will be responsible for meeting the research needs of these students and faculty, often without the "content knowledge expertise to teach discipline-based information retrieval skills" (Scarmozzino 2010). As librarians, we excel at finding the best possible resources for the question at hand. Using our existing skill set and knowledge base as well as adopting an assignment-specific and step-by-step approach to teaching research skills to STEM students will best meet the needs of the novice researcher.

WORKS CITED

Carmichael, Ronald. 2012. "Interview with Ronald Carmichael, Executive Officer, Prince William Operations."

George Mason University Libraries Library Advisory Team. 2005. "Liaison Librarian Program: Statement on Library Roles & Focus and Liaison Program."

Scarmozzino, Jeanine M. 2010. "Integrating STEM Information Competencies into an Undergraduate Curriculum." *Journal of Library Administration* 50 (4) (June): 315–33. doi: 10.1080/01930821003666981.

IV

Collection Development

THIRTEEN

How to Get Science Going

Keary Bramwell

Over the past several years, libraries have seen an increased demand for materials to help develop young patrons' skills in science, technology, engineering, and mathematics (STEM). To meet the community demand for materials in these STEM subjects, and to make science more accessible to children, the Mount Prospect Public Library (MPPL) designed and developed Science-to-Go Kits, which are used in in-house programs and which circulate to the general public.

In 2009, MPPL received a grant from the Institute of Electrical and Electronics Engineers–Chicago Section (IEEE) to purchase science equipment for library circulation. The IEEE's generosity allowed the library to develop seven "kits," as well as a collection of related print and audiovisual materials. Each Science-to-Go Kit includes all the elements needed to carry out a science experiment or activity. MPPL designed its kits for use by children in kindergarten through grade six; however many of the kits interest children older than grade six.

There are two target audiences for the Science-to-Go Kits. First, MPPL uses the kits for in-house science programming. Second, the kits circulate to home-schooled children, scouting troops, daycares, teachers, and the rest of the general public. The public benefits from the kits, which provide access to expensive material that might otherwise be unavailable.

MPPL's kits predominantly teach about electricity and electronics due to the IEEE's involvement in their creation. Given the Science-to-Go Kits initial success, MPPL is considering expanding its program to other topics including kits on weather or magnets. But, ultimately, a library seeking to create its own kits must consider the needs and interests of its patrons.

FUNDING

MPPL created its kits through a grant; however, grants are not a library's only source of funding. An easy way to fund the creation of Science-to-Go Kits might be to assign funds from the general collection budget to cover science kits as a new area of the collection. Another way to fund Science-to-Go Kits would be to approach a Friends of the Library group. A library seeking nontraditional sources of funding might also approach a local business or organization to provide funding, especially one that hires individuals with science degrees.

WHAT MPPL INCLUDES IN ITS KITS

Along with the scientific equipment detailed below, each kit includes a binder with supplemental material containing directions for experiments, background information, teacher guides, and a glossary of technical terms. Instructions for the science equipment are particularly important because patrons using the kits may not have science backgrounds. Parents who were initially intimidated by the prospective of having to conduct science experiments, were relieved to find the detailed instructions. The teachers' guides contain entire lesson plans and connect the activities to national science standards. This makes it easier to use the kits in the classroom and makes the kits more appealing for teachers to checkout.

In addition to specific subject matter information, each binder contains an investigation log that students can photocopy and complete. This log covers the scientific process and has sections for children to write questions, predictions, procedures, materials needed, and investigation notes. It also doubles as a worksheet for teachers.

Finally, each binder contains a list of websites where interested patrons can learn more about the topics explored in the kits or look for a list of additional activities. Most of the websites are government sites, including NASA Education, NEED (National Energy Education Development) Project, and Energy Kids from the US Energy Information Administration. An alternative option would be to include a book or two on the topic in the kit.

MPPL'S SCIENCE-TO-GO KITS

1. VAN DE GRAAFF GENERATOR KIT

- Topic covered: static electricity
- Description: A Van de Graaff Generator creates static electricity. Frequently seen in museums, it is best known for making some-

one's hair stand on end. Directions for other experiments, such as a minivolcano and flying saucers, are included. The kit includes six 6-inch aluminum pie tins for use in one of the experiments.

- Cost: MPPL purchased a VG200 200-kV Van de Graaff Generator from Ramsey Electronics for $139.95, and a discharge wand from Science First for $42.95. Other sources are available for both items. It is easiest to purchase a Van de Graaff preassembled. Some are sold as kits that require assembly. To take full advantage of the Van de Graaff Generator's capabilities; we found that the discharge wand is a necessity.
- Storage: the Van de Graaff Generator is kept in a large plastic container with foam padding.
- Usage: Adult supervision is necessary for all Van de Graaff experiments. The kit is used for demonstrations as well as hands-on experiments and is good for large or small groups. It also works well for in-house library programs. And at least one of our patrons used the Van de Graaff in a science fair project.
- Feedback: Not everyone will be comfortable using a Van de Graaff because it could shock the user. Typically, the shock is uncomfortable. There are steps you can take to ensure you are not shocked. This is where the discharge wand comes in very handy. It is important to have very clear directions included in this kit so patrons can operate the generator without a shock, unless they desire one.
- Overall: This kit impresses patrons. If you plan on purchasing just one kit to start, this is a good option. It is showy, obviously science, patrons would not have easy access to one otherwise, and it can be showcased at programs.

2. ENERGY LAB KIT

- Topic covered: energy sources
- Description: This kit demonstrates different ways to produce electricity, including the production of electricity by wind power, solar power, and chemical power. Users select an energy source and then use it to power either a buzzer or a light. Children see just how much electrical power it takes to accomplish each task and can compare the efficiency of each energy source. Additional information about alternative energy is included in the binder.
- Cost: Since MPPL purchased an ELENCO Alternative Energy Lab for $53.95 from Discover This, the model has been discontinued. An alternative model to consider would be the Thames & Kosmos kits on solar power, wind power, or hydropower.

- Storage: The shape of the energy lab makes storage challenging. We keep it in a plastic container with foam padding customized to fit its unique shape.
- Usage: The ELENCO Alternative Energy Lab works best for small groups or individuals. Children would have difficulty seeing the various experiments in larger groups; however, children generally do not need adult assistance when using it. MPPL does not use this kit in our science programs.
- Feedback: While this kit is popular with patrons, durability is a concern. After fixing the kit multiple times, it failed completely after two years. The chemical cells (which patrons use to test liquids) frequently did not work properly. The wires connecting energy sources also broke easily and needed to be replaced or repaired on several occasions.
- Overall: Alternative energy is popular and patrons want more on the topic. This kit does that for a low price, but breaks frequently.

3. SNAP CIRCUITS KIT

- Topic covered: circuits
- Description: SNAP CIRCUITS are small components that snap together to create working electronic circuits. Two sets of SNAP CIRCUITS make up this kit. They are SNAP CIRCUITS Jr. 100 Electronics Set and SNAP CIRCUITS Green Alternative Energy Set. The instructions are color coded for easy to follow projects.
- Cost: MPPL purchased SNAP CIRCUITS Jr. 100 Electronics Set for $29.95 and Green Alternative Energy Kit for $67.95 from Discover This. SNAP CIRCUITS can be purchased from numerous sources, including Amazon and most toy stores.
- Storage: The SNAP CIRCUITS are kept in their original boxes inside a canvas bag. Once the boxes wear down, MPPL plans to transfer the components to a tackle box or other plastic container with numerous sections. This will keep the parts separate and easy to access.
- Usage: SNAP CIRCUITS work best for individuals or small groups of children ages eight and up. They are not used for library programs.
- Feedback: Missing or broken pieces have been an issue with this kit. Purchasing two sets of each kit to start limits the need to reorder lost pieces. However, it has been easy to order replacement pieces from ELENCO Electronics, Inc, the maker of SNAP CIRCUITS.
- Overall: Have a picture of what all the parts look like and where each should be stored in the container. This helps patrons make

sure they return all the parts. It also helps staff inspect the kit when it is returned. While it might take some time to set up, the investment in time will make it easier to track whether the patrons have returned all the pieces after the kit circulates.

4. 75-IN-1 ELECTRONIC PROJECT LAB KIT

- Description: Similar to SNAP CIRCUITS, but more advanced. The 75-in-1 Electronic Project Lab is a board that uses the wire-and-spring method to teach about electronics and electricity. The lab comes with directions for seventy-five projects. Children connect wires to complete the projects.
- Cost: MPPL purchased the ELENCO 75-in-1 Electronic Project Lab for $47.95 from Discover This.
- Storage: We keep it in the original box placed inside a canvas bag to make transport easier.
- Usage: The kit is best for upper elementary school children. Younger students might have trouble with the directions and the concepts could be beyond them. The kit is best for individual usage. It does not work well with small groups or as a demonstration and has not been used for any library programs.
- Feedback: Fixing the kit is difficult. The wiring is all inside and hard to access unless you take apart the kit. It is easier to just replace the kit than to try and repair it, unless you are familiar with electronic repair.
- Overall: Teachers have trouble using this kit for classes since it works best one-on-one and children do not gravitate to it the same as they do to the SNAP CIRCUITS. If you had to choose either the Electronic Project Lab or the SNAP CIRCUITS, then choose the SNAP CIRCUITS.

5. EARLY STRUCTURES KIT & EARLY SIMPLE MACHINE KIT

- Topics covered: structures/simple machines
- Description (early structures): 107 LEGO DUPLO bricks including a mix of specialty and traditional pieces. Problem-solving cards and teacher notes guide children on basic structure concepts, including balance, and stability. Children can also design their own structures using ideas found in the *Story Starters* (LEGO Group 2007) book included.
- Description (early simple machines): 102 LEGO DUPLO bricks including a mix of specialty and traditional pieces. Problem-solving cards and teacher notes guide children on how to build simple models, including a seesaw, spinning top, and rolling vehicle. Chil-

dren work with pulleys, levers, gears, and wheels and axles while building the models. They can also construct their own models using ideas found in the *Story Starters* (LEGO Group 2007) book included.

- Cost (early structures): MPPL purchased the DUPLO Early Structures Set for $96.95 and Story Starters (LEGO Group 2007) for $29.95 from LEGO Education.
- Cost (early simple machines): MPPL purchased the DUPLO Early Simple Machines Set III for $116.95, along with the teacher's guide for $9.95, activity pack for $30.95, and Story Starters (LEGO Group 2007) for $29.95 from LEGO Education.
- Storage: The sets come in large plastic tubs that we placed inside a canvas bag for easier transport. A picture of all the parts is included.
- Usage: Teams of 2–3 children or individuals use the kits best. Both kits were demonstrated in library programs.
- Feedback: Both kits connect to many science units in school and are popular with teachers. Some patrons also checkout the kit just to play with the LEGO bricks. Do not be discouraged by this. It still serves a need in the community and provides access to items patrons want.
- Overall: Both kits are popular with patrons, but not with staff. The many pieces can make it difficult to check-in. Pieces do get lost, but not as often as expected considering the number included.

6. STRAW ROCKET LAUNCHER KIT

- Topic covered: ballistics
- Description: The Straw Rocket Launcher does just that—you create rockets out of straws, modeling clay, and paper. Then you launch the straw rockets using pneumatic force. It works best outdoors or in a room with high ceilings. Patrons can adjust the launch angle and the force used to launch. The combination of variables creates nearly endless launch possibilities.
- Cost: MPPL purchased the Straw Rocket Launcher for $169 along with the teacher's guide for $24.95 from LEGO Education.
- Storage: The launcher is kept in a large trunk with wheels. Staff cut foam to fit in the bottom and cushion the launcher. It also keeps the launcher from moving during transport.
- Usage: The launcher works with individuals, small groups, or as a demonstration. Age is not as much of a concern with this kit since younger students can make the rockets and an adult can launch the rockets. MPPL demonstrated the launcher at an indoor library pro-

gram successfully. When demonstrated indoors use caution and make sure the ceilings are high enough.

- Feedback: This is the largest kit, so size is a concern. While the launcher does not weigh much, the size makes it awkward to carry. It can still be carried by one person, but a young child would have trouble. The wheels do help with transport. Maintenance has not been as issue. While the launcher rod came apart once, our staff fixed it.
- Overall: Popular with patrons and easier to use than the Van de Graaff Generator. Patrons would not normally have access to this impressive piece of equipment. MPPL highly recommend purchasing this kit.

CATALOGING

MPPL designed original cataloging for its kits based on Anglo-American Cataloguing Rules, Second Edition (AACR2). It was important to make the kits easy for patrons to find so Science-to-Go was included in the title and "science kit" became part of the call number. The kits come up first when patrons search for "science kit," "science-to-go kits," or "science-to-go."

CIRCULATION AND STORAGE

Kits circulate to MPPL cardholders only for three weeks with an overdue charge of $0.10 per day. The kits are not available for interlibrary loan or for nonresidents to checkout. Holds and renewals are allowed. There is a limit of one kit per library card. Teachers may checkout kits on their school card.

MPPL stores the kits in a staff area that is not accessible to the public. When a patron wants to checkout one of the kits, they need to ask the youth desk to get the appropriate kit for them. The kits are too large to fit easily on a shelf making public storage dangerous. There is also nothing on the kits to stop patrons from opening them on the shelf, which could lead to in-house usage and lost pieces.

MAINTAINING THE KITS

Maintaining a collection is not expensive. Replacement parts do not always cost very much, and range from $0.50 to $19. Most pieces cost between $1 and $5. On average five to ten pieces have been lost per year. The main cost is actually staff time maintaining the kits. Generally very little staff time is involved, but when a problem comes up, such as lost or broken pieces, it may take 2–3 hours or more to solve it depending on the complexity of the problem. On average, problems come up six to seven times a year.

The youth services staff inspects the kits when they are returned after usage. This is not a task we delegate to circulation staff. To streamline care of the kits there is a youth science kit point person. She takes care of fixing problems and is the go-to person for issues that may come up. If the point person is present, she will inspect the kits. All youth services staff know how to inspect the kits and do so if the point person is not present when a kit is returned. To aid the check-in, guidelines were created that spell out what staff needed to look for on each kit. Some of the kits also include a picture of all the parts. Staff matches the parts in the kit to those in the picture to see if any are missing. This especially helps with the kits that contain numerous or specialty parts, such as SNAP CIR-CUITS.

DEALING WITH PROBLEMS

MPPL created a science kits problem form to assist staff after finding a problem when checking in a kit. The problem can range from broken parts to missing pieces or any other reason the kit might not work. The problem form lays out the steps for staff to take and has a place for them to check off once each step is accomplished. There is also space for staff to record the nature of the problem, list missing pieces, or make any other appropriate notes. Once the form has been completed, the kit can be left for the youth science kit point person. He or she will fix the problems with the kit and get it circulating again.

Try to get someone with technical skills to help fix the kits when possible. Custodial and building services staff may be excellent resources. Ours have fixed a number of problems that initially looked hopeless.

Unfortunately, some parts cannot be replaced. For example, some special LEGO pieces are hard to find or unavailable. Often it is necessary to use creative sourcing methods to replace missing parts. Continuing the example, BrickLink sells used LEGO bricks, and has been an excellent source for replacements parts. You may also replace an unavailable piece with a similar piece. Be careful when you do this and make sure that you update the check-in notes and any pictures so staff do not get confused. When possible, purchasing a spare kit to use for replacement parts also works.

Not every problem is worth fixing. Sometimes it is better to replace the entire kit. This is especially true of kits like the 75-in-1 Electronic Project Lab where there is only one item and not a lot of parts. If a kit breaks but has not been popular, you may consider replacing it with an entirely new kit.

MARKETING

Storing the kits out of the public's view creates an accessibility issue. If patrons do not see them, how do patrons know we have them? We solved this by making the kits easy to find in the catalog and by promoting the kits at in-house science programs and school open houses. We also displayed the kits at homeschool fairs and school visits to the library. Using the kits in programs also makes them more visible to patrons.

MPPL created two different versions of a flier to hand out. One is geared toward schools, and the other is directed at children. These fliers explain the science kits and include pictures. Slides advertising the kits also run on monitors throughout the youth department.

Patrons will also market the kits to each other. After a student used the Van de Graaff Generator at her school science fair, teachers, other students, and parents all wanted to check it out. Another parent checked out a different kit every week over the summer and had neighborhood science activities for all the kids on her block. Like all good programs and products, the best marketing is always word of mouth.

Circulation of MPPL's science kits has increased since they were added to the collection in September 2010. During the four month the kits were available in 2010, there were only nine checkouts; however, in calendar year 2011, there were fifty-four checkouts. In 2012, checkouts increase by 61 percent from calendar year 2011, with a total of eight-seven checkouts. This rapid increase in circulation suggests both a demand for STEM materials and that the Science-to-Go Kits are helping to meet that demand. Looking at the numbers differently, in 2011, there averaged 4.5 checkouts of Science-to-Go Kits every month. In 2012, the average increased to 7.25 checkouts per month. That is an increase of 2.75 checkouts per month. Between October of 2011 and December of 2012, there were nine months where the kits were checked out eight or more times. This means that during those months at least one of the kits was checked out twice.

This demand for STEM materials in Mount Prospect can hardly be unique to that community. The library is the perfect place to meet the demand and Science-to-Go Kits are one way to do so, as they make science more accessible to the public and are popular with patrons.

WORK CITED

LEGO Group. 2007. *Story Starters*. Denmark: LEGO Group.

FOURTEEN

Graphic Novels Ignite Imagination in the Sciences

Melanie E. Hughes and Gary Pinkston

Few things can enrich the mind and spirit of an individual more than arts and reading. Few things can lift the heart of a teacher more than seeing a struggling student make a connection to an idea, concept, or understanding. How can libraries interest these young readers in science, technology, engineering, and math (STEM) subjects and careers? A possible solution is to use the genre of STEM-themed graphic novels.

Young library patrons are already entertained by the real or imagined inventors, engineers, and scientists like Tony Stark/Iron Man or several of the other Avengers characters, as well as with other contemporary comic book heroes. These stories showcase scientific topics and engender curiosity and imagination (Karlin 2009). Through the use of this format, which students enthusiastically enjoy, STEM-themed graphic novels can easily be used to advance students in their learning.

The importance of STEM careers on the US and global economy cannot be underestimated. Societies depend on the skill and creativity of scientists, technologists, engineers, and mathematicians to advance all aspects of our daily lives. Our country has a severe shortage of STEM-qualified graduates needed to fill both current and future job openings. Currently in the United States, three million STEM jobs are vacant, while simultaneously there are fourteen million people who are unemployed (Sheehy 2012). The US Bureau of Labor Statistics forecasts 123,000 annual computer science jobs openings each year which require a bachelor degree, while there are less than 60,000 computer science graduates per year for all higher educational degree levels (Microsoft 2012). Forecasts of 1.22

million openings for the years 2012–2020 further illustrate the great demand in these areas.

GRAPHIC NOVELS AS AN INSTRUCTIONAL TOOL

Through the use of graphic novels as an instructional vehicle, students can "explore complex and sometimes confusing topics" (Bucher and Manning 2004). The advantages of reading graphic novels over watching movies or videos is that it can be conveniently reviewed in very finite detail (Hogan 2009), and the reader can readily move forward and backward in the book. Library collection development of STEM-themed graphic novels can offer support to STEM teachers, and provide students with a means of reading something visually appealing, informative, and emotionally engaging.

Individualization of learning is embedded in graphic novels because each reader has a unique emotional involvement with the text and imagery, which can enhance their educational experience. The reader can sometimes "hear" the dialogue of main characters as they engage in titanic struggles with ideas, ethics, and intrinsic motivation. The illustration of internal dissonance experienced by the characters provides an emotional connection the reader can relate to. Positive feelings are key to higher levels of student engagement and learning (Reschly 2008). Even though graphic novels are static like their textbook counterparts, they help develop important skills, such as how to "decode facial and body expressions" and the "symbolic meanings of certain images and postures" (Simmons 2003). They allow the reader to observe the body language and movement of characters and objects. This feature may also make graphic novels more appealing to kinesthetic learners. Images and content get embedded into the child/reader's brain due to the multisensory and emotional contexts found in the format of graphic novels; readers remember the story, and they remember the concepts of how they might be applied.

STEAM: GETTING ART AND DESIGN INTO STEM

Librarians need to be aware of the "STEM into STEAM" movement that aims to broaden the science, technology, engineering, and math curriculum and industries to include the arts and design. Real-life examples of STEAM include Leonardo Da Vinci, Steve Jobs, artist-in-residence programs in scientific labs (Lamont 2010), and the more relevant case of an art teacher helping students create watercolor paintings of cells in a biology class (Robelen 2011).

One way of taking advantage of the rich combination of art and text in graphic novels is to use the instructional tool of Harvard University's Project Zero—the Artful Thinking palette: Questioning & Investigating,

Observing & Describing, Comparing & Connecting, Finding Complexity, Exploring Viewpoints, and Reasoning (Project Zero 2010). Students can create a framework for better understanding intricacies of the arts, literature, and more relevantly, STEM subject content through the use of this technique. When students create original comic works of art in their classroom or on their own, the graphic novel format contributes to the enhancement of their art, perceptual representation, writing, communication, and language skills. Graphic novel creation provides opportunities for the students to reveal their deeper understanding of the subject matter and for the instructors to differentiate their teaching. The combination of all aspects of graphic novel creation generates stronger and more permanent neural connections to the subject matter explored. Art and science go hand-in-hand with STEM-themed graphic novels.

DIVERSITY AND STEM

Hispanics, African Americans, and Native Americans are historically underrepresented in STEM careers. As minority children, especially Hispanics, become a demographic majority in the coming decades, it is imperative that teachers and librarians support and encourage ethnic minorities to pursue STEM subjects, starting in middle and high school, and then college. English as a second language/English as a Foreign Language students who struggle with acquiring English language skills or others with low levels of literacy can find a bridge between their reading comprehension skills and the subject matter with the supporting visual content provided in graphic novels. Additionally, "street language" used in graphic novels helps students deal with the complexities of spoken English that textbooks do not address.

An example of a diversity-themed graphic novel series involves the fictional character Max Axiom, super scientist—an athletic African American male who utilizes a variety of science fiction methods, such as shrinking to the size of bacteria, to facilitate his adventures (Biskup 2010). The series, with an African Ameican hero, is an especially rich resource for younger, diverse students with its visual richness. Diversity and science-themed comics can also easily be found in characters such as Marvel Publishing's X-Men and the newly rebooted Spiderman, a Hispanic character named Miles Morales. DC Comics has its own diverse comic book heroes: Batwing the "Batman of Africa," and the Muslim, Arab American crime fighter, the Green Lantern. They demonstrate that diversity can be more empowering than excluding individuals or groups that are different.

CONVINCING REASONS TO EMPOWER READERS WITH GRAPHIC NOVELS

Quality comics and graphic novels often are not recognized as educational resources, so it is important for librarians to convince administrators and parents of their literary and educational value. Consider the following arguments as talking points: Research shows that comic book readers tend to enjoy reading more, and thus read more of all kinds of literature than their peers (Ujiie and Krashen 1996). In a graphic novel, readers not only decode the words and illustrations, but also identify events between the visual sequences (Simmons 2003). From a literacy point of view, the average comic book introduces kids to twice as many words as the average children's book, and exposes readers to five times as many words as the average child-adult conversation (Hayes and Ahrens 1988). Supporting studies show that "graphic novels may require more complex cognitive skills than the reading of text alone," (Lavin 1998). Finland, the nation with the highest proportion of comic book reading students (nearly 60 percent), also has the highest literacy rate (99 percent), as well as the highest library usage (Flying Colors Comics 2011).

Comics, which started as a fleeting amusement in newspapers, have now matured into a diverse, insightful, and entertaining form of literature. This new format of graphic novels is respected and enjoyed by millions. Librarians, English, language arts, and STEM teachers who use them have the opportunity to help students appreciate and understand STEM subject matter and perhaps get them started on the road to a STEM career.

GIRLS AND STEM

There is a shortage of women in STEM careers: only 18 percent of graduating engineering students are women (Sheehy 2012), and only 27 percent of computer science jobs are held by women (Huhman 2012). Lower numbers of female students in STEM careers may be triggered by negative attitudes toward these subjects because of a perceived lack of human and societal applications. Girls and women are stereotypically drawn to careers in which they can help others in a socially significant manner, and they may erroneously believe that STEM careers lack that ability. STEM-themed graphic novels can overcome these obstacles with their conversational style, emotionally laden story plots, and rich visual resources.

We need to get young women interested in STEM subjects before they graduate from high school, when foundational prerequisites are needed to prepare for applications to these college majors. If graphic novels in the curriculum and library are a proposed solution to increasing interest in STEM careers, teachers and librarians need to include materials that will engage all students, including girls and young women.

In Ujiie and Krashen's (1996) influential survey of middle school students, the researchers discovered that boys at both a chapter 1 school in a city near Los Angeles and students in a suburban middle school read more comic books than girls. When asked, "How often do you read comics?" girls at the chapter 1 school said 1 percent "always," 44 percent "sometimes," and 55 percent "never"; girls at the middle class school said: 5 percent "always," 50 percent "sometimes" and 44 percent "never." The researchers based their analysis on the boys, because "the girls' responses would not produce enough variability to reveal relationships between comic book reading and other variables" (Ujiie and Krashen 1996).

Robin Moeller (2011) observed in her school library media center that the majority of graphic novel readers were boys. When she encouraged girls to read them, she was told, "Those are boy books." Moeller conducted research with male and female students reading three works from the *Great Graphic Novels for Teens* list selected by the Young Adult Library Services Association (YALSA 2012). A major discovery was that students attributed graphic novel reading to "nerds," typically defining nerds as male (and white), which illustrated a gender and race connection. Both genders believed they would be criticized by their peer group and perceived as "nerds" if seen publicly reading graphic novels. Girls enjoyed reading them, but stated they preferred traditional novels, which allowed them to imagine more. Moeller suggests that girls were willing to see graphic novels as a supplemental part of curriculum, but their format made students question whether or not they were "real books."

Girls read more manga because of its focus on relationships between characters. Japanese manga novels often have teenagers as the main characters, allowing students to easily identify with the protagonists (Bucher and Manning 2004). The *Manga Guide to Calculus*, for example, presents lots of reasons why and how to do calculus, but the topic is blended in with a subtle romance between a recent journalism graduate and her young boss (Kojima 2009).

A poignant and humorous illustration of the societal and gender bias is that of a fictional female child who was expressing her interest in STEM subjects occurred in the July 18, 2011, edition of the widely syndicated *Baldo* comic strip by Hector Cantu and Carlos Castellanos. Gracie, a young girl of eight, tells Tia Carmen in the first frame that when she grows up and goes to college she will focus "on a STEM area of study." Tia replies "Qué bueno!" (Very good!). In the second frame, Tia's thought bubble pictures Gracie with plants or crops. In the third and final frame, Gracie, who is reading a thick textbook with a pencil, thinks: "Science, technology, engineering, and math." Cantu learned about the STEM initiative at the White House earlier that summer and received several e-mails from readers thanking him for covering the topic (Moorefield 2011).

CREATING, MAINTAINING, PROMOTING, AND UTILIZING YOUR GRAPHIC NOVEL COLLECTION

To ensure security of graphic novels in your collection, mark covers in an identifying way:

- Affix a brightly colored library sticker (Gorman 2003).
- Write the library's name with permanent marker.
- Hole punch covers, using a standard or decorative punch.

To prevent excessive wear of paperbacks:

- Use clear library tape for spines and edges.

Avoid the mixing of adult-rated graphic novels with the children's and young adult collections:

- Presume "any given title is geared for adults, until proven otherwise" (Lavin 1998).
- Check language use, depiction of women, and depiction of violence (Bucher and Manning 2004).
- Access professional librarian resources for title recommendations.
- Read online reviews.

Build relationships with local comic book shops to enhance the library's graphic novel culture:

- Ask owners about community purchasing patterns.
- Create connections with local comic artists.
- Cohost events with guest authors.

Create excitement about your graphic novel collection:

- Prominently separate and display graphic novels.
- Start a graphic novel club.
- Use social networking such as Pinterest or Twitter to book talk new titles.
- Post students reviews to a blog (Carter 2011).
- Encourage students to submit nominations for the *Great Graphic Novels for Teens List* (YALSA 2012).
- Encourage teens to e-mail their favorite author/illustrator (Carter 2011).
- Have a film festival of anime and comic book films.

Encourage the creation of original graphic novels and comic art:

- Display "how-to-draw comics" books with the graphic novel collection.
- Invite an art instructor to teach students how to draw comics.
- Post a list of suggested drawing resources used in the creation of comics.
- Make comic desktop publishing applications available on the library's computer by purchasing desktop or iPad applications, such as ComicLife from www.plasq.com (used to create the dog comics illustrating this chapter), and have links on the library's website to free online publishing applications (e.g., www.makebeliefscomix.).
- Create an appealing graphic novel webpage or LibGuide (springshare.com/libguides) with cover images and links to age-appropriate, web-based comics (e.g., libguides.ius.edu/stem).
- Help classroom teachers integrate STEM-themed graphic novels for their own instruction as well as student-generated content (Wilson 2013).

GRAPHIC NOVEL RESOURCES

Graphic novel series are sold by many publishers and are regularly on display at national library conference exhibit halls and in graphic novel specific catalogs. "Comics and Graphic Novels" is a faceted browsing category on Amazon, with age appropriate divisions. National conventions such as the San Diego Comic-Con and APE (Alternate Press Expo) are great places for librarians to meet authors, illustrators, and smaller publishers, as well as see what fans are reading and collecting. Further afield are larger, international conferences such as Comiket in Tokyo and the Angouleme International Comics Festival in France.

Collection development resources include YALSA's (2012) *Great Graphic Novels for Teens* compiled using suggestions from public and school librarians and teens, as well as the *Best American Comics* annual anthology, edited by comic artists Jessica Abel and Matt Madden (2012). The Eisner Awards, the "Oscars" of the comics, are awarded each year in many categories at the San Diego Comic-Con. Academic librarians have website pathfinders to steer students toward resources, including a *Graphic Novels* LibGuide by Aurora University's information services librarian, Lauren Jackson-Beck (2012). Mike Lavin, a business management librarian at the University of Buffalo, has an extensive guide to *Comic Books: Internet Resources* (Lavin 2012) for collection development, locating comic book stores, and other aspects of the comics industry. *No Flying No Tights* is another graphic novel review website by librarians (Brenner 2012). The *Periodic Table of Comic Books* is an index of elements featured in comic books curated by the Department of Chemistry at the University of Kentucky (Selegue 2012).

For background knowledge and theory on the aesthetics of comics and graphic novels, refer students and teachers to Scott McCloud's works *Understanding Comics: The Invisible Art* (1994) and *Reinventing Comics: How Imagination and Technology Are Revolutionizing an Art Form* (2000). Another classic is Will Eisner's *Comics and Sequential Art: Principles and Practices from the Legendary Cartoonist* (2008).

SUGGESTED STEM GRAPHIC NOVELS AND TEACHER RESOURCES

To help with your library's collection development needs, your authors have created a LibGuide, *STEM Graphic Novels and Comic Books*, at libguides.ius.edu/stem (Hughes and Pinkston 2012). You will land on a listing of serials, but there are other tabs with single titles, teaching resources, and then a grouping of graphic novels by STEM subject area. The LibGuides' "Books from the Catalog" widget populates the author/illustrator and publication date fields. Librarians can then add a call number and location for your library plus a summary or an annotation. The LibGuide is printable so that a librarian can work through the list for collection development, or a patron can come with a shopping list of call numbers. Also featured are many teacher resource books showing how to incorporate graphic novels into the classroom.

AND BEYOND

New graphic novels are being created daily by traditional publishers, and many comics are being independently published and financed through Kickstarter, a crowdfunding website that allows individuals to raise capital for creative projects (Allen 2012). Perhaps as a result of your collection development and programming efforts some of your library patrons will become comic book artists and create their own STEM-themed graphic novels, encouraging others to explore science, technology, engineering, math, and beyond!

WORKS CITED

Abel, Jessica and Matt Madden, eds. 2006–2012. *Best American Comics*. Boston: Houghton Mifflin Harcourt.

Allen, Todd. 2012. "Is Kickstarter the #2 Graphic Novel Publisher?" *Publishers Weekly*. July 10, 2012. http://www.publishersweekly.com/pw/by-topic/industry-news/comics/article/52925-is-kickstarter-the-2-graphic-novel-publisher.html (accessed November 27, 2012).

Biskup, Agnieszka. 2010. *The Surprising World of Bacteria with Max Axiom, Super Scientist*. Mankato, MN: Capstone Press.

Brenner, Robin. 2012. *No Flying No Tights*. http:/noflyingnotights.com (accessed September 30, 2012.)

Bucher, Katherine T. and M. Lee Manning. 2004. "Bringing Graphic Novels into a School's Curriculum." *Clearing House* 78 (2): 67–72.

Carter, James Bucky. 2011. "Graphic Novels, Web Comics, and Creator Blogs: Examining Product and Process." *Theory Into Practice* 50 (3): 190–197.

Eisner, Will. 2008. *Comics and Sequential Art: Principles and Practices from the Legendary Cartoonist*. New York: W. W. Norton.

Flying Colors Comics. 2012. "Food for Thought for Parents, Teachers, Librarians, and Comic Book Skeptics," *Flying Colors Comics*. http://www.flyingcolorscomics.com/revision8/education.html (accessed October 26, 2012).

Gorman, Michele. 2003. "What Teens Want." *School Library Journal* 48 (8): 42–44, 47.

Hayes, Donald P. and Margaret G. Ahrens. 1988. "Vocabulary Simplification for Children: A Special Case of 'Motherese'?" *Journal of Child Language* 15 (2): 395–410.

Hogan, Jon. 2009. "The Comic Book as Symbolic Environment: The Case of Iron Man." *ETC: A Review of General Semantics* 66(2): 199–214.

Hughes, Melanie E. and Gary L. Pinkston. 2012. *Stem Graphic Novels and Comic Books* (LibGuide). http://libguides.ius.edu/stem (accessed November 26, 2012).

Huhman, Heather R. 2012. "STEM Fields and the Gender Gap: Where Are the Women?" *Forbes*. June 20. http://www.forbes.com/sites/work-in-progress/2012/06/20/stem-fields-and-the-gender-gap-where-are-the-women (accessed September 30, 2012).

Jackson-Beck, Lauren. 2012. *Graphic Novels LibGuide*. http://libguides.aurora.edu/graphic (accessed August 21, 2012).

Karlin, Susan. 2009. "The Design and Engineering of Superheroes: Behind Every Man in Tights Stands an Engineer," *IEEE Spectrum*. June. http://spectrum.ieee.org/at-work/tech-careers/the-design-and-engineering-of-superheroes (accessed September 30, 2012).

Kojima, Hiroyuki. 2009. *The Manga Guide to Calculus*. San Francisco: No Starch Press.

Lamont, Tom. 2010. "John Maeda: Innovation Is Born When Art Meets Science," *The Observer*. http://www.guardian.co.uk/technology/2010/nov/14/my-bright-idea-john-maeda (accessed October 14, 2012).

Lavin, Michael R. 1998. "Comic Books and Graphic Novels for Libraries: What to Buy." *Serials Review* 24 (2): 31–45.

Lavin, Michael R. 2012. *Comic Books: Internet Resources*. http://library.buffalo.edu/asl/guides/comics.html (accessed September 30, 2012).

McCloud, Scott. 1994. *Understanding Comics: the Invisible Art*. New York: Harper Perennial.

McCloud, Scott. 2000. *Reinventing Comics: How Imagination and Technology Are Revolutionizing an Art Form*. New York: Perennial.

Microsoft. 2012. *A National Talent Strategy: Ideas for Securing U.S. Competitiveness and Economic Growth* (White paper). http://www.microsoft.com/en-us/news/download/presskits/citizenship/MSNTS.pdf (accessed October 9, 2012).

Moeller, Robin A. 2011. "Aren't These Boys' Books?": High School Students' Reading of Gender in Graphic Novels." *Journal of Adolescent & Adult Literacy* 54 (7): 476–84.

Moorefield, Kesha. 2011. "Girl Power: The STEM Issue Branches Out to the Funny Pages." *Diverse: Issues in Higher Education* 28 (16): 4–5, September 15 .

Project Zero, Harvard University School of Education. 2010. *Artful Thinking Palette*. http://www.pz.harvard.edu/at/atp_palette.cfm (accessed October 9, 2012).

Reschly, Amy L., et al. 2008. "Engagement as Flourishing: the Contribution of Positive Emotions and Coping to Adolescents' Engagement at School and with Learning." *Psychology in the Schools* 45 (5): 419–31.

Robelen, Erik W. 2011. "Building STEAM: Blending the Arts with STEM Subjects." *Education Week* 31(13): 8–9.

Selegue, John P. and F. James Holler. 2012. "The Periodic Table of Comic Books." http://www.uky.edu/Projects/Chemcomics (accessed September 30, 2012).

Sheehy, Kelsey. 2012. "STEM Disconnect Leaves Women, Minorities Behind," *U.S. News*. June 28. http://www.usnews.com/news/blogs/stem-education/2012/06/28/stem-disconnect-leaves-women-minorities-behind (accessed October 14, 2012).

Simmons, Tabitha. 2003. "Comic Books in My Library?" *PNLA Quarterly* 67 (3): 12, 20.

Ujiie, Joanne and Stephen D. Krashen. 1996. "Comic Book Reading, Reading Enjoyment, and Pleasure Reading Among Middle Class and Chapter 1 Middle School Students." *Reading Improvement* 33(1): 51–54.

Wilson, Eydie. 2013. *SeriousComix: Engaging Students with Digital Storyboards.* International Society of Technology Educators (ISTE).

YALSA (Young Adult Library Services Association). 2012. *Great Graphic Novels for Teens.* http://www.ala.org/yalsa/ggnt (accessed September 30, 2012).

V

Research and Publishing

FIFTEEN

Showcasing Scientific Research Output: New Audiences for Science Libraries

Alvin Hutchinson

As academic library services move to a self-service model, science library users require less and less assistance in identifying and obtaining scholarly material for research. Scientists at most universities today can search literature indexes and access articles from their office or lab and can find and purchase affordable books via a well-developed online market. For these and other reasons, scientists visit their library (and perceive a need for their librarian) less and less each year (Niu et al. 2010). University and other research librarians who want to avoid irrelevance must develop new services and find new audiences.

The Smithsonian Libraries began a new set of services in 2006 in response to this growth in self-service. The Smithsonian Research Online (SRO) program documents the published research output of Smithsonian scholars and fills a longstanding but inconsistently managed need for a master list of books, chapters, and articles resulting from institutional research. Standardization of digital publishing and the availability of bibliographic management tools have made compiling a list of publications by a given research institution possible with relatively little manual data entry required. Administrators, webmasters, public affairs, and other groups at the institution have expressed enthusiasm for this nontraditional service, which grew in part out of the recent emphasis on evidence-based research assessment.

One of the more realistic strategies for twenty-first-century science librarians is participation in the research process outside of simply acquiring and storing reading material in anticipation of future user needs. It is clear that scientists do more than simply collect and analyze data, and some of this work can be supported by librarians. The management of a scientist's bibliographic data and advising on data management planning and scholarly publishing alternatives are among the nontraditional services which librarians are increasingly providing (Kroll and Forsman 2010).

But many research organizations have needs that science librarians can fill outside of direct researcher support. One is in assisting with the research evaluation exercise that every scholar faces during their professional career. Because the publication record of a scientist is a key component of his/her evaluation, the compilation of an institution's publication output is a highly valued service and one that librarians can provide easily and reliably thanks to automation in scientific publishing.

IDENTIFICATION

One primary appeal of this kind of service is the low initial costs. The availability of bibliographic data in a standard format for easy collection makes starting a research publication registry something that can be undertaken immediately. The first step is to identify the publication data from among the vast body of literature available online. There are many licensed and freely available sources which allow users to search and find publications emanating from a particular organization. Commercial publisher websites, along with sites like Google Scholar, BioOne, and Highwire Press allow the capture of bibliographic data without charge while subscription resources such as Web of Science provide a single site with comprehensive coverage and more elaborate search features. Most useful are those databases that allow a field-specific query to restrict the search term to an author affiliation or author address field. In this way the university or institution, department, research center or even zip code can be used to filter out "noise" from general keyword searches.

Where the affiliation or address fields are not searchable themselves, a general keyword search is still useful although with the understanding that the results will contain some false hits. For example, a general keyword search on "Ohio State University" in Google Scholar may return extraneous results but whose bibliography includes a reference to a book published by the Ohio State University Press. Additional false hits may occur when the university name appears in the acknowledgement section of the paper. However this information can be forwarded to interested parties on campus who may want to be notified of and collect acknowledgements by outside authors.

After an accurate search strategy is developed, most online bibliographic services allow users to create and save alerts so that e-mail notifications are automatically sent when new publications are added that meet the specified search criteria. Some also allow for the creation of RSS feeds as an alternative system of notification.

It should be noted that most of the online sources listed here cover journal literature extensively, but books and chapters are frequently overlooked. However, in recent years commercial publishers are giving books and chapters a digital object identifier (DOI) and their own web page which includes exportable bibliographic data. This trend suggests that the automated identification of books and chapters in the sciences will become easier in the near future.

CAPTURING

The proactive search detailed above is the first step in automating the process of data collection, and fortunately there are several free and low-cost methods to get the data from the publisher or aggregator website to a database on the librarian's workstation. Most web resources that allow search and alert services also publish their data in a format, which conforms to standard bibliographic management software. Since the 1970s, there have been few options in this class of software, but in the past five to ten years, the options have expanded greatly. Both Zotero and Mendeley, for example, are freely available resources which capture, format, and permit sharing of publication data. Both allow data to be stored or mirrored in the cloud that permits simultaneous access so that multiple users can edit records. The ingest of citations via web browser plugins makes capture very easy.

There are also several commercial products for managing bibliographic citations, but because multiple library staff members work on editing the data, the SRO requires a networked solution. One commercial option, RefWorks is web-based and therefore allows access from different workstations. We use RefWorks to compile, edit, review, and de-duplicate records both because it is web-based and because it allows library staff to globally edit author names, journal titles, and descriptors via an easy-to-use interface. Fortunately the transfer of data between and among these systems is standardized today so that citations captured from web sites via Zotero or Mendeley are easily exported to RefWorks, which serves as a master copy of the database.

Once the data is reviewed and edited in RefWorks, we use a customized output format to migrate new and modified records into an SQL database, which is mounted on an institutional web server. It is impractical to export the entire collection when refreshing the website database therefore the date of last modification for all records is critical to maintain as it helps in identifying which records to move from RefWorks to the web server. This website (research.si.edu) allows anyone to search and filter publications authored by Smithsonian staff.

PROACTIVE COLLECTION

Collecting publication data for a research institution would not be possible if it were left up to authors to contribute and enter the data themselves. The recent experience of institutional repositories for example, shows a general unwillingness by authors to enter their publications into a repository. But for the SRO, the automated search, filter, and capture of this data results in approximately 75 percent of science publications being added to the database without any effort from or notification by the scientist.

Publisher/aggregator websites alone will not provide a comprehensive list of publications for an institution—even in the sciences. Inevitably there has to be some manual data entry for publications which are not online or which are not formatted for reference management software capture/import. The SRO includes a form on our intranet to manually capture the publications not picked up via regular stored searches. Using web scripting language, the data elements entered into this HTML form are sent to library staff in a standard format called RIS which reference management software can read. The RIS format is importable by all major bibliographic software packages and at the same time easily understood by library staff when viewed as a text file. Data appears as one field per line, each using a standard two-letter prefix identifying the data type. For example, PY is publication year and VL is volume, and so forth. Formatting manually entered data in this way is not difficult as the RIS data fields and their prefixes are documented on the web.

FALSE HITS

Although some online sources retrieve false hits as noted above, this is not always useless information. The university press and/or the public affairs office among others, frequently like to hear of the university, its labs, or museum being cited or mentioned in an acknowledgment, and since the information has already been retrieved, it takes little effort to forward the citation to the appropriate staff person thereby cultivating support from another potential library user group.

DUPLICATES

One burden of freely available bibliographic sources is that there is often duplication. HighWire press, Google Scholar, and other aggregators cover a wide swath of literature and often pick up the same citation, sometimes weeks apart. The Thomson Reuters product, Web of Science, often includes items after they appear on a publisher website or a Google Scholar e-mail alert. As with all standard library practice, every citation should be checked for duplication prior to being added to the database. And while not always practical for large institutions, having a single person oversee this kind of service allows him/her to become individually familiar with the stream of papers and often identify suspected duplicates from memory.

PREPRESS

Automatic capture of this data, while a relief to authors, presents some policy issues that influence workflow. Aside from duplication as noted above, alerts provided by many bibliographic systems often identify publications as soon as they appear online—not necessarily when they are issued in print. It should be decided whether an "online-first" version is collected and whether the item should be followed up with enumeration and pagination after appearing in print. On the one hand, a DOI provides an unbreakable link to a paper so that volume/issue/pages information can always be retrieved when needed. But many scientists prefer to have as complete a citation as possible, and this means a subsequent identification and cleanup of these "incomplete" records should be built into the workflow. The SRO includes items immediately after appearing online but has established a workflow to identify them for follow up so that enumeration and pagination can be added later.

EDITING

Once collected, citations can be tagged in a number of ways depending on the desired reports to be generated. Among the most obvious is reporting by the department with which the author is affiliated. The SRO database is tagged with museum and/or department name (e.g., National Museum of Natural History). Additionally, tags could be assigned for the status of all institutional coauthors (e.g., postdoc, fellows). They might also be tagged with grant funding source (e.g., federal v. private), collaborating organizations, a particular lab name or other relevant data. Unfortunately identification of other aspects of authors, coauthors, and sponsors is often unknown by library staff.

While it is helpful for a single person to review all citations coming into the database, at some level of publication output it is impractical and the work needs to be distributed among a larger pool of staff. Ideally a subject specialist, selector, or reference librarian who works directly with certain departments would assume oversight of the data, tagging as appropriate and monitoring publication trends among their direct library user group. This also has the effect of embedding librarians further into the research lifecycle beyond collection development and reference. Serendipitous identification of duplicates would also likely occur assuming that a subject librarian reviews all publications authored by the same set of scientists and develops some familiarity with their work.

USAGE/REPORTING

Beyond collection and reporting for research evaluation purposes, the SRO service is leveraged to serve additional audiences without much effort. Because it is stored on a SQL database on an institution web server, Smithsonian webmasters can reuse the data to create dynamic publications lists on web pages for individual scientists or their labs. Institutional web pages are updated in real time, relieving both web content editors and scientists from the chore of adding publication data to these pages which may have been in static HTML format before. This kind of resource has strengthened the relationship between library staff and webmasters along with the central IT office—groups that traditionally have not been regular users of library services.

While data reuse is a positive development, it should be noted that for those scientists or labs where their publication data is drawn directly from the SRO database, there will likely be a higher level of corrections and feedback given to the librarian(s) who compile the data. Higher visibility means greater scrutiny, and library staff should bear this in mind.

Of course, many scientists would like their web pages to display the entire corpus of their publications beginning when they were in graduate school and including those written while at other institutions where they worked prior to the Smithsonian. For this reason the SRO began accepting publications issued prior to a scientist's arrival at the institution if they wanted to include the data. However, for purposes of metrics and to avoid artificially inflating the publication statistics for past years, a certain keyword was assigned to these that identified it as being published prior to affiliation with the Smithsonian. That way the full list can be retrieved/displayed, but metrics reports for publication totals can exclude these records.

As mentioned earlier, public affairs staff of many scientific organizations are interested in recent activities of the research units and they use the SRO to keep abreast of recent activity. Where in the past they may have had to actively seek content for press releases, the publication registry now serves as a source of regular reports on the latest papers reflecting recent research.

Research Metrics

Bibliometrics is a primary component of research evaluation and a master list of publications is essential for this kind of review and analysis. But the research evaluation process extends beyond publications to include elements such as grants and awards and it is hoped that the SRO could one day be integrated with a database listing grants or funding for scientists. This takes on a greater importance in light of the recently growing trend of some funding bodies to require open access to the publications and/or the data sets resulting from awards. Collecting an institutional publications list is the first step in creating a unified research registry which could include information about publications, grants, scientific data sets and more.

Alternative Metrics (Altmetrics)

The SRO data is useful for collecting bibliometric data for the institution's scholarly output, and while the impact factor and h-index are available for most publications, there are altmetrics to measure readership and access to SRO publications without waiting for formal citation counts. Altmetrics includes a variety of measures including a count of the number of times an item has been downloaded or viewed, mentioned in blogs or on Twitter, bookmarked, or included in other social media, all of which might offer an additional perspective on the individual papers of a scholar. The SRO program's popularity has earned enough support to hire a vendor who specializes in altmetrics to demonstrate readership and usage of Smithsonian publications beyond standard citation rates.

Repository Metadata Generation

Like many research libraries, the Smithsonian Libraries manages an institutional repository of scholarly reprints authored by Institution staff. Learning from the experience at other institutions, we knew that asking authors to enter and upload reprints to the repository would not be met with a high rate of participation. We decided to implement the more realistic "mediated deposit" strategy whereby library staff would collect and upload reprints on scientists' behalf, and the SRO has provided a base for the service. With metadata collection already captured and "databased," it is possible to generate XML-formatted records for batch import into our repository (currently using the DSpace platform) and circumvent manual data entry that might otherwise have been required. A web script takes the SRO data and returns it in a format which DSpace can accept for bulk upload. The only additional step is for library staff to match the digital reprints (provided by scientists) to the appropriate record in the database. This emphasis on batch processing of repository content has resulted in an above average number of items in the repository compared with many other library-managed repositories. By creating a custom metadata field in DSpace, which corresponds to the unique identifier for each record in the SRO, the data as displayed on institutional websites contains links (where applicable) to reprints in the repository.

SYSTEM ARCHITECTURE

Ideally, SRO data would reside on a single server (backed up of course) rather than as different versions (e.g., RefWorks, SQL web server, DSpace). Multiple copies of any database easily become unsynchronized and edits made in one place must be made to the others. The primary obstacle to establishing a single, unified database instance is the absence of bibliographic management software with a user-friendly interface that would allow a wider group of staff to simultaneously log in and edit/ update records, including batch updates to multiple records, standardizing author and journal names, and so forth.

It has been difficult to find such a bibliographic management system as most reference management software is not created for this scale of work. For example, while some allow simultaneous login and edit, they do not allow a user to perform global operations. There are repository platforms that offer metadata management, which may be suitable for the SRO and some include the ability to create web pages highlighting individual scholars, but because the SRO program began as a separate effort from the repository, the two systems were well-established and SRO services dependent on the SQL database before the opportunity to easily integrate them had passed. The consolidation of the data onto a single platform is something which will have to be more carefully coordinated sometime in the future.

SRO program staff is currently evaluating options for a bibliographic management system that can accommodate multiple users and accounts so that the work of editing data can be shared more widely among Smithsonian staff. Were a more robust system identified and implemented, this data review and editing could be crowdsourced so that authors themselves (or their support staff) could tag records with appropriate descriptors identifying funding sources, sponsorship, departments, collaborators, and other information that the Smithsonian research community would find useful but that library staff are not in a position to provide.

STAFF

The SRO has approximately 2.5 full-time employees collecting, and reviewing more than 2,000 items annually. In addition to current publications, there are legacy projects to add books, chapters, and articles which have appeared in printed bibliographies from past Smithsonian annual reports, and other historical publications lists. The program has grown from one professional staff person in the digital services division to now include several others including paraprofessional staff who work in what has traditionally been bibliographic control of the library's online catalog records.

FUTURE IMPROVEMENTS

Recent efforts to create unique identifiers for scholars, their institutions, and grants awarded are similar to DOIs used in scholarly publishing. Incorporating these into the SRO would undoubtedly help to monitor Smithsonian scholarly activities more consistently and comprehensively.

Many open-access publishers offer discounted article processing charges for institutions which pay a membership fee. A number of SRO publications in journals for which publishers offer institutional memberships provide information on the cost-effectiveness of a Smithsonian membership.

A number of Smithsonian-authored papers appear in open access journals but are not included in the digital reprint repository (despite being freely available). Harvesting from sites like PubMed Central, PLoS, or BioMed Central for articles where we lack a reprint could help to populate the repository further. Additionally, the body of text in the repository could be mined for a variety of data such as place names, personal or corporate names, geographic coordinates, museum specimen numbers, species names, and so forth. This data could be plotted using Google maps or used to generate a list of funding sources, previous collaborations, links to museum specimen databases, and more.

CONCLUSION

The SRO program is extremely popular primarily because it serves audiences which have previously been somewhat overlooked at the Institution compared to traditional researchers/readers. The primary drivers of the program—institutional administration and those involved in science policy—do not typically use library resources as regularly as scientists themselves and the SRO is a way to remind them of the value of library services.

WORKS CITED

Kroll, Susan, and Rick Forsman. 2010. A Slice of Research Life: Information Support for Research in the United States. Dublin, OH: OCLC Research. http://www.oclc.org/research/publications/library/2010/2010-15.pdf

Niu, Xi, Bradley M. Hemminger, Cory Lown, Stephanie Adams, Cecelia Brown, Allison Level, Merinda McLure, Audrey Powers, Michele R. Tennant, and Tara Cataldo. 2010. "National Study of Information Seeking Behavior of Academic Researchers in the United States." *Journal of the American Society for Information Science and Technology* 61(5): 869–90.

SIXTEEN

Embedding Librarians into the STEM Publication Process

Anne Rauh and Linda M. Galloway

Scientists and librarians both recognize the importance of peer-reviewed scholarly literature to increase knowledge and improve understanding of the world. Scientists' contributions to their field are reflected in these publications and are important, not only for the greater good, but for peer recognition, promotion, and tenure. Librarians strive to provide access to and communicate the importance of this literature. Bridging the gap between information producers and consumers, librarians can guide STEM faculty through various stages of the scholarly publication process. Librarians can assist by helping scholars study existing resources, providing publishing advice, and finally by promoting publications and assessing the impact of scholarly communication. While this mediation may require some library professionals to step outside of their comfort zone, it is important to remember that librarians already have the skills necessary to help. They know how to find, organize, and disseminate relevant information. Applying these skills to the STEM publication process can be very rewarding, both personally and professionally. In doing so, librarians will gain a better understanding of faculty and institutional research, the scholarly publication process, and learn how to increase scholars' visibility. In addition, they will learn new tools, acquire new skills, and enhance their library's service to the institution.

This chapter highlights techniques the authors have used to support STEM faculty at various stages of the publication process. We will discuss ways in which librarians can help faculty organize a literature review and target a journal for publication and the best practices for doing both. For the postpublication stages, we outline the variety of ways librarians can help increase and enhance access to scholarly works using both free and institutional resources. This chapter will also address methods for assessing the impact of a work using both traditional and emerging scholarly metrics. Using the resources and tools described in this chapter, librarians can become active participants in the STEM publication process.

ORGANIZING A LITERATURE REVIEW

When researchers consider writing and publishing an article, one of the first steps that they take is studying existing resources. Ideally, keeping up with the literature in the field is something that scholars do on a regular basis, but doing a systematic review of literature is important before publishing new work. Efficiently and effectively organizing the search results are tasks that researchers at all levels may struggle with, and this task of organizing literature is a natural place for researchers and librarians to collaborate. The authors have found that researchers are typically eager to receive support in this capacity.

There are a number of tools that allow researchers to collect, organize, and cite literature, websites, images, graphs, tables, and charts within their writing. Many of these tools are supported in academic libraries throughout the country. Merinda Kaye Hensley, associate reference librarian and associate professor of Library Administration at University of Illinois at Urbana-Champaign, provides an overview of the features offered by these tools. She describes how the access models to these tools affect libraries' support of these resources (Hensley 2011). For a more detailed comparison of the features of these tools, visit the University of Wisconsin–Madison libraries' citation manager comparison (University of Wisconsin–Madison Libraries 2012).

Syracuse University Library supports five citation management tools including EndNote, EndNote Web, RefWorks, Zotero, and Mendeley. All of these tools assist researchers in organizing scholarly literature. The tools are accessed in a variety of ways, which range from desktop applications to browser extensions. Some of these tools are freely available, some are paid for by institutional subscriptions, and others are paid for by individual researchers or through their laboratory technology funds. Regardless of how they are accessed and paid for, all of the tools allow researchers to download citation information from literature databases, electronic journals, library catalogs, and websites into their own personal research library. Once they have collected that information, they are able to organize it into folders, assign keywords or tags to the citation information, and attach full text documents of the literature for easy retrieval.

All of the tools also allow researchers to automatically create fully formatted citations in manuscripts with varying degrees of customization.

While these tools work differently from one another, they all allow researchers to collect, organize, and cite scholarly information. Peforming a literature review is an imporatant step in the scientific research and writing process and is a natural opportunity for librarians to utilize their expertise.

TARGETING A JOURNAL

Scholarly communication via academic journals remains the most widely accepted method of disseminating STEM information. The peer-review process required by academic journal publishers provides a measure of authority and quality control to reported research findings. The acceptance of a manuscript by a respected journal indicates that the authors' work is valuable and verifiable. Helping authors decide where to publish requires basic knowledge of the publishing process, the ability to assess journal prestige, and an understanding of authors' motivations. While it is the newer faculty who most often request assistance, more experienced authors publishing outside of their usual venues may also seek guidance. Decisions about where to publish are dependent on scholars' particular field, their motivations, and the quality of their research and writing. For example, the impact factor of a journal is considered a good measure of scientific quality. While it may be desirable to publish in a journal with a high impact factor, the rejection rates for articles may be very high, or the journal may not be suited to certain types of documents. It is at this junction, the matching of an author and potential publisher, where librarians can help.

It is not unusual for an author to consult a librarian for help deciding where to submit an article. Presumably, a librarian is familiar with and has the tools and knowledge to evaluate journals within a discipline. Before suggesting journals for an author to target, it is important to gain an understanding of the type of work to be published, its intended audience, and the author's publication goals. Librarians should ask authors about their goals for the publication. Does the author want the work viewed by as many readers as possible even if the readers are not in same field of study? Does the author want to publish their work in a special issue of a journal where all of the work will be on a similar topic? Does the author have a specific group of journals that they must target for promotion? Does the author want to retain rights to the work once it is published? The importance of discipline-specific knowledge and understanding of the publishing landscape in a particular field cannot be underestimated. In addition to conferring with the librarian, the author might want to ask other practitioners in their field for publication advice.

Furthermore, a faculty member on the tenure track may need to consider time factors that a seasoned author is not aware of. Institutional knowledge and conversations with the author should help the librarian understand how best to assist in the publication process.

There are a number of tools to help gauge the impact and authority of a publication. The factors that are most often considered are the journal's importance and how quickly and frequently an article is cited after publication. The most well-known suite of journal and article impact metrics is Thomson Reuters Journal Citation Reports (JCR). Of the various tools and metrics JCR provides, arguably the most useful are the journal impact factor and the immediacy index. The impact factor measures the average number of times articles from the journal published in the past two years have been cited. The immediacy index is the average number of times an article is cited in the year it is published (Thomson Reuters 2012).

A freely available alternative to JCR is SCImago Journal Rank (SJR indicator). The SJR indicator is populated with information from Elsevier's Scopus database and the ranking algorithm is based upon Google PageRank (González-Pereira, Guerrero-Bote, and Moya-Anegón 2010). The SJR indicator attempts to compute both the quality and quantity of citations received by a publication. The SJR indicator and Thomson Reuters' Impact Factor were found to correlate well when compared (Elkins et al. 2010). SCImago also provides a type of immediacy index—the average citation per document in a two year period. In addition, SCImago includes country scientific indicators which "can be used to assess and analyze scientific domains" (SCImago Lab 2012).

Librarians should also point faculty to open access journals and self-archiving resources in their conversations about publishing venues. Major funding agencies, such as the National Institute of Health, require open access publishing in either open access journals or institutional repositories, and dissemination of articles through open access channels can help increase their readership and visibility. A recent large-scale study of citation patterns revealed that open access journals indexed in either Scopus or Web of Science are approaching the scientific impact of subscription journals. The data supporting these conclusions were discipline-dependent and also dependent on the open access journal funding model (Björk and Solomon 2012), so no broad conclusions should be drawn. However, increasing exposure to one's scholarship is desired and may prove to be more important as the scientific community begins to embrace alternative metrics used to evaluate impact.

PROMOTING RESEARCHER'S WORK

Librarians can assist with the scientific publishing process by promoting a scholar's work after it has been published. Promoting the monographic work of scholars is something many librarians embrace and are familiar with. Librarians suggest books for purchase to colleagues at other universities, consult with authors in deciding where to solicit book reviews, and help authors determine the number of libraries that have purchased their titles. Promoting scientific journal literature is not inherently different from these practices, though the tools authors have available to promote their work do differ.

One tool that librarians at Syracuse University use for promoting faculty work, especially publications in journals, is the institutional repository, SUrface. The goal of the repository is to archive the scholarly work of the university and make it globally accessible. While the widespread distribution of this work for free is at odds with the copyright policies of some journals, many publishers allow a postprint (the revised manuscript version of the work accepted by the publisher) of the scholar's work to be archived rather than the publisher's PDF version. Librarians can use the alert services of library databases to receive notification of new publications from university-affiliated authors. They can then use tools such as SHERPA/RoMEO, a searchable database of publisher's archiving policies, to determine if and how an article can be archived. Adding scholarly works to the institutional repository allows researchers around the world to access articles published in journals to which they may not subscribe.

Google Scholar Citations is another way to collect and promote a scholar's work and is a viable alternative for authors who do not have access to an institutional repository. This tool creates a profile based on searches in Google Scholar for works attributable to the author, displaying the citations along with information about the work. Several citation metrics are also shown on the author's profile including citations per article and historical citation information about the author's body of work. Authors verify that the work is their own and are given the option to manually enter citations not found by Google Scholar. This is an effective tool for promoting one's work because it is easily found in Google searches and it offers a venue for authors to display all of their work in one location.

A powerful new tool that is designed to disambiguate authors' names is ORCID (Open Researcher and Contributor ID). This initiative assigns an alphanumeric code to each researcher and is used to provide every author with a unique identifier. Currently, many journals only list last names and first initials in the author fields. Researchers with common names or those whose names have changed during their professional career are also hard to distinguish. ORCID is a system that assigns an author's unique number to each work rather than relying on matching names to locate all of an author's work. This identifier has been adopted by numerous publishers "including Thomson Reuters, Nature Publishing Group, Elsevier, ProQuest, Springer, CrossRef, the British Library and the Wellcome Trust" (ORCID Inc. 2012), which will allow for consistent use throughout literature databases, libraries, and funding agencies.

ASSESSING IMPACT

In theory, assessing the impact of an individual's publication record should be very straightforward: simply calculate the number of citations articles receive in peer-reviewed journals. This should be an objective and unbiased exercise. However, citation metrics are not consistent across platforms, are often available only via subscription resources, and also take a long time to accumulate. In general, traditional citation metrics evaluate an article's influence only on a specific scientific community.

How does one measure a scholar's impact? Traditional tools, like Web of Science and Scopus, calculate author influence by measuring several factors including times cited, indices such as the h-index, and journal impact factors (described earlier in this chapter). The times cited count is perhaps the most recognized measure which determines the number of citations to an author's publications, generally in a specific time frame. Librarians who understand how citations are generated and counted can help faculty calculate these important metrics. It is crucial to stress that comparisons of results across tools should be avoided due to the different pools of data mined, proprietary ways in which publications are included (or excluded), and the various time parameters used.

A well-regarded bibliometric parameter, the h-index attempts to measure both productivity and impact of an author. Described in Hirsch's seminal work (2005) the h-index is simply the number of a scholar's papers, h, that have been cited at least h times by other publications. The h-index is calculated by many citation metric tools including Web of Science, Scopus, and Google Scholar and is considered a good measure of scholarly impact.

Both Web of Science and Scopus are selective scholarly citation databases that include information from highly regarded journals. Google Scholar is freely available and includes more types of publications than the two databases previously mentioned. More information about these databases may be found in the authors' online guide that details the procedures and metrics used to calculate publication influence.

Attempting to gauge impact beyond citation counts, altmetrics, is an emerging field that "focuses more narrowly on scholarly influence as measured in online *tools and environments*" (Priem, Groth, and Taraborelli 2012). Altmetrics can complement existing citation metric tools, uncovering the impact and reach of research in new media for evidence of connections and influence that are not represented in the traditional modes. For example, a measure of a paper's influence might include the number of times this paper has been saved in a Mendeley library or the number of times it has been downloaded from an institutional repository. While these numbers do not represent tangible citations to these works, they may more effectively capture the influence that a work wields. There are many emerging altmetrics websites, tools, and programs, some of which will certainly prove to be more useful than others.

Assisting STEM faculty in the publication process requires an awareness of the various tools and resources that can be used to assess the impact of an author or an article. The established tools, such as Scopus and Web of Science, can be complemented by the existing and emerging altmetric tools. If one does not have access to the paid subscription resources, these alternative metrics may also be used to provide a demonstrated measure of academic success.

CONCLUSION

This is an important time for librarians to be involved in both the organization of research as well as how that research can be promoted and measured. Many academic libraries are expanding their services to include assistance to researchers in organizing and storing their research data. While helping authors organize their literature is not as challenging as working with large data sets, assisting researchers at this phase of their work is a natural starting place for libraries that are interested in becoming involved in data management. Scientific researchers understand our expertise with literature. By becoming involved in the steps of the publishing process in which we offer unique expertise and support, we can demonstrate our value and gain trust in our capacity to understand and meet their data management needs in the future.

This is also a very important time for librarians to become involved in the discussions taking place on new metrics and ways of assessing scholarly works. As metrics are refined to extend beyond traditional journal publications and take into account new modes of scholarly communication, librarians need to share their expertise in this area and take part in these conversations. Engaging with the traditional tools and metrics that we have outlined will help you to understand their strengths and weaknesses to better suggest improvements for these new metrics.

The authors believe that all librarians have the necessary skills to embed themselves into scientific publishing. The ability to organize information and assess credible sources is something that all librarians possess. The activities that librarians perform in our library may be slightly different from ways that you have previously applied these skills but all librarians have the skills and ability to successfully assist in the STEM publication process.

WORKS CITED

Björk, Bo-Christer, and David Solomon. 2012. "Open Access Versus Subscription Journals: a Comparison of Scientific Impact." *BMC Medicine* 10(1): 73, doi: 10.1186/1741-7015-10-73.

Elkins, Mark, Christopher Maher, Robert Herbert, Anne Moseley, and Catherine Sherrington. 2010. "Correlation Between the Journal Impact Factor and Three Other Journal Citation Indices."*Scientometrics* 85(1): 81–93.

González-Pereira, B., V. P. Guerrero-Bote, and F. Moya-Anegón. 2010. "A New Approach to the Metric of Journals Scientific Prestige: The SJR Indicator." *Journal of Informetrics* 4(3): 379–91.

Hensley, Merinda Kaye. 2011. "Citation Management Software: Features and Futures."*Reference & User Services Quarterly* 50 (3): 204–8.

Hirsch, J. E. 2005. "An Index to Quantify an Individual's Scientific Research Output."*Proceedings of the National Academy of Sciences of the United States of America* 102(46) (November 15): 16569–16572. doi: 10.1073/pnas.0507655102.

ORCID Inc. 2012. "ORCID." http://about.orcid.org/.

Priem, Jason, Paul Groth, and Dario Taraborelli. 2012. "The Altmetrics Collection." Ed. Christos A. Ouzounis. *PLoS ONE* 7 (11) (November 1): e48753. doi: 10.1371/journal.pone.0048753.

SCImago Lab. 2012. "SCImago Journal & Country Rank." http://www.scimagojr.com/.

Thomson Reuters. 2012. "Journal Citation Reports." http://thomsonreuters.com/products_services/science/science_products/a-z/journal_citation_reports/.

University of Wisconsin–Madison Libraries. 2012. "Citation Managers Comparison." http://library.wisc.edu/citation-managers/comparison.html.

VI

Outreach

SEVENTEEN

How Not to Reinvent the STEM Wheel: Using Crowdsourcing and Community Partners

Jennifer Hopwood

WHAT TO DO IF YOU ARE NOT AN EXPERT

When I first heard about the acronym for the science, technology, engineering, and mathematics (STEM) fields, I really wasn't sure how to start incorporating it into my library programs. I have always been interested in computers and technology, but my little LEGO block houses simply can't compare to the elaborate designs of today. I can handle simple algebra, but forget about geometry. Plus, while science was something I was relatively good at, it was more something that I fell into because I had to rather than because I wanted to. I chose to be an English education major after all, what did I know about STEM? Turns out, I was already doing it and didn't even realize it.

Within three months of my promotion to the head of youth services at my library, I was given the opportunity to participate in a lunar workshop for librarians being hosted at the Kennedy Space Center. Immediately I had flashbacks to the tenth grade astronomy class; other than getting to examine moon rocks, it really wasn't that great of an experience. Incorporating science into library programs? I was sure it would be more of the same, and no kid wants to go to a library program that is just a rehashing of what they learned in school.

Working with NASA was different. The workshop was full of hands-on experiments that incorporated science elements across the curriculum. There were songs, crafts, games, and stories all about the moon. We weren't just bombarded with mind-numbing facts. The workshop was fun, fascinating, and very far from boring. When the Kennedy Space Center came to the library that summer to do a program for us, the kids were excited to participate in all the activities and touch the materials that the education liaisons brought with them. The best part was that they were learning while having fun.

Flash forward five years later: science, technology, engineering, and math are still something that I incorporate into my regular library programs. Only now I make a point of referring to them as STEM. No, I am not a STEM expert, but that's okay. When a child comes to us at the library and asks about a subject we are not familiar with, we find the answer by looking it up or referring to other sources. The same strategy applies to STEM collaboration. If you are not a STEM expert, then find a STEM expert. Since STEM covers the fields of science, technology, engineering, and mathematics; there is a good chance there are people right in your community who would be willing to lend their assistance. There are actually advantages to not being a STEM expert. It means I am able to relate better to the new learner. In other words, there is no technojargon to bog down our understandings. I can keep things simple.

PLANNING

Many STEM projects can be completed using materials already on hand or patrons can be asked to donate items such as those building blocks their kids are no longer playing with! Using recyclable materials is a great idea because it is freely available and is helping the environment. For example, a bin of paper towel tubes is a great start toward planning a marble-run contraption for the engineering part of STEM. Use paper towel tubes to create a maze of tunnels and shoots to propel a marble from point A at the top to point B at the bottom. It can be as simple as connecting tubes together at angles or having the marble drop down into a different set of tubes. The goal is to make sure the marble does not get stuck anywhere in the maze; that is where engineering comes into the planning. This is a great project to tie-in books about levels and mining. It can also be tied into real-life experiences by showing clips from amusement parks, such as log fume rides and water park slides.

Books, blogs, and listservs are great resources for ideas. Make sure to test ideas found on the Internet before using them in an actual program. When planning this past summer reading program, I found a great idea from the popular Pinterest website for a glow-in-the dark project. The project involved using a certain highly caffeinated, neon-greenish carbonated beverage, baking soda, and hydrogen peroxide. The concoction was supposed to glow in the dark when mixed together, sealed, and shaken. I tried the experiment three times. I even checked videos on the web to make sure I was doing it right. Still nothing happened. Turns out if I had continued searching the Internet, I would have eventually discovered that the project was a hoax. Thankfully, my unsuccessful attempts at replicating the project took place at home and not in front of a room full of patrons. Lesson learned: not everything on the Internet is true or reliable, although several experiences like these could make for a great future library program debunking the information found on the net.

Finding resources and projects can be very time consuming. It is hard to do when you are short staffed or busy with other programs. It is good to have some go-to projects. However, even if they are new to the patrons, it can get stale for the presenter. Enthusiasm is very important when presenting as it can make a huge impact on the audience and increase their enjoyment of the program. Finding new ideas is a great way to keep things interesting.

COLLABORATION

Once a theme has been decided on, it is time to gather all the information available on the topic and get down to planning. The best way to do this is through collaboration, working together with another person or a group of people with the same goals. It is a partnership toward creation. There are many different ways to collaborate.

If you are just starting out with your collaboration task, you may not have a readily available pool of experts to call upon. The term "crowdsourcing" refers to a strategy when a group of people, sometimes strangers, are asked to complete a task. Wikipedia is a great example of crowdsourcing at its finest. Known as a free online encyclopedia that anyone can edit, Wikipedia is a resource to which anyone can add their expert knowledge.

Try free wiki services like PBWorks to create your own wiki sites for any topic you choose. It can be used for collaborating on topics related to STEM where everyone has access to editing and contributing. It can also serve as a locked resource that others may read but cannot edit. If you are crowdsourcing, you can share a link to the wiki you have created with other people and they can input their information directly there.

The best way to find partners for collaboration is to network. I have found the Association for Library Services to Children (ALSC) and Young Adult Library Services Association (YALSA) listservs to be very helpful. Generally, I use listservs to get help with specific questions about a project. Usually within five minutes I have already received two or three suggestions. However, listservs can also be used as a source to get the word out about your STEM project by sending a link to the wiki you have created. Although this makes it a little less private, you can also post a link to the wiki with a brief explanation using Twitter.

Social networking tools provide a great opportunity to share ideas. Skype allows you to conference with other individuals in a manner similar to a conference or a phone call. Of course you can still use the phone, but this can be difficult if your schedules don't match up. This is where technology comes in not just as a STEM topic, but as a valuable tool to have in your bag of tricks.

GOOGLE DRIVE

Cloud computing sounds a little scary at first, what with having all your information floating out there in cyberspace. However, it is one of the best ways to collaborate in a world where almost everything has gone digital and where people find themselves in need to connect and are unable to do it face-to-face.

Google Drive consists of all those wonderful creativity apps that Google offers, such as word processing documents, spreadsheets, presentations, frms, and even drawing: 5GB of space is available at no charge; more can be purchased if needed. What makes this a great tool for collaboration is that files are saved in the cloud; in other words on the servers at Google. Therefore, these files can be shared with anyone, anywhere. An example of how this can be applied to STEM library programs would be the STEM Children's Book Recommendations list which was created using Google Spreadsheets (http://bit.ly/STDXVq). This spreadsheet was built as a way for librarians to maintain a list of children's books related to STEM. The spreadsheet has open access for anyone with that URL who is interested in editing or adding titles to the list.

Here is an example of the STEM children's book resource list (table 17.1).

The example in table 17.1 does not really exist, but it demonstrates the purpose of the list. Include the author's name, the title of the book, the ISBN number; S,T, E, or M to stand for the field or fields represented in

Table 17.1.

Author (last, first)	Title	ISBN	Field (i.e., science, technology, Engineering, math)	Age range	Comments
Smith, Joe	Building Dreams	x-12345-123-1	Engineering	10 and up	This fiction book is about a boy who decides to enter his school's soap box derby race. Great to pair with a library program on building vehicles.

the book; an age range, and any comments about the book. Comments can include recommendation on how to use the book in programs or a brief sentence detailing what the book is about. This is a crowdsource project, so it is still a work in progress, but feel free to enter your own favorites on the list.

BLOGS

When a new product is ready to be launched, it has already been through many trials and retrials. It has been tested to make sure it has customer appeal and certainly we would hope it has been tested to make sure it works. Sometimes these products are given to people who get to test them either right before they are released to the general population or sometimes right after. It depends on the goal the company has in mind: is it for promotional purposes or is it to test the product in a real world setting?

Collaboration can also be viewed as such testing. Remember the episode with the glow-in-the-dark soda experiment? This is why it is important to test projects out before a program. Knowing if something will work or not is the reason I love to read blogs, particularly blogs written by homeschooling parents or fellow librarians. For example, STEM Friday is a good blog to look at for book suggestions associated with STEM topics.

Blogs are almost a form of one-sided collaboration; the blogger posts the information, then the reader takes that information from the blog and adapts it to a particular setting. The blogger can see that someone is visiting the site, but they don't know if the information was helpful. Most bloggers post because they want to share their experiences or knowledge with others. Next time when you are visiting a blog, take a moment to leave a comment to let the blogger know how much the information was appreciated. If you are using the information found on the blog, take a moment to drop back by and tell the blogger about it. Bloggers love hearing from their readers and such feedback can go a long way toward inspiring more great ideas. It may become a starting point for a future two-way collaboration project.

Internet searches on a topic can result either in perfect matches that correspond to your chosen topic or in a lot of garbage. If you are trolling for ideas, then take a look at some blog directories like Technorati. Technorati often serves as a starting point for finding blogs that correspond to specific topics. I recommend that you search using keywords like "science and children" for better results. My search using STEM as a keyword resulted in a lot of blogs related to stem cells.

PINTEREST

Pinterest allows websites to be bookmarked using images instead of the traditional URLs. Images are "pinned" to boards that have been created for various topics. Text boxes associated with the images allow users to add descriptions and hash tags to make searching easier. When you click on an image pinned to a board, it will redirect you to the original website for further details. Pinterest also allows adding collaborators to existing boards. This means that collaborators may pin items to boards originally created by other people. A great place to get started on Pinterest for STEM links would be to browse the Education category. There are also several STEM boards that can be found using the "search" feature.

DISCOVER COMMUNITY OF PRACTICE

STAR_Net has developed a website called Community of Practice (CoP). It serves as a collaboration resource for professionals such as librarians, scientists, educators, museum staff, engineers, and others interested in supporting or providing STEM programs in libraries. Access is restricted to registered individuals only, but contact information can be found at the Discover Exhibits Community of Practice website. Once login information is established, members will have access to documents related to STEM as well as discussion boards. Contact information can be also uploaded to their databases as a way to reach out to others in the community of STEM.

STEM IN LIBRARIES LINKEDIN GROUP

LinkedIn is commonly known as a website for professionals to network. There is also a large librarian presence on the site. The STEM in Libraries interest group is a place for librarians interested in STEM to share ideas, discuss topics, and of course, network for future collaborations.

NATIONAL GIRLS COLLABORATIVE PROJECT

The National Girls Collaborative Project (NGCP) is another great resource for libraries. NGCP is focused on providing resources for organizations that implement STEM programs geared primarily toward females. NGCP is also a good resource for webinars and grant opportunities. The website hosts several free webinars a year where you can make contact with others who are also interested in STEM.

COMMUNITY PARTNERS

Working with community partners is a great opportunity for you to collaborate on programs using knowledgeable people in your own backyard. Contact a local club, college, or university for guest speakers. Many groups will be more than happy to bring visual aids like telescopes and slides for an astronomy club or robotic vehicles for a robotics club. Experienced community partners, such as outreach educators, will also have knowledge of what will work for your particular area or needs. This is a give and take, so make sure that there is open communication between you and the organizer. If something about the program didn't work for your group, let the presenter know about it. If they are not aware about a concern, then they are not able to address it.

I have collaborated with representatives from NASA on several occasions to offer space-based programs at our library. An example of this partnership was a program about Mars conducted as a part of our summer reading activities. First, I e-mailed my contact from previous joint programs to determine if they had a speaker available to present the topic. Many groups, such as government agencies or universities have speakers bureau pages on their websites that you can use as a starting point for contact if you do not already have an existing relationship. Then using the speakers' contact information, we e-mailed back and forth on the needs of the program as well as the format of the presentation. The guest speaker presented slides and videos about Mars. Our staff also presented interactive experiments which were adapted for the program from education materials available on NASA websites. A local supermarket participated by providing supplies for the experiments.

KEEPING IT REAL: EXAMPLES FROM THE FIELD

When researching the ways to incorporate STEM into library programs, it is very easy to find subjects to include. If you take a look at the STEM children's book recommendation list mentioned above in connection with Google Drive, you will see that science is the predominant STEM category. Many libraries use technology in their programs, especially with teens. Engineering can sound intimidating, but think of it more in terms of building. What do children build with? LEGO blocks! LEGO blocks are an affordable way to include the engineering component into your programs and examples of successful LEGO programs can be found throughout the country. Every library does it differently, but usually they give children about an hour to create either a defined building project or one using their imagination.

STEM is also a great way to incorporate programs targeted at home-schooled students. If you do not have a large enough homeschooling community in your area to make this type of program beneficial, consider holding it as a school outreach event. Paring the story *Bartholomew and the Oobleck* by Dr. Seuss, followed by making a batch of green oobleck, is also a wonderful sensory activity for students with special needs.

Paring STEM with story time provides an opportunity to include small children in your STEM planning. This can be done through group projects related to STEM, such as a demonstration activity or even a take home craft. It is a great way to connect your fiction picture books to your nonfiction collection. Young children love to ask why, so make sure you have a display of nonfiction titles on hand when you incorporate science, technology, engineering, or math themes into your story-time programs. Remember, you do not have to be an expert, but you should be able to find the answers if needed. In other words, be ready for those teachable moments when you can show your story time groups how to use the library resources. Even if you have a younger story-time crowd, their parents or caregivers will appreciate the information. Using STEM with teens can be a little trickier. Typically, you will get smaller crowds for a teen program when compared to a program targeted at younger children. However, remember that moms or dads usually bring children to the library for programs; teens come to the library because it was their choice. Having a teen advisory group can help you out with planning because its members can act as your sounding board on what they and their friends might enjoy. Teens are not interested in sitting through a lecture or a slide presentation, so make sure that there are hands-on activities available where they can interact with their peers.

CONCLUSION

While it may at first sound intimidating, incorporating STEM into your regular library programming is not difficult. By using social media resources such as blogs, you can find out firsthand what has and hasn't worked for others. You may discover that you already utilize some aspects of it.

Reaching out to your community for STEM experts is a winning partnership because it will provide word of mouth advertising from friends and family. It also creates community connectivity allowing for a richer library experience. Teens and children not only learn from the program but can also establish relationships with future mentors.

Planning a great library program can take a lot of work when you are starting from scratch. By reaching out to others you are not only cutting down on the workload, but are also discovering new ideas and inspiration for future library projects. Maybe the ideas you find are not flawless, but after a few modifications, you might just achieve a perfect fit.

EIGHTEEN

Girls' Night Out: STEM Programs for Girls Only

Kathleen J. Clauson

"Girl power" has become part of our national dialogue, particularly in regards to science, technology, engineering, and mathematics (STEM) as educators explore creative ways to spark girls' interest in STEM-related fields. Women make up 50 percent of the workforce and earn the majority of college degrees, yet only 25 percent of the STEM work force is represented by women (National Science Foundation 2012). Schools are looking for exciting ways to improve math and science programs and to offer memorable and inspiring STEM classroom experiences, yet they find their pockets aren't deep enough, nor are there enough hours in the day to cover the units required for each grade level, much less offer special programs for girls only. Libraries, determined to add programming to their repertoire, offer hopeful solutions and alternatives.

Libraries are "poised for creating lasting memories for girls" (O'Dell 2002, xi). By offering special STEM programs with hands-on activities, libraries can work with teachers and parents to give the girls a sense of accomplishment and ignite their interest. Libraries can be exciting places, far away from the pressures of the traditional classroom, a place where girls can go with their friends, siblings, and parents. Sometimes they have so much fun, they actually forget they are learning! Spending an afternoon or an evening at a library on a college campus is particularly thrilling for enthusiastic third and fourth graders, especially when the library itself is unusual and interesting. Our library (Physical Sciences Library at Western Illinois University, Macomb, Illinois) is a round two-level, space-age delight built back in the 1970s, and children who have visited have declared our library "truly awesome" and "cool."

Planning special STEM-related programs can be beneficial for everyone; not only can special events offer extraordinary hands-on learning opportunities, but these events promote the library and its services as well. Books and reading are often mentioned by women in science as the common denominators in their success stories (Karnes and Stephens 2002; Pritchard 2006). With the turn of the page or the click of a mouse, the library can magically transport girls to another world where the sky is the limit.

PLANNING LIBRARY PROGRAMS

In the last five years, our academic branch science library has hosted a variety of successful STEM programs, all free of charge for both the university and the local community, including two four-week-long series for college students on forensics and astronomy, a collaborative event with the physics and biology departments for preschool children and special "girls' night out" programs. Like many libraries, we do not have a budget for programming, yet we are still able to offer successful, quality events by utilizing resources we already have by collaborating with local schools, organizations, and agencies, and by using our campus network of faculty, staff, and students in various departments and library branches. Our programming initiatives are designed to increase the library's visibility and traffic, inspire interest in science, support multiple academic disciplines and student learning, and engage the community. The guidelines included below can be used by any library—school, public, or academic—to plan successful STEM programs.

Careful planning is required for events of any size. A plan should include a detailed description of the proposed event, the goals and objectives, a proposed date and a place for the event, information about the target audience and their interests, budget requirements, marketing needs, and evaluation methods. After each event we write up an evaluation, noting strengths, weaknesses, challenges, attendance, total amount of money spent, and feedback.

LIKE BAKING A CAKE

Planning special library events is like baking a cake. You have to determine what you can make, when you will make it, who will eat it, where it will be served, and how much time, money, and effort it will take to go from being just a plain cake to becoming a memorable dessert.

I get started by compiling a list of ideas. Ideas may be submitted by students, library staff members, and faculty. They could be a result of brainstorming with my colleagues or based on activities that have been used elsewhere in the classroom, or by other organizations and libraries. Some are directly associated with particular units that take place in the classrooms. Others come about because of opportunities that present themselves on campus.

By spring, several weeks before the end of the semester, I start the process by organizing a planning team. My team includes student library assistants and one or two members of the departments with which I collaborate. From the list of possibilities, we select four to six ideas. For each idea, we write a brief description of the event with a list of activities, displays, and exhibits, possible dates, target audience, budget requirements, and marketing needs.

THE TARGET AUDIENCE

The next important step in planning library events is to collect information about the target audience's background and interests. Getting feedback from this group is one of the cardinal rules for successful marketing whether you are planning a library program or launching a new consumer product. The main obstacle that prevents organizations from achieving success with new products, services, and programs, is their failure to do the groundwork. You may think that everything you plan will be fully embraced and well-attended, but that is not always the case. You may generate some interest "by default," but the opportunities for success are greatly enhanced by knowing the interests of your patrons, their backgrounds, their expectations, and their perceptions.

How can you find out pertinent background information in a timely manner and still have enough time to properly plan your event? Start several months in advance. Gather information in a variety of ways—informal discussions with members of the target audience, focus groups, surveys, and pilot programs. For planning the college-level forensics and astronomy series, we gathered information by having discussions with students in the library, meeting with faculty who were teaching related courses, and by reviewing past library programs. Instructors of relevant chemistry, psychology, and law enforcement courses were asked for dates they would be willing to bring their classes to a presentation. This was directly related to the success of our programs. We discovered that we had significantly higher attendance rates by scheduling a guaranteed audience and by promoting the events with posters, news releases, our blog entries, and mass e-mails. Word of mouth generated even more excitement and these events became the place to be.

COLLABORATION AND NETWORKING

Networking and collaboration are essential in planning library programming. Few libraries have large programming budgets, so reaching out to colleagues and community leaders is important. By collaborating with teachers, professors, local organizations, and community agencies, you will often find many local STEM professionals who are willing to donate an hour or two for presentations. I am usually able to schedule eight to ten presenters for each series, half of whom are out-of-town guest speakers just by asking. Make contacts with multidisciplinary university faculty members and outside agencies, and then cultivate your network by keeping in touch with them and supporting events in their departments.

Asking female college students in STEM programs is another great way to introduce girls to role models who can relate to them and the challenges they face. College students find working with young students refreshing and it's a great experience for them too. Middle school girls relate well to college students since the age gap is not that wide.

Working with a local Girl Scout troop is an easy way to begin a successful library outreach program because the girls already have regularly scheduled meetings after school and troop leaders are genuinely delighted to find programs for which the girls can earn badges. Since the troop is "girls only," this is an easy way to have a girls' night out program without making boys feel left out. Hosting a library outreach becomes easy as pie when collaborating with Girl Scout, 4-H, and other leadership organizations. We have also hosted similar programs for Boy Scouts.

GIRLS' NIGHT OUT

When planning future girls' night out events, we decided we would work with Girl Scout troops of nine- or ten-year-olds for several reasons. A review of the literature revealed that girls begin to lose interest in math and science by the time they are eleven years old and we felt our program would have a positive influence on this age group (Goetz 2007, 1–2). Troop leaders and parents had approached me asking if we would be willing to sponsor programs and opportunities for earning badges.

Planning events around the Girl Scouts' schedule and STEM objectives was ideal because girls already had meetings scheduled twice a month; their parents were actively involved with the troops and demonstrated a higher level of dedication and interest in extracurricular library programs. After our initial discussions, we met with the troop and asked them to complete a short survey about their interests. In the following discussion, parents provided information from the teachers regarding upcoming classroom units. Based on the information collected, we decided to schedule girls' night out events about forensic science, astronomy, and women in science. We already had a framework for forensic and astronomy-themed events. Utilizing what we had on hand eliminated the need to purchase special items. We also found speakers who presented at other events and were more than happy to do the same for our girls' night out programs. Promotional costs for our events are normally minimal because we produce posters internally, post events on the library website and our blogs, and ask a marketing librarian to send out mass e-mails to the university community and news releases to local media.

GIRLS' NIGHT OUT: FORENSICS

Our first girls' night out event was a one-hour forensic-themed outreach event for local Girl Scouts. We conducted a short presentation and a hands-on activity about online safety, including a demonstration about how computers, cameras, and cell phones can make it easy to identify a person's location with an IP address and Google Earth. This was particularly shocking to most of the parents. The second part of the program was a short fingerprint demonstration of basic fingerprint patterns by one of the students in the forensic chemistry program, followed by a quick fingerprint identification activity. My student assistants served fun fingerprint cookies as a snack. This event was attended by nearly all parents and we provided packets of information about online safety and recommendations for keeping children safe with a list of resources for emergencies and further information. We also designed a fun newsletter for the girls, highlighting important things they had learned that evening. This was very successful and we received great feedback from parents, who were thankful for the candid information about cyber-security.

GIRLS' NIGHT OUT: ASTRONOMY NIGHT

For our second girls' night out event we focused on astronomy. Although we had no budget, we wanted to create a clever "out of this world" exhibit that would wow the girls. We used mostly repurposed or recycled materials, including a giant-sized papier maché moon, almost five-feet tall and five feet in diameter, complete with a rocky surface full of craters and a banner of well-known constellations such as the Big and Little Dipper.

Activity stations, displays of books about astronomy and space travel, and interactive models of planets were set up near the moon, some of which were loaned to us by our sister branch library that specializes in children's books and teaching resources. Our physics department loaned us a rare brass telescope from the 1950s for display, as well as constellation globes, and brilliant color posters, mostly photos from the Hubble

Telescope. We created information cubes with facts about the moon and other fun astronomy facts.

A colleague in the physics department was happy to make a short presentation about the night sky and a brief explanation of how telescopes work. After the presentation, the physics professor and physics graduate students set up the telescopes outside. In the meantime, my library assistants served a space snack, "green martian cupcakes" and "space juice." The cupcakes were frosted with green icing and decorated with candy alien faces. The space juice was an ordinary juice box covered in foil and a little green man on the label. When the telescopes were ready, every girl received a glow-stick bracelet to help us keep track of everyone in the dark. We took a few girls at a time to the telescopes, while the others enjoyed the books, displays, and space toys. Everyone had a chance to "stargaze" using three big telescopes and was able to see Venus, Saturn, and the moon. Gift bags of fun astronomy activities, puzzles, brainteasers, and solutions were also given out. All of these items were created by student library assistants.

OUTREACH ON A SHIRT TAIL

Budgeting is one of the biggest obstacles in creating great events, yet libraries shouldn't let having no money stop them. Collaborating and networking opens up the possibilities. "Outreach on a shirt tail" is a concept I coined which refers to creating library programs by taking advantage of events planned by another organization. Because of a library lecture series, it was possible to plan another girls' night out event. When a permanent lecture series for the libraries at our university was established by an endowment from a former faculty member, I was asked to help find an accomplished woman in a STEM profession. This series was designed to highlight accomplished women, as a reminder to girls and women that they can be or do anything they want. To pursue this avenue, you must contact the responsible organization, provide a detailed proposal, and the speaker's agent will review their itinerary and contract.

To find a suitable speaker, I made a few calls to an agency that books speakers, and I received information about two or three women who had done some groundbreaking work in science. I had also contacted our own physics and chemistry departments. A few days later, in a wonderful example of networking, one of the chemistry professors offered to help me make contact with his cousin, former NASA astronaut Dr. Linda Godwin, who had spent about forty days in space.

Our Girls' Night Out with Famous Women in Science event was designed to support student learning by complementing the girls' classroom unit on women in science, inspire girls to get involved in STEM, promote our library services, and contribute to opportunities for the Girl

Scouts to earn badges. We set two dates for this program, a week apart. The first week the Girl Scouts met at the library for a short presentation about women in science, an activity, and a snack. The following week, the girls were invited to attend Dr. Godwin's lecture on campus.

For the first part, we prepared a display of books about famous women in science and a photo exhibit of well-known female scientists, past and present, from all over the world. We included a number of age-appropriate books from our sister branch library as well. Our presenters included female faculty members from chemistry, physics, and biology departments, emphasizing how they got hooked on science. Small groups of girls were given the name and biography of a female scientist and were asked to perform a five-minute skit using a few props, including a lab coat which the girls loved, test tubes, and other science items, but without saying the name of their scientist. The others were asked to identify the scientists, which included Ada Byron, Marie Curie, Dr. Shirley Ann Jackson, and Sally Ride. The girls enjoyed playacting and improvising. The final skit was about Sally Ride, the first American woman in space.

One of my students talked about what it takes to become an astronaut, how math and science are used, and what astronauts do at work. We designed spaceship invitations for Dr. Godwin's lecture and personally addressed one for each girl. Last but not least, we served special snacks, freeze-dried astronaut space ice cream, which I ordered online.

No formal marketing was required by us for this event. The committee for this lecturer series publicized Dr. Godwin's lecture with posters, mass e-mails, and announcements in local newspapers and on television. We sent our own follow-up e-mails to parents about the lecture and provided directions for parking at the university. Since Dr. Godwin had already agreed to answer questions after her presentations and attend a public reception, no formal agreement was required for our program.

A week later, the Girl Scouts were mesmerized by Dr. Godwin's lecture as she talked about growing up in a small town in Missouri, traced her steps to the space program, and showed photos from her space flights. The girls had a chance to meet her in person, get her autograph, a photo, and ask questions. Dr. Godwin was especially wonderful with the girls and no one was too shy to approach her. With very little effort, we created an outreach activity which became a once-in-a-lifetime opportunity for these girls.

MORE STEM PROGRAMS IN THE WORKS

Evaluation of girls' night out programs demonstrated that they were successful and should be continued. We are in the process of planning future girls' night out events, including Powder-Puff Trebuchet, Chess for Girls,

The Chemistry of Baking, Fibonacci Magic in Nature, Speed-Cubing with Rubik's Cube, and All about Kittens. For each event, we are planning a short presentation by a female STEM professional, a fun hands-on learning activity, a brain-teaser, a list of books girls can read for more information, and a STEM-themed snack. By providing fun, inspirational outreach programs, challenging girls to think outside the box and to jump on the STEM bandwagon, our library continues to offer unique opportunities to the future successful generations of girls.

STEM FOR GIRLS

When planning STEM events, libraries can do their part in encouraging girls in STEM fields by incorporating some of the insight and strategies included in this chapter. Library outreach programs "for girls only" offer girls a kaleidoscope of opportunities—presentations by female scientists and role models, special exhibits, inspirational films, and eye-opening, hands-on activities with real-life applications, especially for girls.

STEM role models can easily convince girls that math and science are hard work but with practice, they will get better at it. Hearing about the childhood and school experiences of a female scientist, their challenges, their struggles, and their feelings, which often mirror what the girls are experiencing, is a wonderful way to show girls that their dreams are within reach.

School libraries, public libraries, and academic libraries can work hand-in-hand with teachers, parents, community leaders, and each other, to develop spectacular, memorable outreach programs, guaranteed to stir the imagination of girls and to create life-long learners.

RECOMMENDED READING ABOUT GIRLS AND STEM

Ambrose, Susan A., Kristin L. Dunkle, Barbara B. Lazurus, Indira Nair, and Deborah A. Harkus. 1997. *Journeys of Women in Science and Engineering: No Universal Constants.* Philadelphia: Temple University Press.

American Association of University Women. 2010. *Why So Few: Women in Science, Technology, Engineering, and Mathematics.* Washington, DC: AAUW.

Dempsey, Kathy. 2009. *The Accidental Library Marketer.* Medford, NJ: Information Today.

Eliot, Lise. 2009. *Pink Brain, Blue Brain: How Small Differences Grow into Troublesome Gaps and What We Can Do About It.* New York: Mariner Books.

James, Abigail Norfleet. 2009. *Teaching the Female Brain: How Girls Learn Math and Science.* Thousand Oaks, CA: Corwin.

McKellar, Danica. 2007. *Math Doesn't Suck: How to Survive School Math Without Losing Your Mind or Breaking a Nail.* New York: Hudson Street Press.

National Science Foundation. 2006. *New Formulas for America's Workforce 2: Girls in Science and Engineering* NSF 06-60. http://www.nsf.gov/pubs/2006/nsf0660/nsf0660.pdf

Rosser, Sue V. 2004. *The Science Glass Ceiling: Academic Women Scientists and the Struggle to Succeed.* New York: Routledge.

Sommers, Christina Hoff, ed. 2009. *The Science on Women and Science.* Washington, DC: American Enterprise Institute.

WORKS CITED

Goetz, Susan Gibbs. 2007. *Science for Girls: Successful Classroom Strategies.* Lanham, MD: Scarecrow Press.

Karnes, Frances A. and Kristen R. Stephens. 2002. *Young Women of Achievement: A Resource for Girls in Science, Math, and Technology.* Amherst, NY: Prometheus Books.

National Science Foundation, *Science and Engineering Indicators,* 2012. http://www.nsf.gov/statistics/seind12/

O'Dell, Katie. 2002. *Library Materials and Services for Teen Girls.* Greenwood, CO: Libraries Unlimited.

Pritchard, Peggy A., ed. 2006. *Successful Strategies for Women in Science: A Portable Mentor.* New York: Elsevier.

NINETEEN

Celebrating Geographic Information Systems through GIS Day @ Your Library

Carol Patterson McAuliffe

GIS Day celebrates geographic information systems (GIS), a technology that incorporates elements from all four STEM subject areas. Not only does GIS provide a valuable multidisciplinary tool for STEM educators, it is also an opportunity for libraries to highlight their GIS resources for STEM students and professionals. Organizing a GIS Day event at your library will educate the general public, schools, and academic communities about GIS technology and applications, which make a difference in their lives.

GIS: AN INTRODUCTION

GIS technology is a multidisciplinary tool used to organize, manipulate, and analyze spatial information. Any data that has a spatial component can be visualized using GIS. Here are a few basic facts to help you understand GIS technology and its importance.

1. GIS utilizes layers of geographic data. These data layers are linked to tables, which include specific attributes in addition to geographic coordinates. Multiple layers of georeferenced information allow the user to identify and study spatial relationships.
2. GIS is a problem-solving tool. Almost every major issue we are facing today is spatially relevant. Crisis management, environmental modeling, urban planning, and wildlife conservation are among

the many diverse fields that use GIS to study and solve crucial issues.

3. GIS is on the rise. The use of GIS in interactive online maps, such as GoogleMaps, has increased interest in geography-based technologies. GIS puts the power of map creation into the hands of the public, including educators and students. The wide use of global positioning systems (GPS) in smartphones and other navigational devices has also increased public awareness. One common misconception is that GIS and GPS (global positioning system) are interchangeable terms. However, GPS is a specific technology which uses transmitters and trilateration to get exact locations on the earth via a network of satellites. GPS is used for navigation and to collect location-based data. The geographic data that is used in GIS is often collected through the use of GPS technology.

MAKING THE CONNECTION BETWEEN GIS AND STEM EDUCATION

Advancements in science, technology, engineering, and mathematics were vital to the development of GIS technology. However, GIS also gives back to each of the STEM fields by creating new avenues for study and advancement. For instance, Gilbrook (1999, 34) highlights the importance of GIS to engineering: "GIS can help engineers analyze vast amounts of data from a variety of disciplines to create comprehensive, accurate, and efficient environmental reports for transportation projects."

Studies also suggest that GIS enhances the understanding of STEM subjects by students (Wai, Lubinski, and Benbow 2009, 817) and that "spatial thinking is associated with skill and interest in STEM fields" (Newcombe 2010, 29). GIS is STEM applied. GIS allows practical application of STEM subjects in a problem solving context while encouraging critical and analytical thinking. GIS enables STEM students to practice what STEM professionals do in their jobs everyday (Baker 2012).

GIS DAY AT YOUR LIBRARY

GIS data collections and services are now being offered in many libraries. As purveyors of information, libraries have the responsibility to educate their users about GIS technology and its application. According to Weimer, Olivares, and Bedenbaugh (2012, 42), "Global events like GIS Day . . . afford excellent opportunities to promote both the library itself and specific services where they exist."

Every November, the Wednesday of Geography Awareness Week is dedicated to celebrating GIS and educating the public about its application. This is an opportunity for libraries to take the lead in introducing

STEM students to GIS technology. Libraries can be a central place for many in the community to learn about GIS.

THE STEPS

First of all, you do not have to be an expert in GIS to organize a GIS Day. You just need to (1) understand why GIS is an important tool, (2) build your team (including experts), and (3) focus on learning goals and having fun. Everyone has to start somewhere and it is the same for organizing your own GIS Day event.

Phase 1: Defining the Scope of Your GIS Day Event

Step 1: Goals

The objectives of your GIS Day event should align both to the intended purpose of GIS Day as well as the mission of your library. Some common goals are

- To increase awareness of GIS, including how it is being used in research and in practical applications to improve the community
- To provide a forum where local companies, organizations, agencies, and those who use GIS can share their work
- To provide educational outreach to schools and to build GIS technology knowledge and skill sets in students
- To highlight the usefulness of GIS to STEM students and professionals
- To promote GIS and geography-related collections and services to your library patrons

Step 2: Audience

In addition to the primary population you serve, you may consider broadening your audience to include other user groups in your community. For example, a university event could invite K–12 classes to attend. Defining your audience will guide your planning for specific activities and venue requirements for the event.

Step 3: Stakeholders

Understanding who the stakeholders might be will help determine your planning team and community partners. Gather information about who in your community uses GIS and would potentially be interested in participating in the event. If you are focusing your GIS Day event on STEM subjects, remember to ask STEM professionals about how they use

GIS. Stakeholders can be those who are directly or indirectly impacted by GIS.

Phase 2: Planning Your GIS Day

Step 1: Get Administrative Support

If possible, talk to your supervisor in person about your GIS Day proposal. Having a one page summary outlining the scope (goals, audience, and stakeholders) will help.

Step 2: Recruit Your Planning Committee

The research you put into defining your stakeholders comes to fruition when recruiting your planning committee. It is important to get as wide a representation of interests on the committee as possible. Possible members to include

- Other library staff
- Academic faculty or graduate students interested in GIS
- Teachers who are interested in using GIS in their classrooms
- Members of special interest groups, such as a Geography Student Association or a geocaching club
- Volunteers from the public who are interested in GIS

Once you have recruited your planning committee, set up a planning meeting. During your meeting explain the scope of your project as defined during phase 1.

Step 3: Brainstorming

There are multiple elements to your GIS Day which require input from your committee including who your community partners will be and which events you would like to include in your GIS Day. Below are just a few examples of community partners, potential activities, and other details that you need to consider for GIS Day at Your Library.

Community Partners
- Schools: Education plays a central role in any GIS Day celebration. For that reason, no matter what kind of library you work in, a GIS Day celebration often involves participation from one or more educational sectors, either primary, secondary (including AP classes), and/or higher education. Students can be invited to submit digital mapping projects or posters. Professors at universities can be encouraged to give their students extra credit for attending GIS Day events.

- Commercial: Local businesses can be helpful partners for GIS Day. Surveyors, GIS specialists, geologists, archeologists, civil engineers, and landscape engineering firms are just a few of the commercial professions that have an interest in GIS and furthering GIS education. Increasing awareness about what they do and how they do it can be a compelling reason to them to get involved.
- Government: Local city and county planners, water management districts, and other government agencies such as the United States Geological Survey and the Fish and Wildlife Service have GIS experts on staff who are often willing to be involved with a local GIS Day event.
- Community groups: There may be special interest or student groups interested in participating in a GIS Day celebration. For instance, many communities have local geocaching groups. Geocaching has become a popular activity with the rise of smartphone and GPS technology and local groups involved in the hobby can help you plan a geocaching activity for your GIS Day. Student groups interested in STEM subjects are also a good source for collaboration.

Activities
- Speakers/presentations. Your stakeholders and community partners are good potential speakers and presenters. Remember that if you do not have money in the budget for honorariums, then your presenters will most likely have to be local. When thinking about what kinds of presentations you would like to include, be sure to consider your audience and their knowledge level and ask speakers to tailor their presentations to meet your needs. Consider giving them a theme that will connect all the speakers together, such as how GIS is used in STEM fields.
- Career fair. With interest in GIS jobs on the rise, career and information fairs can generate a lot of interest. Contact businesses that employ GIS professionals well in advance if you would like to invite them to set up a booth at a career fair.
- Games. Fun and interactive elements for your GIS Day celebration could include geocaching (a scavenger hunt carried out using GPS units) and/or geodashing (a race using GPS units to a find a predetermined location).
- Poster sessions and map contests. Invited poster sessions from university students and faculty can be used to showcase a wide range of GIS applications in research. Maps contests are a great way for students to show off their work in GIS—but be sure to budget some money for prizes!
- Workshops. Workshops can be a helpful way to serve a wide range of user needs. They can be used for a basic introduction to GIS or to

cover more advanced topics. Libraries can also take advantage of workshops to highlight their GIS services and resources.

Step 4: Consider Logistics

Once you have brainstormed events and partners and decided whom and what you want to include, it is time to figure out the venue, refreshments, and your budget.

Venue   When considering a venue, the anticipated size of your audience and activities you will want to include are key factors. If you are having a speaker series, you will need a venue that includes a computer, projector, and screen along with presentation software. Workshops will need a computer lab with GIS software installed (see helpful resources). Remember, every activity does not have to happen in the same location and some things can happen simultaneously. For example, you may want to schedule a beginners GIS workshop and an advanced GIS workshop at the same time since the intended audiences don't overlap. Also, if possible, reserve the venue for your GIS Day the afternoon before. That way setting up chairs and hanging posters can be done beforehand.

Refreshments

Refreshments can be a good way to draw in crowds and to offer a nice break for participants. If you have the money, consider getting a large cake with the GIS Day logo printed on it. Cakes can feed a lot of people at an affordable price.

Budget

Money will be a limiting factor in your GIS Day celebration. Because GIS has a lot of support in various fields, seek corporate or local business partners to cosponsor the celebration with the library.

Step 5. Establish a Timeline

Officially, GIS Day is celebrated on the Wednesday of Geography Awareness Week every November. It is helpful from a marketing standpoint to tie it to the international event date, but if another date works better for your library, then do what works for you! Once you have decided on a date, it is best to begin the process up to six months in advance. The main considerations when forming your timeline are scheduling your speakers and venue(s). Additional time requirements will vary depending on what events you have decided to include.

Phase 3: Implementing Your Plan

Step 1: Contact Stakeholders and Form Partnerships

As soon as possible, let your stakeholders and partners know about your plans. The quicker they can get an event onto their calendars the more likely it is that they will be able to participate. Continue to build support as you go along and continue to contact new stakeholders as you discover them. You never know who your biggest champion will be!

Step 2: Marketing

Similar to listing books in a library catalog so that they can be found, marketing is necessary for your audience to find out about your event. Marketing ideas include

- Webpages. Having a dedicated page on your library website will naturally increase awareness of your event. Weimer et al. (2012, 52) suggests the following for GIS Day webpages: Write the pages in HTML so that they are accessible to search engines. Include pictures and/or videos of people interacting with GIS technology. Keep past GIS Day pages live once they have been created so that people searching for GIS Day events have a better chance of finding out about yours.
- Register your GIS Day event on the official GIS Day website (search worldwide GIS Day celebration).
- Create a geocache. Having a geocache hidden on library grounds which people can find using clues and GPS devices is a good way to increase interest in GIS and related technologies. If you can, relate the "treasure" that they find to GIS Day. Be sure to register it on "Geocaching: The Official Global GPS Cache Hunt Site" so that interested people can find it!
- Mobilize your stakeholders. Don't forget to reconnect with your stakeholders and remind them to spread the word to other interested parties. More than half the battle is getting information about your event to the right eyes and ears.

Step 3. Organize and Delegate

Organization and delegation should be occurring throughout the planning and implementing phases. However, here are some tips to help keep you on top of the event.

- Keep a contact list. A running list of names, contact information, and affiliations will help you keep in touch with the right parties as well as be a valuable resource for years to come.

- Continue to update your timeline. An established timeline is necessary in the planning phase (see phase 2) but it doesn't end there. As more specific information comes to light about deadlines, keep your planning team updated through a shared calendar.
- Printing. Remember to print out signs, flyers, and evaluation forms well in advance of your event. Also, individualized itineraries for teachers who are bringing along classes of children can be helpful and cut down on confusion.
- Extra credit. Provide teachers with an example extra credit assignment on your webpage to further encourage participation.
- Speaker needs. If you are having a speaker series, make sure you get the presenters' biographical information before the big day. Ask them to send you their presentations via email as a backup and so that they can be preloaded onto the presentation computer.
- Delegate. Divide up responsibilities for specific activities among members of your team, such as the speaker series and geocaching game.

Step 4: Tackling the GIS Day Celebration

Finally, the big day arrives! There are always last minute things to take care of on the morning of a big event but at some point you just have to hold on and enjoy the ride. Tips for the day:

- Have business cards ready.
- Provide name tags and water for the presenters as well as for your helpers.
- Make sure you test out AV equipment.
- Don't forget the evaluation forms and assign someone to count attendees hourly rather than just once the entire day.
- Have fun! It is very rewarding to see all your hard work come together.

Phase 4: Wrap Up

Step 1: Thank You Letters

Send out thank you messages to those who actively participated in your GIS Day soon after the event. Stakeholders will appreciate your acknowledgement of their help and it will pave the way for future collaborations.

Step 2. Assessment of Feedback

Thoroughly analyze the feedback given on the evaluation forms to understand your audiences' reaction to the event and to get ideas for the future.

What to ask on the evaluation form:

- Which event activities did you attend?
- How did you hear about GIS Day?
- What information did you find the most useful? Least useful?
- What kinds of activities would you like to see at future GIS Day events?
- Did the event meet your expectations?
- How could this GIS Day event have been improved?

Step 3: Wrap-Up Meeting

Conduct a wrap-up meeting with your planning team. Discuss successes along with failures. Being able to admit shortcomings will help you improve your GIS Day event in the future.

Step 4: Preplanning For the Next Year

Since GIS Day is an annual event, look toward planning for next year. A one-page write-up of the event will help inform library administration about your successful outreach and will be a good marketing tool for next year's GIS Day.

HELPFUL RESOURCES

There are resources available to help you feel fully prepared for your GIS Day event. One primary need is access to GIS, especially if you want to have hands-on workshops. The major provider of GIS software is Esri. They offer individual, student, and institutional site licenses for ArcGIS, their primary GIS software. Check with your institution to see if you already have access to ArcGIS. If it is not available, you can sign up for a personal account that will give you access to Esri's online resources including free-to-use GIS programs. The Esri website says that "with a free ArcGIS Online personal account you can create, store, and manage maps, apps, and data, and share them with others. You also get access to content shared by Esri and GIS users around the world" (ArcGIS Online Free Personal Account, 2012). Another option is to use other free online apps such as GoogleEarth to demonstrate GIS principles.

For additional help, visit the official GIS Day website and search "worldwide GIS Day celebration." On the website, you will be able to

- Register your GIS Day event

- Get the official GIS Day logo for use on promotional items
- Get additional activity ideas
- Find information on past GIS Day events at other institutions around the world

Geocaching is a fun GIS Day activity. If you would like to conduct a geocaching game or set up a permanent geocache on your library grounds, look up "Geocaching: The Official Global GPS Cache Hunt Site." You will be able to find a helpful introduction to geocaching called "Geocaching 101," information on how to register your geocache, and other geocaches in your area.

Finally, to further study the connection between GIS and STEM subjects, check out these online resources.

- "GIS is STEM" from Esri Education Community. Information about the relationship between GIS and STEM, including examples of projects from STEM fields using GIS http://edcommunity.esri.com/stem/
- "Exploring GIS and STEM" from Esri Education Community. An educational map gallery showing "how GIS can be used in any STEM field." http://downloads2.esri.com/EdComm2007/gallery/STEM/index.html
- "Geospatial Technologies" from National Center for Rural Science, Technology, Engineering & Mathematics Education Outreach. Lesson plans "designed to introduce and use GIS as a tool for middle school science and mathematics." http://www.isat.jmu.edu/stem/curriculum.html

CONCLUSION

While undertaking an event like GIS Day can seem daunting, there are many valuable outcomes that make it worthwhile. GIS Day at Your Library will allow you to highlight GIS technologies as well as any GIS or geography-related services offered by your library. It will also show the value of GIS as a tool for STEM fields. Students studying STEM subjects will greatly benefit from understanding GIS and how they can utilize it in their research projects. Celebrating GIS through GIS Day at Your Library can be a welcome addition to your library's educational outreach programs.

WORKS CITED

"ArcGIS Online | Free Personal Account." 2012. Esri, accessed 09/20, 2012, http://www.esri.com/software/arcgis/arcgisonline/features/free-personal-account.

Baker, Tom. 2012. *Advancing STEM Education with GIS*. Redlands, California: Esri. http://www.esri.com/library/ebooks/advancing-stem-education-with-gis.pdf.

Gilbrook, M. J. 1999. "GIS Paves the Way." *Civil Engineering* 69 (11): 34–39.

Lisichenko, Richard. 2010. "Exploring a Web-Based Pedagogical Model to Enhance GIS Education." *Journal of STEM Teacher Education* 47 (3): 49–62.

Newcombe, Nora S. 2010. "Picture This: Increasing Math and Science Learning by Improving Spatial Thinking." *American Educator* 34 (2): 29–35.

Todd, JL. 2008. "GIS and Libraries: A Cross-Disciplinary Approach." *Online* 32 (5): 14–18.

Wai, Jonathan, David Lubinski, and Camilla P. Benbow. 2009. "Spatial Ability for STEM Domains: Aligning Over 50 Years of Cumulative Psychological Knowledge Solidifies Its Importance." *Journal of Educational Psychology* 101 (4): 817–35. doi:10.1037/a0016127.

Weimer, Katherine H., Miriam Olivares, and Robin A. Bedenbaugh. 2012. "GIS Day and Web Promotion: Retrospective Analysis of U.S. ARL Libraries' Involvement." *Journal of Map & Geography Libraries* 8 (1): 39–57. doi: 10.1080/15420353.2011.629402. http://dx.doi.org/10.1080/15420353.2011.629402.

TWENTY

Fun Is Learning: Making an Interactive Science Café Series

Karen Lauritsen

Making is memorable. When you make something, you have a story to tell—a muscle memory of the experience. Moving beyond the lecture series gives people the opportunity to collaboratively build a vibrant, interactive learning community together. It becomes an open invitation to anyone, regardless of related expertise, to explore STEM topics that delight and inspire. This chapter offers practical guidance about how to develop, host, extend, and sustain an experiential Science Café series that feels inclusive and welcoming.

Cal Poly Science Café is an interactive and fun public program that brings people together for stories, demonstrations, hands-on play and casual conversations with an expert at the Robert E. Kennedy Library at California Polytechnic State University in San Luis Obispo. When the event is over, you haven't just learned something new; you've experienced it. Our program is offered as a model for developing your own series, at your own library, no matter the type.

Informal science education is a well-documented need and public education priority in the United States, supported by organizations such as the National Science Foundation (NSF) and the Alfred P. Sloan Foundation. By offering hands-on activities with experts in a welcoming setting, Cal Poly Science Café is part of a growing international movement to expand informal STEM education. As an example of its effectiveness, two members of the founding Science Café team discovered that 85 percent of people who attended an event discussed it with friends, family, or colleagues (Scaramozzino and Trujillo 2010).

In addition to designing memorable events we also document them, giving them a life beyond the day they happen and a reach beyond the people who were able to attend. It's because of this storytelling that our series has been featured on Boing Boing, the internationally popular technology blog; NOVA Science Café at sciencecafes.org; and on our campus' home page, updated live as part of an interactive gaming event. Our stories are a powerful way to extend the educational experience, invite others to share that experience with their communities, and show how libraries, in their interdisciplinary and inclusive nature, can inspire collaborative learning and doing.

BUILDING A MEANINGFUL FUTURE THROUGH INCLUSIVE COMMUNICATION

In August 2008, the library invited a dozen faculty and staff to offer their ideas as the program was being developed. Since the library is a comprehensive and neutral hub for all disciplines, it's in a unique position to host a program that invites interdisciplinary exploration. It's also a welcoming place for members of the community, since libraries are a familiar part of every city.

In January, a few short months later, the first event was launched. While the advisory group no longer meets, we have grown a valuable network of informal advisors via reputation and collaboration, who continue to shape the program through their ideas.

IT'S NOT JUST STEM: CONNECT WITH CAMPUS CULTURE

At Cal Poly, we're big on "Learning by Doing." That's one reason why we started emphasizing hands-on experimentation. Science Café is also a great way to engage the community, which is another explicit strategic imperative at Cal Poly. In addition, one of the many payoffs as an organizer is observing a community of people coming together to figure something out.

If you're launching Science Café at an academic library, connecting to the campus culture means that the program will fit into larger themes that have already been identified as priorities. Among many benefits, this connection can translate into help with program promotion and the sense that the program belongs to everyone. Finally, knowing that Science Café is connected to what's important to the university helps everyone answer, "Why are we doing this?"

Now that you have created a foundation, you are ready to develop the day. This can be both the most exciting and the most daunting part of the process, especially since you may be working on a tight budget. Being an academic library we are lucky to have lots of local on-campus experts who are willing and excited to share their expertise. If you are not an academic library—reach out to your local colleges and universities. Since it is often a requirement of faculty tenure process to do outreach activities, you can create a win-win situation.

INVITE ON-CAMPUS COLLABORATORS AND OFF-CAMPUS GUESTS

It's time to identify experts and a topic to explore. I find mixing it up with a combination of campus faculty and out-of-town guests is the way to go. In terms of identifying experts, you can use a combination of methods:

- Ask faculty, staff, and students whom they would invite.
- Select someone who can speak about a hot topic in the news.
- Identify a star on campus that has recently been recognized.
- Ask your Science Café community once it's up and running.

Experts are already interested in sharing their research with the public, but they need to know that they are in capable and organized hands. On my end, I want to know that we are forming a partnership. I set this tone from the outset by framing our relationship as a collaborative one. An invitation to be an expert for Science Cafe is not an invitation to a time slot. I take the initiative to float ideas, ask questions, and suggest formats. I share past experiences and experts via our Science Café channel on Vimeo for inspiration. All that said, I keep the initial invitation very general, rather than launch into all the possible details immediately.

In terms of payment, we are able to offer a modest honorarium for out-of-town experts, along with an evening in a hotel. Admittedly, our location helps attract experts since we're in a beautiful small city, halfway between San Francisco and Los Angeles. If you are at a university, other departments on campus may be able to offer sponsorship in exchange for partnering on the event. Sponsorship can be defined in a variety of ways, including financial; for us, it usually means help with publicity through their direct channels.

IT'S NOT A LECTURE; IT'S AN EXPERIENCE

Most experts will want to give a lecture using a PowerPoint presentation. Sometimes it is okay, but it is not a real interactive experience. It may be helpful to frame the event as a workshop, although that has its pitfalls too, since you don't want the guests who show up at Science Café to feel that they are required to do anything. Some may simply want to observe and they should be comfortable doing that.

There is also a balance in setting the tone for the audience. You and the expert want to assume that the audience is smart, while providing enough scaffolding that they can understand topics that may be outside of their experience. This is where interactivity can bring people together.

Here are a few examples:

- We built simple circuits at group tables before moving to the library's grand staircase to create a large-scale, computer-based, interactive game. Guests designed and built the game using Arduinos (an open-source electronics platform) and breadboards (reusable electronic test boards analogous to circuit boards). They also determined the strategy and layout of the physical game board (the library's staircase) culminating with a tennis ball target competition. The scoring was automatically updated to the library's digital displays, the campus home page, and guests' mobile devices.
- We transformed the open café area of our library into a kitchen, using outlets that usually power student laptops for powering water kettles. We poured three coffee samples for guests while an expert introduced intersecting issues around soil science, sustainability, business, and world affairs in the coffee industry. That weekend, we partnered with a local coffee shop to host an additional tasting in the community.
- We invited a bookbinder and author, who brought handmade kits for a hundred people to bind their own books with recycled materials. This event tied in with our opening celebration for a major exhibit featuring fine press printing and book arts.

Our events are scheduled to run no more than 1.5 hours. One guiding rule is that a minimum of half of that time should be spent interacting with the expert. Here are a few ways we've experimented with the time we have:

- Experts introduce themselves and an activity in ten minutes. For the next half an hour or so guests participate in an experiment. Then we regroup for questions.
- An expert demonstrates how to make something, like a handmade book. Then, using provided materials, guests make their own book while the expert interacts with them during the process.
- An expert spends half an hour talking. Guests then have an hour to interact and ask questions.

I develop a detailed timeline that I share with the experts and our team so that we are all confident about what's expected and when.

We host one event in the busy fall quarter, then two events each in the winter and spring quarters. We have found that 11:00 a.m.–12:30 p.m. on Thursdays is a good time for our campus, so we try to stick to that pattern. Perhaps a time after school or during the evening will be best for your community. Definitely check for conflicts that may impact your audience! Scheduling an event before a long holiday weekend, for example, is probably not a good idea.

BEAUTY ATTRACTS

We are a visual culture. Design plays a crucial role in promoting events and great promotion begins with excellent design. It's not just about making something beautiful. It's about instilling confidence that you're going to offer an inspired program that is worth everyone's time.

Every year the library hires a team of students who are studying design. With guidance, they develop systems of awesome and coordinated posters, flyers, video titles, Facebook banners, online event pages, and case displays for Cal Poly Science Café and other events and exhibits.

Our promotions contain just enough information to hook someone and make them feel welcome. We cover the who, what, where and when with a link and QR code to more information. You can see them on the Robert E. Kennedy Library website if you search for Cal Poly Science Cafe.

PERSONAL CONNECTIONS MATTER MORE THAN FACEBOOK CONNECTIONS

Promoting your event is a big deal. It's one thing to have an intimate audience because the topic appealed to just a few; it's another to share a great experience with a handful of people because the word didn't get out there. That said, one of the biggest mysteries is always, "How many people will come?"

In keeping with the casual feel, we don't require any sort of registration. The event happens in the open in the library (you don't have to open or close a door), and we offer a variety of seating options—groups around tables, theater seating or a mix–depending on what we are planning.

If not many people attend, it's a chance to make it an intimate occasion for those who are there. If more people attend than anticipated, we do our best to accommodate everyone. I like to think that it is not about the headcount, but about the experience for those who are present. Besides, there is always a chance to extend the event with online media. More on that later.

So, how do we get the word out?

We keep a list of e-mail addresses from the sign-in sheets used at events and add those names to an online marketing system. We also

- Enter the event to online community calendars in the area.
- Add a blurb to campus and departmental newsletters.

- Write a press release.
- Create an event page for the library's website and share on the home page.
- Invite related student groups and facilitate other student-to-student outreach.
- Put up a stanchion at the library's entrance.
- Contact related departments for help on how best to get the word out.
- Write a preview of the event for our blog and include photos.
- Deliver print promotion to departments and post on campus boards.
- Ask invited experts to promote using our links and materials.
- Really *use* Facebook.

Having a living Facebook page is a good thing (and we do; please join us!). You can create events (although only those who have a Facebook account see them), and invite interaction. On Facebook, we also

- Ask experts to invite their network using our Facebook event.
- Build audience by buying ads that promote our page. I found the "friends of friends" option works best, which means we advertise to friends of those who already like us.
- Create event banners to feature at the top of the page.

In addition, the student assistants who work with Science Café have vast networks with which they can share events. Students are coadministrators of the Cal Poly Science Café page, with explicit parameters about what to share and how to encourage a conversation. They post using a conversational but detached tone, asking questions and including a link.

While Facebook is a useful tool, personal invitations in the hallway, via e-mail, phone, and flyers are even better. Finding people who are totally into the topic and who will share their enthusiasm with others, also helps spread the word. Those enthusiasts can also offer suggestions on how to reach interested audiences in new ways.

PUT EVERYONE AT EASE TO CREATE AN OPEN SPACE FOR EXPERIMENTATION

Finally, after your preparations, the day has arrived and it's time to host a good party. Your role as organizer is a visible one. Like people do at a wedding, guests will look to you for cues. If you're having a great time, rolling with the unexpected and making it look easy, it sets the tone for others to relax and enjoy themselves.

Sugar and caffeine are key for our community. We always serve pastries, tea, and coffee. I encourage experts to grab a cup and croissant as well, and mingle with people as they arrive. That way they're not hidden behind the "fourth wall," and there isn't an intimidating separation between them and the guests. We also like to welcome people with music playing in the background; there are some great party songs about science out there.

The café environment keeps it feeling informal and fun. Sometimes it's even possible to tie specific food into the topic. For example, we had jars of gummy worms out during a Science Café on vermicomposting. These fun gestures remind people it's a low-key crowd. Nothing is high stakes at Science Café. This encourages questions.

Finally, if there is an interactive element, we try to provide written as well as verbal instructions. Or, if a topic doesn't lend itself well to interaction, there may be an opportunity to give something away. For example, a signed book by the featured expert. Or perhaps a vermicomposting bin, full of real worms, used in a demonstration on soil science.

SHARE EXPERTS WITH THE WORLD VIA VIDEO STORIES

We're lucky to have a small team of people who work together to capture our experts on video. At first, we experimented with capturing the series for podcasts, but since things are so interactive it didn't work well. Now we ask experts to arrive early to sit down for a short interview with a student on camera. The student and I develop the questions in collaboration with the expert to highlight their specialized knowledge.

Ideally within two weeks of the event, a short 2–5 minute video is released. It highlights the expert, what they're working on and what we did together at Science Café. We have created a channel for these videos, which you can find if you search for Cal Poly Science Café on Vimeo.

IDEAS FOR GOING BEYOND HEADCOUNT

Our series typically attracts 50–100 (sometimes as many as 140!) students, faculty, staff, and members of the community. Assessment and documentation isn't easy for a program that identifies itself as a casual, drop-in interaction. As soon as you start measuring and doing surveys, things begin to feel less casual, fast.

A few less-invasive assessment options:

- What are people saying on your Facebook page? Ask them.
- What do you overhear at events?
- What does the expert have to say about his or her experience?
- Put up oversized blank paper near the sign-in, and visually invite comments.
- Do people return, regardless of topic? Ask familiar faces why they come.

BUILDING GOODWILL BEYOND THE EVENT

It's not over when it's over. Showing thanks and appreciation is a chance to reflect on how the event unfolded and what made it meaningful. We follow up with experts and guests in a variety of ways that include the following:

- Thanking the expert with a framed poster used to promote their event.
- Sending a thank you note that highlights memorable moments.
- Sharing a write-up about the event on our blog.
- Posting the video interview to Facebook and tagging the expert.
- Acknowledging how experts, staff, faculty, students, and guests made the day.

HOW TO KEEP IT FRESH IF YOU GET TIRED

Sometimes it is difficult to sustain an ongoing program for a variety of reasons. Turning to one's colleagues for inspiration can help get things going. They may have ideas that range from whom to invite, what to call the event, to what to do that day. It can also be useful to consider what else is happening at the library. For example, it was a lot of fun to create a Science Café that tied in directly with a book arts exhibit.

What about working with a friend or colleague who is an expert? Or borrowing from an event you loved as a guest? Perhaps attend a maker faire, a "festival of invention."

It's also useful to leave behind the "should" in researching possible topics and allow for serendipity. Sometimes I jump down a rabbit hole online and follow my interests without Science Café in mind, only to discover something inspiring.

We have explored many STEM topics, including

- DIY: Physical computing at play: "Join us for a morning of making, strategizing and playing as we extend computers into the physical space to create a large-scale, interactive game in the library. Arduinos, breadboards, circuits, and code all factor into the equation in this hands-on workshop."
- Hypersonic speeds! How you can fly to space in the not-too-distant future: "Richard Branson is selling flights to the edge of space that you can soon take (for a fee). Find out how technology is making commercial travel to space possible with our featured speaker, Professor Dianne DeTurris, who specializes in propulsion and high-speed aerodynamics."
- Bionics: Merging man and machine: "Technology has reached a point where we can now effectively merge man and machine. Learn

about bionic devices that are designed to both augment ability (HULC) and facilitate walking (eLEGS) from a Cal Poly alumnus."

Science Café also explores topics outside of science, so that all disciplines taught on our comprehensive polytechnic campus are included. I'm particularly interested in exploring the intersections of art and design with other disciplines. This attention to interdisciplinary play emphasizes the power of collaboration and integrated thinking.

A COMMITMENT OF RESOURCES

Kennedy Library's commitment to offering vibrant public programs is reflected in its budgetary, advisory, and participatory support of these and other events, including staff who manage the facilities setup, food ordering, A/V coordination, and postproduction. Without this close collaboration, this program wouldn't be as successful or fun to run. In addition, while it's possible to operate Science Café on a modest programming budget, it's important to acknowledge that a significant portion of my full-time position and a part-time student assistant position are dedicated to the program. You may want to pick and choose what's doable for your Science Café depending on your resources.

ADDITIONAL RESOURCES

To learn more, search for Cal Poly Science Café at the Robert E. Kennedy Library. Discover an archive of events, including photos, videos, blog posts and more that illustrate how things happen. You can also watch the Cal Poly Science Café channel on Vimeo, which includes a slideshow about how to host the series. It's called Coffee + Cookies = Science Communication.

Science Café is an international movement. Check out NOVA Science Café as a resource for launching your own cafe. You may also want to visit the Center for Advancement of Informal Science Education and Visitors Studies Association.

WORK CITED

Scaramozzino, Jeanine Marie, and Catherine Trujillo. 2010. "Developing a Science Café Program for Your University Library." *Issues in Science and Technology Librarianship* 63. Accessed October 10, 2012 . doi: 10.5062/F4QC01D6.

VII

Partnerships

TWENTY-ONE

How to Make Library Workshops Popular with Science and Engineering Students

Giovanna Badia

Science and engineering students at McGill University can choose to attend a wide variety of instructional workshops by the Schulich Library of Science and Engineering, covering diverse topics such as library orientation, literature searching, citation analysis, current awareness, and bibliographic management software. How do librarians convince STEM students to attend these library workshops? Motivating students to attend extracurricular activities can be a challenge when they have demanding course loads. This chapter will discuss strategies for creating popular library workshops that engage the audience, writing student-centered advertising to increase attendance, obtaining advocates for library instruction among organizational support staff, and convincing faculty to make time for information literacy instruction in the classroom.

CREATING AND DELIVERING IRRESISTIBLE COURSE CONTENT

Library workshops are more likely to attract students if they

- Teach searching for information that cannot be easily found by using Google
- Include scenarios that are relevant to students
- Incorporate active learning exercises to keep the audience engaged
- Allow participants to take away something tangible at the end of the session

"UNFORTUNATELY, YOU CAN'T GOOGLE EVERYTHING"

This is what I tell students at the beginning of my literature searching workshops. Google is the proverbial elephant in the room that I address in my introduction. I explain in the first few minutes why Google or Google Scholar do not contain everything needed to do research for term papers. Students need to search other sources as well, since Google and Google Scholar have problems; for example, they include unauthoritative sources so that students need to spend additional time trying to identify those peer-reviewed scholarly articles among their search results that are appropriate to use for their papers. Research databases, such as Web of Science and Scopus, are then presented as the solution to these problems. My mention of Google elicits laughter from some of the students, but they all wait to hear what comes next. Google becomes the loveable villain, and Web of Science and Scopus turn into the heroes. Using the villain–hero dichotomy to create an attention-grabbing introduction is an idea that I obtained from reading Carmine Gallo's book, *The Presentation Secrets of Steve Jobs* (2010). Gallo describes how Steve Jobs delivered show-stopping lectures by presenting a problem and then proposing a solution to the problem raised in the form of an Apple product.

Telling your audience why Google cannot be their sole resource for researching a topic will not hold their attention throughout a workshop. During a literature searching class, I put aside some time to teach students how to search at least one type of information that is not easily found via a Google search, such as finding the most frequently cited articles on a topic, government reports, data and statistics, images with Creative Commons licenses, and so forth. My literature searching workshops also include timesaving resources, such as how to use bibliographic management software, (e.g., EndNote), to save their search results, cite their sources, and create bibliographies in Microsoft Word. Students leave the workshop having learned that Google is not the only quick and easy option. There are other resources that exist, which can easily help them research their topics, save them time, and that may also contribute to a better assignment grade.

Make It Relevant

Comparing and contrasting research databases to Google is only one way of engaging the audience and convincing them to use these resources. Another method is to present problem-based scenarios or examples that demonstrate why they would use a specific database. These scenarios should be relevant to the discipline or subject area that the students are studying since they play a major part in keeping students interested during a workshop and contribute to the audience's perception of the librarian. If the search examples presented are relevant, the students are more likely to think that the librarian understands their needs and can teach them something useful. It increases the likelihood of the presentation being well received.

The following are examples of scenarios that I use to teach a workshop on resources for Earth and Planetary Sciences:

1. Find publications that discuss whether a bolide impact hastened the extinction of the dinosaurs. (This scenario is used to show how to search for articles in Web of Science.)
2. Identify key papers that discuss the effects of thermal tides on the climate of Mars. (I demonstrate sorting search results by "Times Cited—Highest to Lowest" in Web of Science with this example.)
3. You are going on a field trip to Marguerite Bay in the Antarctic Peninsula. You would like to know what has been published about this area or what studies have been done. (I use this scenario to show browsing for articles in GeoScienceWorld.)
4. Find images for a presentation, or to help you study, about the hydrothermal features of igneous rocks and processes. (With this example I present a few websites listed on the library's Earth and Planetary Sciences online subject guide which have Creative Commons licenses for the use of images.)
5. Find government reports about climate change in Quebec. (To answer the question in this scenario, I take students on a tour of useful and free search tools and publications on the Natural Resources Canada website.)

Relevant teaching examples can be obtained by gathering background information about the subject area. I read review articles and chapters from basic textbooks, scan the publications of researchers in that department, as well as look at my notes, when available, on past research consultations with students and faculty. If a professor requests that I provide in-class library instruction, I ask the professor for a copy of the term paper assignment and for sample search topics. For in-class library instruction, I make direct links between what I am teaching and the course assignment, as well as anticipate problems that students may run into and present solutions. For example, I show students how to complete an interlibrary loan request in the event that the library does not own the book or subscribe to the journal they need. I also share my own personal searching experiences with the students to emphasize how the workshop content applies to a real-life situation.

Incorporate Active Learning Exercises

Presentation of the most relevant content will often be insufficient to prevent students from doing or thinking about other things during a workshop. Incorporating active learning exercises into the workshop content can help keep students focused.

Below are some sample active learning activities that I integrate into my teaching:

Open-Ended, Matching, Multiple-Choice, and/or Rank-Order Questions

Put in the correct order:

__Combine search terms (AND/OR)
__Identify the appropriate resource(s) to search
__Evaluate your results and modify your search strategy if necessary
__Break down you question into its separate concepts
__Apply limits
__Brainstorm synonyms, or search for subject headings if available
__Define your question

Hands-On Practice Search Exercises

- What are the leading candidates to replace chromium in making aerospace materials? Find journal articles to support your answer.
- Small group discussions, (e.g., Prepare a conference, elevator speech about your research topic and share it with the person next to you).
- Verbal quizzes to recap the workshop content, (e.g., i. Where can you find references to journal articles?; ii. How would you search for *planets* or *planetary*?; iii. How would you obtain journal articles or books that are not available at the library?; iv. How would you find who cited an article?; v. Where can you find references to books on a topic?

Allow a Head Start on Assignments

Setting aside some time for students to research their own topics—in combination with acknowledging Google pros and cons, presenting relevant content, and including active learning exercises—should increase the attractiveness of a library workshop and ensure satisfaction among participants. Students are more likely to feel that attending a library workshop will be worth their time if they are able to accomplish something, (e.g., complete part of their assignment, during the session). The theory is immediately put into real-life practice. Anything tangible that students can take away at the end of a session, such as having found and saved journal articles on their topics, having downloaded citation software on their laptops, and so forth, will lead to a greater appreciation of the instruction given.

ADVERTISING INSTRUCTION

Creating great content is only half of what makes a workshop popular. The other half involves advertising, (i.e., convincing the intended audience to attend). The course outline provides the basis for writing the advertising material. Summarizing the workshop outcomes in the advertisement and including what would make it worthwhile for students to attend, such as learning search techniques that will save them time or getting a head start on researching their assignments with the help of a librarian, will create a compelling ad copy. Advertise in as many venues as possible, both in print and online, for instance, create posters and flyers, send e-mails, publish ads in newsletters, and/or post on listservs, blogs, and websites. Send your announcement to the intended audience, but also contact those who can convince your audience to attend, (e.g., professors, departmental secretaries, etc.) A well-advertised instructional session will increase participation and the chances of generating positive buzz before the event.

Below is an example of a workshop announcement that was e-mailed to all undergraduate and graduate students in chemical engineering at McGill University.

Hello all,
I am e-mailing to tell you about a workshop, called "Literature Searching: How–to Strategies for Chemical Engineering," that I will be offering this month, where participants will learn how to

- identify where to look for references
- build an effective search strategy
- find the most influential papers on a topic
- use Endnote to save time and cite their sources

Participants will also have time to perform searches on their own topics, thereby giving them a head start on doing research for their own assignments or theses.
The same session will be given at two different times to accommodate as many people as possible:

- Thurs., **October 11** from 2:30–4:00 p.m. in the Schulich Library, room 313
- Wed., **October 17** from 4:00–5:30 p.m. in the Schulich Library, room 313

All are welcome to attend. Registration is required. To register for one of the sessions above, e-mail me at giovanna.badia@mcgill.ca.
I look forward to seeing you there.

Regards, Giovanna
[e-mail signature]

Gifts and Prizes

Giving away gifts or prizes at the end of an instructional session can also entice students to participate. McGill Library branches offer an orientation program at the beginning of each autumn and winter semester. The orientation program consists of: (1) a thirty-minute tour of the library; (2) a one-hour "getting started" workshop about how to locate books and journals, login to your library account, renew library materials, recall items that are loaned out, and access electronic resources from home; and (3) a one-hour "finding the right stuff" workshop about how to locate appropriate research databases for a subject area, create effective search strategies for finding references on a topic, and request an interlibrary loan. The program is advertised as "Take three, get free memory!" Students are given an orientation passport, in the form of a printed bookmark, on which the instructor places a sticker after an activity has been completed. Once a student has collected all three stickers on his/her passport, the student can submit the passport at any McGill Library services desk to obtain a free 2GB USB bracelet. The program is popular with the students; they rush to complete all three activities to receive their bracelets.

In addition to gifts and prizes, scheduling is important, both for the advertising and delivery of the workshops. Library tours and workshops are being offered two weeks before the autumn semester starts, and one week before the winter semester starts, when the majority of students are available to attend. To receive the widest promotion possible, these activities are included in the advertising for the university orientation that is offered to new students every August. For example, library staff members participate in the McGill Street Festival offered at the end of each summer where different university departments have a table and promote their services and activities. The library orientation program is heavily promoted at this event.

Furthermore, raffles are held at the end of the "getting started" and "finding the right stuff" workshops, in order to encourage students to complete the evaluation forms. The winner of the raffle receives a travel mug. I have also included raffles at the end of my other workshops to reinforce students' positive feelings of the training session and motivate them to attend future workshops. I obtained items that I could raffle off, such as USB keys and water bottles, by requesting free promotional materials from the websites of database vendors like Thomson Reuters.

OBTAINING ADVOCATES AMONG SUPPORT STAFF

If advertising is widely distributed, it increases the likelihood of attracting more students. Organizational support staff can be instrumental in distributing library advertising and convincing students to take advantage of workshops offered by the library. It is, therefore, important to establish a relationship with them. For example, I attend departmental activities with gifts from the library to help ensure that support staff remember my name. I am in frequent contact with administrative staff of various departments to ask them to distribute advertising within their units. My colleagues and I also maintain a good relationship with staff at the McGill Engineering Student Centre, which handles academic and career advising and is located next to the Schulich Library of Science and Engineering, and with members of the McGill Writing Centre, which helps students with their writing skills. We advocate their services and activities, referring students to them when appropriate, and they do the same for us.

Moreover, we participate in other university activities and hire students to obtain as many advocates as possible. For instance, as part of promoting the library's orientation program, library staff participate in a services roundtable for floor fellows in the university dormitories. Floor fellows are undergraduate students that act as role models and mentors for new students living in the residencies. At the services roundtable, each university department has the opportunity to speak with the floor fellows about their services and activities. We give the floor fellows a free USB bracelet to encourage them to promote the library's orientation activities to new students. The library's student employees also give some of the library tours to empathize with our intended audience. Similarly, the library employs graduate students to act as facilitators in our graduate research workshop series to share their own experiences, thus making the content more relevant to participants. These graduate students have already taken the workshop series themselves and have applied it to their work.

APPROACHING FACULTY

Professors or course instructors are the best advocates for library instruction in an academic setting. Providing library instruction during class time reaches the largest number of students. How do you convince faculty to make time for information literacy instruction in the classroom? The following are some successful strategies:

1. When approaching a professor for the first time about in-class library instruction, request a small amount of class time, (i.e., 15–20 minutes). The risk to the instructor of accepting your offer becomes minimal. Once you have delivered the instruction successfully, you will be in a better position to negotiate more time in the future if you need it.

2. Link the content of your instruction to the course outcomes. For example, I propose to teach a literature-searching workshop in those courses that include a research paper assignment. I do not send e-mails to all instructors who are teaching courses in a semester. I read the course descriptions and only contact those faculty members who teach courses where I believe that library instruction would benefit the students in completing their assignments.

3. Provide instructional activities, (e.g., brown bag lectures, webinars, workshops, etc.) for faculty. Seeing you in action may persuade them to invite you to their classrooms.

4. Offer workshops on behalf of the library and send the announcements to those instructors whose students would benefit. I ask these instructors to spread the word among their students. I have also had faculty respond by asking me to give the same workshop during the class time since some of their students said that they are interested, but would not be able to attend outside of class.

5. Distribute feedback forms for students to complete and send copies of completed forms, or a summary of the feedback received, to the instructor. I have used this strategy when I have taught workshops in other courses and students have told me, or written on the feedback form, that they would have appreciated having learned the content in a specific course that they took earlier in their program curriculum. I also send the feedback to professors who do not attend my in-class workshops. It communicates what occurred during their absence, (i.e., shows what students learned and appreciated, and serves as their reminder to include in-class library instruction when they teach the course in the future).

To maximize the impact of any of the strategies listed above, write communications that are unique. Tailor e-mail messages to the professor and his/her course. Below is an example of an e-mail I sent to a faculty member about teaching a workshop in his higher-level undergraduate course, which discussed biological applications of chemical engineering.

Dear Professor X,
I saw in the course calendar that you are responsible for teaching CHEE ### this autumn. I was wondering if I could speak to your class about interdisciplinary literature searching. Some of the content I could cover is how

- To construct a well-defined search question
- Build an effective search strategy to obtain relevant results
- Make the most of core databases in the life sciences (e.g., PubMed, Embase), as well as compare and contrast these with the classic resources in engineering and the physical sciences (e.g., Web of Science, Compendex)
- Use EndNote to cite their sources

Please let me know if this would be of interest to you, or if there is anything else I can do for your class.
Regards, Giovanna
[e-mail signature]

THE FORMULA FOR SUCCESS

Making library workshops popular with science and engineering students involves creating relevant and interactive workshop content that allows participants to take away tangibles at the end of the session, advertising workshops in as many venues as possible, and including incentives to participate, obtaining advocates among organizational support staff and students, and approaching faculty with customized offers to provide in-class library instruction that is tailored to their courses.

WORK CITED

Gallo, Carmine. 2010. *The Presentation Secrets of Steve Jobs: How to Be Insanely Great in Front of Any Audience.* New York: McGraw-Hill.

TWENTY-TWO

Learning About Future Stem Careers

Eileen G. Harrington

The Bureau of Labor Statistics has predicted that the number of jobs in science and engineering fields will grow by 20.6 percent between 2008 and 2018, while jobs in all occupations will only increase by 10.1 percent during the same period (National Science Board 2012). The changing nature of society in the United States over the last few decades partially explains this increase in demand. Technology surrounds us and plays an integral part of our lives. Our current economy is more knowledge based and innovation driven and relies on a workforce with skills and knowledge central to science, technology, engineering, and mathematics (STEM) fields. In addition, climate change, pandemics, and the rapid loss of natural resources present myriad challenges both in the United States and around the world. Science and technology can help combat these problems, but they require a strong and knowledgeable workforce to do so.

Although the number of undergraduate and graduate STEM degrees conferred in the United States over the last several years has steadily increased, many fear that this increase will not meet the projected demands. Also, within these increases, several disparities still remain. While the face of America changes, with many minority groups now becoming the majority, most of the faces found in STEM fields remain white and male. In 2010, of the total number of US bachelor's degrees in STEM fields, only 8.6 percent were earned by African Americans, 9.1 percent by Latinos, and 0.7 percent by Native Americans (COSEPUP 2011). Women have made great strides in fields such as law, medicine and business, but their numbers still lag in many STEM fields, particularly engineering, physics, and computer science (Hill, Corbett, and St. Rose 2010).

Misconceptions about science and scientists, as well as prevailing stereotypes, likely discourage many students from pursing STEM degrees and careers. Exercises where students are asked to describe or draw a scientist often evoke images of a man in a white coat toiling away alone in a lab. They are unaware of the full range of activities that scientists, engineers, and mathematicians undertake. Students might be passionate about nature or finding a way to mitigate the effects of climate change, but do not see a direct way to transform that passion into a future career. Based on how science has been taught in their schools, students might correlate it with memorizing facts rather than an activity that involves questioning, experimenting, and trying to make sense of the world around them. In addition, persistent negative stereotypes and the unconscious bias that boys are innately better at science and math make it hard for girls to envision themselves pursuing STEM careers (Hill, Corbett, and St. Rose 2010).

Given this landscape, many universities and colleges offer summer programs or workshops to encourage girls and underrepresented groups to pursue STEM degrees and careers. Some examples include the following:

- University of Illinois I-STEM summer camps for high school students
- Summer camps for elementary, middle, and high school students through the A. James Clark School of Engineering at the University of Maryland–College Park
- Texas A&M Women Explore Engineering program for female high school students
- The STEM Academy at Oregon State University, which offers various programs for elementary, middle, and high school students

These types of programs give students the opportunity to immerse themselves in the work of engineers and scientists, thereby gaining a deeper understanding of what it would be like to enter those fields. They also might encounter an aspect of a field that they had not originally associated with science or engineering work.

Often science or engineering departments organize these programs with little or no involvement by university libraries. This is a missed opportunity. Involving libraries enables students' discovery of other ways to learn about future careers, as well as the many resources libraries can provide to undergraduate and graduate students and career professionals.

This chapter outlines one way to incorporate the library into a larger STEM career exploration program. It focuses on the workshop *On the Hunt for Your Future Career*, which was part of the 2012 Journeys in Engineering, Technology and Science (JETS) program at the Universities at Shady Grove. This type of activity could be integrated in similar programs in other universities or could be adapted for use by school librarians in middle and high schools.

JOURNEYS IN ENGINEERING, TECHNOLOGY, AND SCIENCE (JETS)

The Universities at Shady Grove (USG) is an innovative model for higher education. It consists of a partnership between nine universities from the University System of Maryland. USG offers 80 upper-level undergraduate and graduate programs from the nine universities on one nonresidential campus. Students are members of their home universities and their degrees are conferred by them, but they attend classes at USG. Its location in a high-density population area creates a more convenient and affordable university environment for many students. USG has also formed many partnerships with local governmental and research organizations, allowing students to gain experience through internships and other programs. The degree programs offered at USG reflect the US job sectors with high growth rates, thus fulfilling future workforce needs.

For the past four years, USG, in partnership with Montgomery County Public Schools (MCPS) and Montgomery College, has delivered the JETS program. USG is located in Montgomery County, Maryland, which has the largest school district in the state and is the seventeenth largest in the United States. Twenty-six percent of students in MCPS are Latino, 21 percent are African American, 14 percent are Asian American, and less than 1 percent is Native American (Montgomery County Public Schools 2012). Montgomery College is a multicampus community college located in Montgomery County that serves nearly 60,000 students. Many Montgomery College students transfer to USG to earn their bachelor's degree.

The overall objective of JETS is to energize middle school students about careers in science and engineering. It is a free, one-day event open to all MCPS middle school students and their parents/guardians. MCPS science teachers and counselors assist with marketing the program, and a key target group for the program is students who might not be planning to attend college or even consider a scientific career. In 2011, approximately 40 percent of those who attended were from this target group. Overall, between 400 and 450 students and about 350 parents/guardians attended the event in 2011 and 2012.

The day begins with two large group presentations by organizations known for their dynamic and interactive presentations, such as Mad Science. These presentations energize the kids and prepare them for a day of fun-filled science activities. Following these sessions, the students are divided into groups of approximately twenty and attend two "technical sessions" in one of three tracks: bioscience and medicine; engineering and environmental science; and computer science. Lasting about forty-five minutes, the technical sessions entail hands-on activities presented by people who work in STEM fields. Through these activities the students gain a better understanding about these different fields and have the opportunity to learn more from the presenter about how he/she got into the work he/she does. USG draws upon faculty and graduate students from its nine different universities to lead the activities, as well as local organizations and businesses, such as the Rockville Science Center, the Tech Council of Maryland and the National Institutes of Health. The activities range from extracting DNA from a strawberry to exploring the inner workings of a computer.

After a full morning, the students and their parents/guardians have lunch and then are free to explore the STEM Pathways Expo. The Expo is a large room full of tables where different universities, organizations, businesses, and science teachers from MCPS high schools provide mini-demonstrations and information about themselves. It offers an informal way for students and their parents to gain an understanding of what types of classes they should take in high school and beyond to pursue a career in STEM. Organizations and business that have participated in the past include the following:

- Discovery Communications
- Human Genome Sciences
- Lockheed Martin
- NASA Goddard Space Flight Center
- National Institute of Standards and Technology

By the end of the day, students leave with a better understanding of the variety of career opportunities available to them in STEM fields and ways to embark on their journey into a future STEM career.

ON THE HUNT FOR YOUR FUTURE CAREER

As part of the 2012 JETS program, the science librarian at USG's Priddy Library developed and delivered a technical session entitled, *On the Hunt for Your Future Career*. During the session, students completed a scavenger hunt, allowing them to explore the variety of careers within the engineering and environmental science fields while utilizing a variety of library resources. Because the session was part of the engineering and environmental science stream, all of the activities focused specifically on these areas of STEM.

To start off, the science librarian introduced the activity by talking about her background and how she ended up in her current career. Using a slideshow, she shared her early interest in nature and the outdoors, as well as her desire to help others learn more about the natural world. Because of this early passion, she studied biology and environmental studies in college and then went into the Peace Corps as an environmental education volunteer. After this, she got a master's degree in environmental studies and did field work in Costa Rica with teachers, students, and coffee farmers. Finally, she decided to continue to help people find the information they need by getting a master's degree in library and information studies. This led her to work in a natural history museum for several years and then later, her current position as a science librarian. She stressed to the students that although they might not immediately associate a librarian with being a scientist, she considers herself a scientist because she has studied science and thinks like a scientist. This is important when doing STEM-related career development activities with young people because often they do not realize the range of science-related careers open to them. Many science librarians at universities and colleges likely have an undergraduate or graduate degree in the sciences and could talk about the path that led them to their current position. This helps students to see that many careers that on the surface might not seem science-related actually are. Also, including a more personal introduction to the activity allowed the students to quickly get to know the science librarian and feel more comfortable in asking questions about her career path. Finally, the librarian told the students that they were going to utilize skills that scientists do during this session, such as seeking information, asking questions, and collaborating. This can help break down barriers that make students think they cannot be scientists.

After this brief introduction, the librarian introduced the scavenger hunt activity, using the following ground rules as a guide:

- Work in pairs to search for information on a scavenger hunt in twenty-five minutes
- Only write answers on one sheet
- Take turns writing answers and using iPad
- Ask for help if needed
- Come back to this room when done

These ground rules were posted on the last slide as part of the introductory talk. As alluded to in the ground rules, each student received a sheet of questions that were part of the scavenger hunt so they would both have easy access to them, but they only had to record their answers on one sheet. Table 22.1 has an example of the text found on one of the worksheets. Often the same questions were repeated across all copies of the sheets, but in a different order to avoid having too many groups working on the same question at the same time. For the book-related question, a few different book titles were given. This was done so that twenty students were not all looking for the same book. The questions were designed so that the students would use a variety of resources when looking for information—the Internet, librarians, books, and a touch-screen monitor.

Prior to the activity, a timer app was installed on the iPads. The timer was set to twenty-five minutes so the students could keep track of the amount of time they had left. We briefly went over the basics of using the iPad, but all of the students were very comfortable using one or had used

Table 22.1 Scavenger Hunt

ON THE HUNT FOR YOUR FUTURE CAREER

You and your partner are on the hunt for information on career opportunities. You have 25 minutes to complete the following tasks. Once you are finished, come back to the room you started in. Remember to ask a librarian if you get stuck! Good luck!

1. *Go to Group Study Room 1200R. It has a touch-screen monitor (smart board). The eGFI (Engineering Go For It) website (http://students.egfi-k12.org/) should be on the screen. In a section of this website called "Trailblazers," watch the video about Natalie Jeremijenko, an engineer. What did you think of the video? What do you think about Natalie's work? Leave a comment or doodle about your reaction to the video on the screen using your finger or the special pen. Save your comment/doodle on the desktop.* **PLEASE LEAVE THE COMPUTER ON THIS WEBSITE WHEN YOU ARE DONE.**

2. *Using the iPad, go to the Engineer Girl website (http://www.engineergirl.org/). Click on the "Try on a Career" link. Choose a career that interests you and click on its tag. How much money would you make if you chose that career?*

3. *Find the book* All in a Day's Work: Careers Using Science *on the shelf. Its call number is Q149.U5 S92 2008. (Hint: The books are on the shelves in alphabetical and numerical order. A book with the call number R200 .U15 2010 will be in the "R" section after the "Q" section and before the "S" section. Once you find the "R" section, look for the books that start in the 200s.) Once you have found the book, scan the table of contents, which lists different careers in the sciences. Choose a career that interests you and go to its page. What kind of advice does the author give students who want to work at that job? Write down the advice below, along with the name of the job. Return the book to its correct place on the shelf when you are done.*

4. *Ask a librarian or JETS volunteer to show you a website with information on any engineering or environmental science jobs that interest you and are in or near the city where you live. Write down the name of the website and a job that each of you would like to do.*

one before so not much time was spent on explaining its functionality. The students were then let loose in the library to complete their scavenger hunt. The parents were instructed that they could explore the library on their own, stay in the room, or shadow the students. If they shadowed the students, they were asked not to help answer the questions, but rather let them work on them on their own or to seek help from a librarian or volunteer.

After twenty-five minutes, the students returned to the instruction room in the library where the session started, if they had not already made it back before then. The students shared the information they found as a large group, using the following questions as a guide:

- What was one new and interesting job you learned about?
- What made you interested in it?
- What would be some skills you would need for that kind of job?
- What resources did you use to complete your scavenger hunt?

The librarian stressed that she hoped they had learned about some new and fun resources they could explore in-depth when thinking about their future careers. They also encountered the variety of resources libraries can provide, whatever their information needs might be. The students gained a sense of what a university library is like, and when they go onto college, they will know what to expect and have a higher comfort level using the library and seeking help.

Prior to the activity, the science librarian purchased items as prizes for the first pair to finish the activity, as well as candy for all of the participants. Since most of the groups finished at the same time, all of the students were given candy, and no "winners" were declared. Prizes were not stressed at the start of the activity so the students were fine with only getting candy. They also seemed to enjoy doing the activity and were very engaged throughout without the incentive of winning a prize.

The collaboration of other librarians and staff at the Priddy Library was instrumental to making this session a success. After creating a draft of the questions for the scavenger hunt the science librarian had her colleagues test them out as if they were students. This allowed her to: determine the timing for the scavenger hunt, decide whether to add or take away questions, make the questions harder or easier, and test the overall clarity of the instructions. On the actual day of the event, in addition to the regularly scheduled reference desk librarian, several librarians and volunteers helped out as floaters. They answered any questions the students had while working on their scavenger hunt. Prior to the event, the science librarian prepped all of the librarians and volunteers about one of the questions on the scavenger hunt. This question had the students ask a librarian or volunteer about a particular website. The website they showed the students was CareerOne Stop, a government-sponsored website. Within this website, the librarian or volunteer did a search with the students in the "Job Search" section. Another librarian was stationed in the room with the touch-screen monitor in order to help orient the students to using it (if they had not used one before) and for any technical difficulties that might arise.

This activity was created for an academic library setting, but it could be adapted for a school or public library setting, as well. A school librarian could deliver the activity in partnership with science teachers who could talk about how they got into their careers. A school librarian could also invite students' parents who work in STEM fields to participate in an event like this by talking about their careers. In addition, science teachers or parents could be incorporated in the scavenger hunt as sources of information for specific questions. In very same ways, public librarians could create a career exploration program and seek out volunteers from the community to help deliver it.

INSPIRING FUTURE STEMITES

Libraries can play an important role in helping to foster young people's interest in science, engineering, technology, and math. By implementing STEM career exploration programming in a fun and hands-on way, students gain a deeper understanding of jobs in these fields, while also becoming more comfortable finding and using library resources. Studies have shown that many scientists first became inspired to pursue science as a career because of experiences they had as children and that exposure to positive adult role models nurtured that inspiration, as well as provided them with guidance along their chosen academic and career paths (Anderson and Gilbride 2007; Maltese and Tai 2010; Royal Society 2004). Even if students do not end up in a STEM career, many of the required skills for STEM pursuits—problem solving, gathering and synthesizing information, being observant, working collaboratively, and thinking creatively—would serve them well in any chosen career. Libraries and librarians have always opened up new worlds and possibilities to youth, and with STEM career programs they can continue to do just that.

WORKS CITED

Anderson, Lisa and Kimberley Gilbride. 2007. "The Future of Engineering: A Study of the Gender Bias." *McGill Journal of Education* 42 (1): 103–17.

Committee on Science, Engineering, and Public Policy (COSEPUP). 2011. Expanding Underrepresented Minority Participation: America's Science and Technology Talent at the Crossroads . Washington, DC: The National Academies Press.

Hill, Catherine, Christianne Corbett, and Andresse St. Rose. 2010. *Why So Few?: Women in Science, Technology, Engineering and Mathematics*. Washington, DC: American Association of University Women.

Maltese, Adam V. and Robert H. Tai. 2010. "Eyeballs in the Fridge: Sources of Early Interest in Science." *International Journal of Science Education* 32 (5): 669–85.

Montgomery County Public Schools. 2012. "Montgomery County Public Schools at a Glance."Accessed January 30, 2013. http://www.montgomeryschoolsmd.org/uploadedFiles/about/MCPS-At-A-Glance.pdf

National Science Board. 2012. *Science and Engineering Indicators 2012.* Arlington, VA: National Science Foundation. Accessed December 13, 2012. http://www.nsf.gov/statistics/seind12/start.htm

Royal Society. 2004. "Taking a Leading Role—Scientists Survey." Accessed January 30, 2013. http://royalsociety.org/uploadedFiles/Royal_Society_Content/Supporting_scientists/Equality_and_Diversity/Scientists_survey.pdf

TWENTY-THREE

"Take It from the Top": Cultivating Relationships with STEM Faculty to Connect with Students

Shawn V. Lombardo and Barbara A. Shipman

In keeping with our library's advocacy of information literacy (IL) across the curriculum, librarian liaisons to academic departments at our institution have historically concentrated on expanding IL instruction for students and, secondarily, on developing the library's print and digital collections. Unfortunately, the librarian liaisons to the science, technology, engineering, and mathematics (STEM) departments were unsuccessful in drumming up faculty interest in the library and its services beyond the occasional book or journal request. While course-related and course-integrated IL instruction thrived in other disciplines between 2003 and spring 2012, librarians taught only one IL session per each chemistry, engineering, computer science, or mathematics course, and the librarian liaison to the biology department fared only slightly better during this same period. Because most of our library's science and technical literature is available online, we rarely saw STEM faculty in the building or encountered their students needing reference assistance. As a result, the library's outreach efforts geared toward these areas stagnated.

Under a new strategic plan and a new library dean, our vision of the librarian liaison role has broadened recently to include promotion of scholarly communication initiatives and concerns, more intensive research support for faculty and students, and more engagement with the department generally. To maximize our efforts, we grouped together liaison responsibilities to create synergies: previously the biology, physics, engineering, mathematics/statistics, and chemistry departments were assigned to multiple librarians; under the new model these areas are now the responsibility of primarily two librarians—us! While we used to call ourselves reference and instruction librarians, we now became the science and engineering librarian and the mathematics and statistics librarian.

We were excited by this new challenge but also a bit fearful. What did librarians with degrees in English and cinematic arts know about providing library services to STEM faculty and students? How could we successfully re-engage with our faculty and students? We're still experimenting, but our early successes have given us confidence that we're on the right track.

GET TO KNOW YOUR STEM COMMUNITY

The first step in devising an outreach plan for your STEM departments is to learn as much as you can about the academic programs and faculty at your institution. Course catalogs and departmental websites are a good place to start. Investigate how faculty and student research is shared within the department too. Are there senior research project showcases or demonstrations? Are there active department student organizations?

In addition, become familiar with the research activities and preferred publication venues of your faculty. Again, departmental websites may link to faculty CVs, personal web pages, or other profiles, and the departmental secretary may be able to supply you with a list of recent faculty publications. Be sure to examine relevant research institutes or centers on your campus to identify the companies or agencies that are funding faculty research.

Additionally, use Google Scholar to identify the top researchers at your institution. Obviously, you can search by author or institution from the main or advanced search options. However, another excellent way to explore your STEM faculty's scholarly output is to search for your institution in the "Author Search" box that appears on your own Google Scholar profile (or that of one of your faculty); this search feature will retrieve a list of other public profiles from your institution (rather than a list of publications), with the most highly-cited researchers appearing first.

For more in-depth information about faculty needs, consider designing and distributing a brief survey. Survey results can identify ideal times to hold workshops or office hours, capture faculty concerns about their graduate students' research skills, and so forth. There are numerous free web-based options for conducting a quick survey; select an option that makes it simple to create, disperse, complete, and track the questionnaire. The forms feature in Google Docs, for instance, allows you to embed a questionnaire into the body of an e-mail so that respondents can complete the survey without leaving their inbox, and survey results can be imported seamlessly into a Google spreadsheet for basic data analysis.

Once you have a good grasp of the teaching and research environment within your liaison areas, explore the library literature for a broader perspective on the information-seeking and research habits of STEM faculty and students in general. For example, there have been numerous studies on engineering faculty library use. Engel, Robbins, and Kulp (2011) found that engineering faculty do not consider libraries as their first source of information; instead, they rely on their students and colleagues for their research and teaching needs, with time constraints and accessibility as the top reasons for this behavior. With all of their information resources at their fingertips, it may be difficult to persuade them to look beyond their colleagues and their computers. Unfortunately, this belief in the library's irrelevance will most probably trickle down to their students.

Like their faculty, engineering graduate students turn first to their professors when they need information (George et al. 2006) and are introduced to most library research skills by their instructors (Hoffmann et al. 2008). And, according to Scaramozzino (2010), undergraduate STEM students are in an even worse position: "Compared with humanities and social science majors, science majors often use the library only for general education, English, and speech classes and then fail to visit the library to use source materials until their senior year if at all. . . . Any way to increase student awareness of the library even for nonacademic reasons can make it easier for them to use the library later" (323).

Our preliminary research, along with past experience, led us to conclude that pushing for formal information literacy instruction in our liaison areas would not yield the results we wanted. We decided to try a different strategy: to make ourselves relevant to STEM faculty first, who could then advocate for the library on our behalf.

ESTABLISHING COMMUNICATION CHANNELS

Librarians looking to promote their services among STEM faculty and students must first establish or, in our case, reestablish lines of communication. In previous years, communication was conducted primarily between the librarian and a department's library coordinator—a faculty member who serves as the main contact for disseminating information about the library to the rest of their colleagues. While this liaison/coordinator model worked well in other disciplines, it never gelled for most of the STEM departments; announcements, database trials, and offers to provide IL instruction generated little response. Our first task in our newly envisioned role was to improve communication! We crafted an introductory e-mail that was brief, focused, and provided a few concrete examples of the services that we could provide. We sent the e-mail to all faculty in our departments rather than relying on the department's library coordinator to disseminate the information, in order to create a critical mass of conversations among the faculty about their library-related research and teaching needs.

In fact, this one e-mail generated more responses in one week than all previous attempts. Almost immediately, we saw an increase in office visits from mathematics graduate students seeking information on graph theory and biology research assistants who were sent by their faculty advisors specifically to learn to search Web of Science effectively; we were asked to give a presentation to the mechanical engineering graduate seminar; and we received the first request in many years for formal library instruction for a computer science class. Throughout the semester, we sent short, informal e-mails about new database trials, lists of recent publications in their field and an occasional reminder of pertinent library services, being careful not to spam them with too many or irrelevant messages. These follow-up e-mails continued to reap benefits. Sending a "thank you" message to the mathematics instructor who referred his students to the library for research assistance, for example, generated a conversation about the possibility of providing IL instruction to his graduate class in future semesters—potentially the first IL session offered for a mathematics class at our institution.

FOCUS ON WHAT'S IMPORTANT TO FACULTY

Why were our communications so successful? We tried to address only a few topics that were likely to generate immediate interest from the faculty:

1. *Their Students*

Because STEM graduate students rely on their instructors for current information, they are most likely to seek out librarian assistance when encouraged to do so by faculty, and because faculty rely on their graduate students and colleagues for information, marketing library services for students in a way that is advantageous to faculty, too, is critical. In the initial e-mail to our departments, we described the support that we could provide specifically to their graduate assistants in using resources and research tools (e.g., Web of Science, RefWorks). To make the referral process seamless, we established office hours and used Google Calendar's appointment slot feature to enable students to sign up for research consultations from their mobile device or laptop. (Our institution employs Google apps for its campus-wide e-mail and calendar services; investigate the calendaring options available at your institution or online, or set up a public appointment calendar with a personal Gmail account.) We included the office hours, along with the link to the public appointment calendar, in the e-mail and on our personal profiles on the library's website. Because many graduate students work full-time, we added Skype widgets to our profile pages to connect with students who were unable to come to campus during regular office hours.

Targeting instructors who serve as advisors to student chapters of professional organizations (e.g., Society of Women Engineers, American Chemical Society) and other clubs and organizations can be another effective inroad into your liaison areas. These faculty are student-oriented and will be receptive to new initiatives that emphasize student success. Keep in mind, too, that student success is not measured by academic achievement alone. Next year, we plan to hold a workshop for graduating seniors on conducting a job search; other workshop ideas include sessions on finding co-op/internship opportunities or selecting a graduate program in the STEM disciplines.

2. Their Academic Programs

Program Development

Initiatives that will clearly improve retention rates, grow academic programs, or help the program meet accreditation standards will resonate with faculty. In our case, a perfect opportunity presented itself: the Department of Mathematics and Statistics developed a new undergraduate actuarial science program. To encourage the program director to be actively involved in selecting library resources for the program and with the library, we decided to name him a "library coordinator"; essentially, the department now has two library coordinators. While the new title is primarily semantic in nature, it gives the faculty member a service responsibility that can be added to the tenure portfolio and, one hopes, cultivate a collaborative relationship. Dialogue with the department has improved: communication with the actuarial science's library coordinator grew from e-mail correspondence to face-to-face meetings in which the librarian liaison was able to highlight library services that can support the growing program's teaching and research needs. The conversation resulted in an invitation for the librarian to speak at a future actuarial science club meeting.

Accreditation

It is likely that some of your STEM faculty may face (and dread) an accreditation visit in the near future. Library participation in the self-study preparation and the site visit will no doubt build bridges between the library and STEM departments. Become familiar with the appropriate accrediting agencies and the timetable for accreditation. Visit accrediting organizations' websites for an overview of the accreditation process and standards; usually the guidelines feature a section on library resources and services.

If possible, review the self-study (and even the visiting team's preliminary or final report) that was compiled for the last accreditation cycle. Did a librarian write the library-related portions or did the department? Were concerns raised about the library's collections? Does the information presented in the self-study seem adequate and only requires updating? Is there a more effective way to present the library data?

Most important; be proactive. Contact the harried faculty members who are tasked with assembling the self-study and offer your assistance in gathering data (and even writing) the portions that address library resources. In addition to creating very grateful faculty, you will also benefit; faculty often forget about the library-related sections in the face of other concerns, leaving the librarian scrambling to meet a tight deadline. This participation can also serve as an opportunity for you to heighten awareness of underutilized resources and services.

3. Their Research

According to a survey conducted on faculty use of current awareness services in databases and e-journals, scientists and engineers preferred to teach themselves how to use research tools (Leatherman and Eckel 2012). STEM faculty usually are technologically adept but they tend to stick with the handful of journals, databases, and organizations (e.g., American Mathematical Society) that are most familiar. They are not always as comfortable with tools—citation management applications, database or journal alerts, and RSS feeds—that can optimize their information flow.

Promoting these tools, especially through the lens of the tenure and promotion process, will likely draw interest from faculty. Use their eagerness to enhance and measure their research impact to establish connections. For example, during an informal conversation, a biology instructor described his difficulty keeping track of how often his work is cited, presenting an excellent opportunity to demonstrate the value of a Google Scholar profile and to set up a Web of Science alert that notifies the researcher when a paper is cited in the database. Other possibilities include

- Review Google Scholar, Web of Science, SCOPUS, and ORCID to identify faculty who have not established profiles on their services. Encourage them to create their profiles as a means of publicizing their work.

- Share with faculty the strengths and weaknesses of traditional impact factors (e.g., the h-index) and introduce them to alternative impact metrics through initiatives like ImpactStory.
- Assist new faculty in placing their research in appropriate venues; demonstrate how to use the "Sort by Source Title" in Web of Science to identify journals that publish research on a particular topic, or introduce them to *Journal Citation Reports'* journal rankings.

These activities can be addressed in faculty workshops and departmental meetings or they can be tackled through discrete, manageable online learning objects that facilitate faculty's self-directed learning. We are creating faculty-centered online research guides for each STEM department, where we will link to tutorials, research tips, and available grant-searching tools. While much of this content may be duplicated from page to page, personalizing the guides for each department will reinforce our roles as their primary library contact.

CHALLENGES IN DEVELOPING RELATIONSHIPS WITH STEM FACULTY

Working with STEM faculty can present challenges for new and experienced librarians alike that must be addressed in order to cultivate a successful relationship. As noted above, the online availability of most STEM literature and the tendency of STEM researchers to turn to their colleagues for information make the physical library superfluous for many faculty. You may encounter other obstacles:

1. Lack of Subject Expertise

At our institution most of the librarians have backgrounds in the humanities or social sciences, leaving a deficit in STEM discipline knowledge. STEM faculty and students might conclude, therefore, that librarians have nothing to offer them. In addressing this perception, be honest! Librarians may not necessarily be experts in a particular discipline, but we are experts in navigating research tools, creating effective search strategies, and organizing and managing search results. Emphasize these skills in marketing services to STEM faculty.

Further, STEM librarians can become more literate in their assigned disciplines and stay abreast of research trends without obtaining an advanced degree. Meier (2010) encourages librarian liaisons assigned to unfamiliar disciplines to read the literature for guidelines. Tomaszewski and MacDonald (2009) recommend librarians attend professional STEM meetings and provide a selected list of conferences (586); these conferences may include presentations on pedagogy and undergraduate curricula that might prove particularly fruitful to your departmental relationships and, in fact, could lead to opportunities for collaborative research with STEM faculty.

Within the library and information science profession, there are organizations, mailing lists, and other resources to help the new STEM librarian. Join the science and technology section of the Association of College and Research Libraries (ACRL) for ideas and advice from other STEM librarians. Or consider enrolling in free online courses related to your liaison assignments: for example, Coursera and other providers host MOOCs (Massive Open Online Courses) on a wide range of topics in technology and the sciences, Peer 2 Peer University (P2PU) facilitates online group-sourced learning, and MIT makes course materials freely available on its OpenCourseware platform. While most of the courses obviously will be geared toward students and researchers in the discipline, an introductory course will give you a basic understanding of the field's structure.

2. Waking a Sleeping Giant

As a result of a successful outreach campaign to STEM faculty, librarians may find themselves inundated with requests for expensive materials, research and grant-writing support, and cited reference searches for tenure and promotion; at least, this has been our experience. Time and resource constraints obviously limit librarians' ability to meet every faculty request, so, when possible, collaborate with other librarians in your institution to develop workshops, online learning objects, and other tools that are relevant to multiple disciplines; for example, as a result of an onslaught of requests for tenure-related cited reference searches, we are developing tools to enable faculty (or their graduate assistants) to conduct these searches on their own. While these initiatives can be marketed to each department separately, the preparation and planning can be shared.

In addition, embrace faculty requests for new resources as an opportunity to reevaluate library collections. Even when these requests are beyond the capacity of your budget, they may provide an opening for dialogues on scholarly communication, open access initiatives and the serials pricing crisis. And maintaining a "wish list" of faculty requests will allow you to respond quickly if additional funding is made available. For years, our chemistry department faculty have asked the library to subscribe to two expensive journals which we could not afford. When the library had an opportunity to submit a proposal for increased funding to support faculty research, we included those two journals (among other faculty requests) into the proposal. The faculty appreciated our continued awareness of their needs.

CONCLUSION

When we began, our primary thought was how to reach faculty and students who seemingly don't use the library. But they do, in fact, use the library's resources. The challenge is to demonstrate our relevance to STEM faculty in a way that also highlights what we can do for their students. We focused our initial efforts not so much on formal instructional opportunities in the classroom, although we did see a jump in requests; rather, we concentrated on the support STEM faculty need outside the classroom. Fortunately, this strategy is not a one-way path from contact with faculty to contact with students: at a workshop for the mechanical engineering graduate seminar, we demonstrated RefWorks and cited reference searching tips; within a few weeks, a faculty member who attended the seminar requested assistance in conducting a cited reference work on his research. While we do hope for increased interactions with students through formal information literacy sessions and research consultations, we plan to move slowly, cultivating the burgeoning relationships with faculty to identify opportunities to support undergraduate and graduate research. Perhaps the most useful takeaway from our experience is the need to use every interaction and every informal conversation with faculty to learn about their research needs and to promote the library's services.

WORKS CITED

Engel, Debra, Sarah Robbins and Christina Kulp. 2011. "Information-Seeking Habits of Engineering Faculty." *College & Research Libraries*. 72 (6): 548–67.

George, Carole, Alice Bright, Terry Hurlbert, Erika C. Linke, Gloriana St. Clair and Joan Stein. 2006. "Scholarly Use of Information: Graduate Students' Information-Seeking Behavior." *Information Research*. 11 (4). http://informationr.net/ir/11-4/paper272.html

Hoffman, Kristin, Fred Antwi-Nsiah, Vivian Feng and Meagan Stanley. 2008. "Library Research Skills: A Needs Assessment for Graduate Student Workshops." *Issues in Science and Technology Librarianship*. 53. doi: 10.5062/F48P5XFC

Leatherman, Carrie C. and Edward J. Eckel. 2012. "The Use of Online Current Awareness Services by Natural Sciences and Engineering Faculty at Western Michigan University." *Issues in Science and Technology Librarianship*. 69. doi: 10.5062/F41V5BWQ.

Meier, John J. 2010. "Solutions for the New Subject Specialist Librarian." *Endnotes: The Journal of the New Members Round Table*. 1 (1). http://www.ala.org/nmrt/sites/ala.org.nmrt/files/content/oversightgroups/comm/schres/endnotesvol1is1/1solutionsforthenews.pdf

Scaramozzino, Jeanine M. 2010. "Integrating STEM Information Competencies into an Undergraduate Curriculum." *Journal of Library Administration*. 50 (4): 315-333. DOI: 10.1080/01930821003666981

Tomaszewski, Robert and Karen I. MacDonald. 2009. "Identifying Subject-specific Conferences as Professional Development Opportunities for the Academic Librarian." *Journal of Academic Librarianship*. 35 (6): 583–90.

VIII

Funding

TWENTY-FOUR

Grant Writing to Support STEM

Susan P. Cordell and Reenay R. H. Rogers

The nuances of locating, requesting, receiving, and evaluating the success of grants are not uniform. Many grant proposals do draw upon a common set of characteristics, such as type of institution or organization making the request, demographics, and other recyclable data and narrative. However, grant requirements vary widely not only in topic or focus but also in range of eligibility, application requirements, proposal detail and direction, even geographical location. This chapter looks at grant-writing for STEM projects and resources on a general level: how to begin, where to look, and tips on drafting, evaluating, and submitting the grant proposal. The second portion of the chapter focuses on major grant clearinghouses and some of the most recognized funding sources that continue to be viable.

THE STRENGTH OF STEM

Science, technology, engineering, and mathematics (STEM) have always existed. The acronym STEM, however, has brought a fresh awareness and sense of urgency to these subjects as an intertwined cluster. The merger of these subjects through the STEM movement has taken once isolated areas, strengthened the importance of each individually, and given prominence to the four areas as a synergistic whole. In the public's eye the term STEM brings together the idea that all of its components are equal and, bound together, can be deployed with the strength of a four-stranded rope.

THE PROBLEM WITH STEM

STEM materials are not inexpensive. Few libraries are flush with cash, particularly school, state-operated university and public libraries. In at least one southern state, for example, PreK–12 school libraries have received zero dollars in state-level funding for at least four years, and this is a state where local tax contribution to education varies widely depending on the socioeconomic region within the state. In fact, some of the state's school districts receive no local government contribution or tax revenue. Complicating matters is the fact that STEM-related materials are often among the oldest, most outdated areas of the library collection. With the newly created Common Core Standards' focus on a 70–30 percent (70 percent nonfiction and 30 percent fiction) daily student reading ratio, what is the librarian to do in the section of the library that, in all likelihood, needs the most attention?

THE BEAUTY OF STEM

With today's budget cuts in all areas of education, including funding for libraries, it may be surprising that one area has clinched the interest and thus the funding of many major organizations. STEM persists in garnering financial support from both government agencies and private sector corporations and foundations. Government offerings that continue to be funded include the US Department of Education's Minority Science and Engineering Improvement Program, National Science Foundation grants, National Leadership grants, and the Laura Bush 21st Century Librarian Grant. These grant opportunities as well as private sector corporate and foundation grants will be addressed later in this chapter.

CREATING NEW SPACES FOR STEM

In grant writing, one good acronym calls for another. Grant writers frequently entitle their potential projects with relevant words or phrases that are folded into memorable acronyms. One current example is Project ENABLE (Expanding Nondiscriminatory Access By Librarians Everywhere), awarded to Syracuse University and supported by a Laura Bush 21st Century Librarian Grant. To set the tone for writing a grant proposal, consider NEW SPACES! The steps represented by NEW SPACES will guide the grant writer through the general considerations required for submitting a winning grant.

What's NEW?

NEW represents three major points to consider before writing a grant. Grant writing is not for the faint of heart. The initial adrenaline rush that fuels the aha! moment of the dream project can quickly slow to a metabolic nightmare. Imagine driving through halcyon days on endless, comfortable roads filled with glorious scenery and the confidence of achieving the dream (your grant project), only to crest the horizon filled with nothing but the Los Angeles freeway during perpetual rush hour (the application process). This illustration is and is not exaggerated: Smaller grants usually require less work (although not less rigor); larger grants can be the eighteen-wheeler filling your rearview mirror.

So what *is* NEW? Need, effectiveness, and workability. When matching a potential project to its most compatible grant, need is paramount. Do the grant description and the library's identified need match? Even the best rationale will land in the rejection pile if it does not fit the purpose or mission of the granting party. Study the need for funding carefully against the evaluation criteria required by the granting organization. Heed the criteria. No matter how much your middle school library needs laptops and wireless access for collaborative student projects, a grantor searching for global collaboration projects among educators will not shift its focus to meet your urgent need.

Effectiveness comes into play at this point. Consider the original need. Could your middle school, and perhaps partner schools, brainstorm a project that would provide for your technology needs, meet the mission of the granting organization, *and* develop a collaborative STEM proposal that could have significant and far-reaching implications? Prove your case by explaining what you intend to accomplish with the funding. Provide specific examples of how needed tools, resources, equipment, texts, and assistants will be used effectively and efficiently. What begins as a simple request can be translated into a vision that becomes a reality that, while providing for those initial needs, also creates a transformative impact for the grant's beneficiaries.

Workability facilitates effectiveness. For your proposal to be workable, it must be one that your library is equipped to administer. For example, a summer reading proposal might fit well into the criteria of a corporate grant (Dollar General Literacy Foundation Grants, for example). Dollar General offers grants in the categories of adult, youth, and family literacy. When writing your library's grant proposal, identify your audience, your goal, and your ability to support the project. Do not write a grant that estimates 200 participants if you only have physical space for 25. Also, be sure to make your goal attainable within the parameters of the staff and resources available. Do not become overly ambitious. Your project may be ingenious, but if it is not workable it will not be funded or, worse yet, it will be funded and you will be unable to show evidence of its success when the time arrives for accountability. Create a proposal that is effective, efficient, important, and workable.

Now, About Those SPACES

Winning a STEM grant will indeed open up those NEW SPACES in the library—through added materials and resources, professional development and workshop opportunities, talented guest speakers, summer programs for children and young adults, international collaboration, research to solve a library-related STEM problem . . . the list can truly go "to infinity and beyond," to quote one brave space adventurer. Every need-turned-proposal must prove its worthiness. To do so, grant writing requires SPACES: search, parameters, application, creativity, evaluation, and submission.

The Search

Although grant opportunities do fall serendipitously into librarians' laps, this stroke of luck is not the norm. Thus begins "The Search." Once you have brainstormed a rough idea of what it is that you need or plan to do, start looking for funding. Obviously, with today's lightning-fast technology, thousands of opportunities are mere keyboard clicks away. Use Boolean operators to broaden, narrow, and tailor searches to your particular needs. Googling "STEM" will return 187 million hits in only 0.25 seconds. Googling "children STEM grants" will narrow the field to 23 million results but will cost 0.04 additional seconds—extra time well spent. Precise search terms will bring more relevant hits, from grant opportunities to granting organizations to tips on applying.

Technology is wonderful, but so are human beings. Consider the foundations, businesses, nonprofit organizations, corporations, industries, and other community entities that operate in your area. Inquire about the possibilities of partnering with them in a local grant effort. If State Farm is in your backyard, be a good neighbor and ask about grant funding. Do you have a college roommate who now works for Boeing? Renew the relationship. Network with colleagues. Research professional organizations—local, state, regional, national, and even international. Serendipity can strike in the most unusual places. Watch for it!

Parameters

The project has been chosen and so the hunt begins. Your grant idea is wonderful, but you cannot find a grant that fits perfectly into your plan. Be clear in your purpose but reasonable in the parameters you set. You are the designer of your project; therefore the boundaries can be flexible to accommodate both your project and the requirements of the grant. Do not let your project become overly ambitious. If your proposal requires a major undertaking worthy of hundreds of thousands or millions of dollars, the parameters will reflect the extent of need. However, if your grant proposal is of a considerably smaller scale, inflating it or giving it more legs than a millipede will result in rejection at best and disaster at worst. Match the grant funds to the project and adapt the project to the grant funds. Keep the original purpose in mind, but feel free to revise your project as necessary. It is during this phase that good proposals can actually morph into excellent ones!

The Dreaded (or Not) Application

Many applicants look at the application with fear and trembling. Sometimes that is justified. More often the dread dissipates with a careful reading of the application. Do it *before* beginning to write. Determining the granting body's criteria regarding demographics, audience, purpose, scope, focus, time limitations, eligibility, and other requirements will save time and effort, particularly if the library does not meet any or all of the stated criteria. (Helpful hint: Many granting organizations maintain an online database of previously funded grants. Read over some of them to gain a better understanding of the organization and its expectations.) Follow instructions to the letter. If the application calls for specific fonts and sizes, margins and other technical considerations, make sure your proposal fulfills the guidelines. Do not state in two hundred words what the granting organization requires that you state in fifty. Your eloquent verbosity may send your proposal to the "reject" pile without the possibility of further consideration. Be succinct, specific, and as brief or detailed as required.

The Creativity Factor

Professional grant reviewers are experts at their job. They cue in on keywords and phrases written into the description of their grant's purpose. Use these words but not in rote mimicry. Write professionally but do not be afraid to interject creative details into the proposal. Be realistic but innovative. Explain why your proposal should be funded using terms that bring to mind fresh perspectives and vital outcomes. It is also helpful to mention the future possibilities of the proposed project. If your grant will provide not only for the current project but will also serve as a foundation for a sustainable, ongoing program, make your case. The longer a grant can maintain a residual impact, the better the chance for becoming funded.

Evaluation

This stage of evaluation should not be confused with the summative evaluation that will be submitted to the granting organization at the end of the funding period. Formative evaluation in the application process is vital. This is the time when other sets of eyes review the proposal. Although grant reviewers are experts, they may not be familiar with highly specialized jargon used in a particular profession or setting. If a university library, a public library, and a school library are competing for a certain grant, even the experts can become entangled in a mass of acronyms and jargon. Define acronyms and limit jargon. Outside readers are useful for spotting these problems as well as serving as proofreaders and editors. The proposal, above all, should adhere to the criteria of the application. Review, accept constructive criticism, and revise, revise, revise. If necessary, cut that sentence you wrote that to you is a transcendent work of art but to proofreaders is a waste of fifty characters!

Finally: Submission!

The deadline looms. The proposal you have so lovingly and carefully crafted is ready for submission. Just a few words of advice here:

- Arrange the application in the order required—for example, application on top in correct page order with supporting documents added as appendices or placed in back.
- Bind the document (or not) as required. Many granting institutions prefer paper clips over staples and no binding over a notebook presentation. Some require packaging the proposal in a box, others in an envelope.
- Submit in the format requested, whether through postal mail, by fax, or electronic attachment.
- Submit before the deadline! While some of us do our best work under pressure, submit as early as possible. This is especially true of electronic submissions. When overburdened with five hundred simultaneous grant proposals that must be logged in by midnight, the Internet can become clogged—and late submission equals wasted effort.
- If the granting organization offers the option for you to follow up or request the status of the application, do so. This indicates your interest and anticipation in receiving funding.

FINDING FUNDING SOURCES FOR STEM EDUCATION

Now that you know the idea behind NEW SPACES and have the basics of grant writing in hand, the next step to grant award success is identifying sources of funding for your STEM project ideas. STEM education is at the forefront of the United States' interest in creating a workforce with the skills needed for success in the twenty-first century. As a result, there are many sources of funding for STEM education for students, increasing teacher effectiveness through professional development, and developing STEM resources.

Government-Supported Grants

Three billion dollars was earmarked in the government's 2013 budget for STEM education with one of the primary areas of focus on K–12 teacher effectiveness. One K–12 area supported by the current government's administration that school librarians can capitalize on is providing resources and professional development for STEM teachers with the ultimate goal of improving both STEM instruction and learning. The funds support two major grant providing organizations: the National Science Foundation (NSF) and the US Department of Education.

The NSF awards grants yearly in support of improving the STEM educational experience. The NSF website provides a searchable database of grants, proposal guidelines, and other relevant information for grant writers, including examples of previously awarded grants. Some grant programs that may be of interest to the librarian are Advancing Informal STEM Learning, Innovative Technology Experiences for Students and Teachers, and Discovery Research K–12.

- The Advancing Informal STEM Learning (AISL) program provides funds for STEM education outside of the normal school environment. The purpose of this grant is to instill a life-long interest in STEM learning through activities outside of the formal school atmosphere. Some examples of STEM activities that have been funded include teen science cafes, robotics clubs, and digital or virtual museum exhibits. For the school librarians willing to open their doors before or after school for STEM-based programs, the AISL grant program offers endless possibilities.
- Innovative Technology Experiences for Students and Teachers (IT-EST) supports the development of models for involving K–12 students in real-life experiences that foster STEM and ICT workforce development for the future. This grant provides the librarian with a great opportunity to design and implement a collaborative project that prepares students for the twenty-first-century workforce. Opportunities exist for establishing professional STEM mentoring programs, developing computer modeling labs, teacher professional development, and much more.
- Discovery Research K–12 (DRK–12) is a research-based grant that intends to enhance STEM learning by a variety of stakeholders including K–12 students, teachers, administrators, and parents. Of the four strands identified in DRK-12 grants—assessment, learning, teaching, and scale-up—librarians can focus on projects that aim to enhance teaching and learning. Teaching emphasizes projects that

seek resources and tools for teachers. Learning is student-centered, focused on new and emerging technologies. This grant is perfect for the librarian who wants to introduce additional technologies to the library or who needs to increase those STEM resources for the teachers.

The US Department of Education also offers numerous grant opportunities. Their website publishes a guide to education programs that includes descriptions of the grant programs supported by the Department of Education, the available dollar amount of funding, and eligibility requirements. Librarians can also search the department's database for grant competitions. Ongoing grants are listed in the "Federal Register Notices" while those that will be available in the near future are listed in the "ED grants forecast." Some of the current grant programs that are available are the Investing in Innovation and the Minority Science and Engineering Improvement Program.

- Investing in Innovation (i3) grants must address one of four key areas: supporting effective teachers and principals; improving the use of data to accelerate student achievement; complementing the implementation of standards and assessments that prepare students for success in college and careers; and turning around persistently low-performing schools. Librarians in low-performing schools can seek funding for innovative projects seeking to improve STEM performance.
- Minority Science and Engineering Improvement Program (MSEIP) is a grant program which supports traditionally underrepresented groups in STEM fields. One aspect of this program, the precollege programs, is aimed at supporting both teachers and students in the K–12 area. Investigate the demographics of your school population. Determine if your school serves a group identified as a minority group in the STEM fields. Funding opportunities also exist for higher education institutions that seek to eliminate barriers preventing the entry of minorities in STEM disciplines. Some ideas for projects include mentoring programs or programs which encourage the use of technologies such as iPads, graphing calculators, or laptops.
- The Laura Bush 21st Century Librarian Program provides grants for five different project areas, ranging from K–12 projects through academic research opportunities. The continuing education tract provides funding opportunities for the K–12 librarian who has identified a need for improving services for the school's special needs population, who wants to develop a program for increasing digital literacy skills, for conservation science and practice, for digitization or any aspect of digital stewardship, or finally, for enhanc-

ing the ability of the librarian to cultivate twenty-first-century skills in their users.

- Other government supported institutions such as the National Oceanic and Atmospheric Administration, the Office of Naval Research, and the National Institute of Health also offer funding for STEM education. Do not limit your searches strictly to the NSF or ED.Gov websites. A smart Internet search can locate sources of funding that you might not find within specific database searches.

Corporation, Foundation, and Private-Funding Sources

Funding opportunities also exist through state and local organizations, power and other public utility companies, manufacturers, and large corporations. Some groups such as environmental protection organizations offer funding for a variety of environment-friendly projects. Legacy, an environmental group in Alabama, offers both "mini" grants as well as larger grants for teachers who want to promote environmental responsibility. Many power companies such as Florida Power Light and First Energy in New Jersey also offer education grants for teachers which can be used to fund STEM programs through the K–12 library. If you are unsure how to locate some of these groups, StemGrants.com is a website dedicated to locating grants for STEM education projects. The site offers a listing of grants for K–12 as well as a free guide to STEM funding.

- Some additional corporations and manufacturers which offer STEM funding are Google, Lockheed Martin, and American Honda Foundation.Google is a large corporation which offers awards to promote STEM and Computer Science education in the K–12 setting. The program referred to as Google RISE (Roots in Science and Engineering) offers the librarian the opportunity to seek funding for technology enrichment in the library with the purpose of increasing student excitement and understanding in STEM and computer science. The school library is the perfect place to create a technology enriched learning environment that students can use to enhance classroom learning or to explore STEM topics outside of the classroom.
- Lockheed Martin is another corporation which specifically supports a K–12 STEM Education Initiative, Engineers in the Classroom. This corporation also supports STEM focused programs that offer their employees the opportunity to engage in the local community. Librarians can take advantage of this company's support of putting its professional employees in the community to develop STEM programs that partner these real-world professionals with students from the community.

- American Honda Foundation offers grants which are intended to support the education of young people in the areas of STEM, the environment, job training, and literacy. Their goal is to assist in meeting the needs of America by funding education projects in STEM for its youth with the ultimate goal of creating a life-long benefit to American communities.

Even in today's budget-cutting era, funding for STEM education exists. The resources outlined above pave the way toward finding that perfect grant opportunity. Combine the NEW SPACES approach to grant writing with the wealth of information on grant funding resources and you have the ideal combination to get your STEM project funded!

TWENTY-FIVE

STEM on a Budget!

Sarah Wright

Science, technology, engineering, and mathematics (STEM) have a number of national initiatives to improve students' comprehension and test scores (Hopwood 2012). As knowledge sources and community partners, libraries need to provide STEM-related materials to students, but they can take it one step further and supplement schools with STEM programming. This provides opportunities to spark interest in students who may not be interested in traditional classroom learning, providing additional STEM coverage (National Museum and Library Services Board Meeting, 2010).

Many library professionals have backgrounds in the arts and humanities so STEM programs may appear daunting to them. Shrinking budgets make it seem impossible to add new programs to the mix.

Never fear! There are plenty of easy, inexpensive STEM programs that anyone can do. Take a look at the mix from the four STEM components that you can build on for your own programs.

SCIENCE

Science is one of the easiest areas of STEM because there are so many resources available. You can recreate the Mentos and Diet Coke rocket (plenty of directions online) or set anything on fire. (The first should be set up outside, and the second should have a fire extinguisher handy, just in case. Safety first, kids!) However, if you have dreams of recreating episodes of Bill Nye, a miniscule budget seems like the end of your mad scientist dreams.

Scaling back can actually do you a favor, though, because it puts the experiments within reach for your customers. If you can suck an egg into a bottle for less than $5, guess what? So can they! Make sure to have books or experiment directions on hand to give out to those kids who just have to try it themselves. You would hate to send home a kid who never realized that your egg was hard boiled and peeled.

How to choose the best option to set up science programs at your library? It depends on your goals and environment. I run a homework help center and a big, one-time program may become a distraction while ongoing passive programs are a great way for kids to explore science on their own.

One-Time Experiments

Who doesn't love a mad scientist? Even if you don't have a great cackle and a lab coat, experiments still add up to a lot of fun. You can even set these up as a mythbuster to increase your connection to pop culture. However you choose to conduct programs and experiments, just be sure to show kids that science can be exciting!

Egg in a Bottle

- What you need: An egg (hard boiled and peeled), a glass bottle, a small piece of paper and a match (or two).
- What you do: Set fire to the paper and pop it into the bottle and immediately place your hardboiled egg on top of the mouth of the bottle. The warm air will push out of the bottle which can make your egg dance. As the air inside the bottle cools, pressure inside the bottle decreases, eventually sucking your egg in. How much to explain is up to you.
- The science: Heat makes air molecules move faster, increasing the air pressure in the bottle. This causes air to escape around the egg. As the air cools, the molecules move slower, and the pressure decreases. The positive pressure from the outside air pushes the egg inside.
- What to watch out for: Be careful about the size of your bottle mouth and egg. You want the egg to be slightly bigger than the opening, so it has a chance to slip through. If it's too big, it will get stuck. Also, sometimes the paper burns too quickly to work. You can find alternate ways to heat the bottle, like hot water, but make sure you practice beforehand. Get the egg back out of the bottle by blowing in the bottle, allowing the egg to roll to the opening before removing your mouth, and then catching the egg as it falls.

- Approximate costs: Eggs (twelve experiments!) $2.00, reused bottle $0, matches (250) $1.50. Total = $3.50, with plenty of leftovers for future experiments

Magic Milk

- What you need: a wide dish, milk (2 percent or higher), food coloring, a cotton swab, and dish soap.
- What you do: Pour enough milk in your dish to cover the bottom. Add a few drops of different food coloring on top of the milk. Dip the cotton swab in the dish soap so that one end is coated. Get everyone excited, and dip the soapy swab into the milk. The milk's surface will then move rapidly, spreading out the colors.
- The science: The cotton swab breaks the surface tension so the colors can move. The bonds in the fat and protein molecules of the milk are weak so the dish soap is able to break them down. This causes the colors to shift as the chemical makeup of the milk changes.
- Approximate costs: Half-gallon of milk $2.00, food coloring $2.50, borrow a capful of dish soap and a couple cotton swabs from home or buy 250 cotton swabs for $2.00, and 25 oz. of liquid dish soap $3.70 for hundreds of experiments = $10.50 or less.

Flaming Death

This experiment is a showpiece element of a fellow homework help center coordinator, Dustin Jolivette's (2012) science programs. While the title is intimidating, this is a favorite demonstration among kids and perfectly safe, if the proper precautions are followed.

- What you need: 90 percent isopropyl alcohol, an empty five-gallon water cooler jug, a match, safety gear like safety goggles, and a hand protector (like a flame resistant/retardant glove).
- What you do: pour a small amount of the alcohol (approximately two tablespoons) into the container and coat the inside by rolling the container around. Put on your safety gear (this step is added by me, though Dustin has successfully performed this program without). Drop the match inside the container and pull your hand back quickly and carefully.
- What happens: You will achieve a flaming fireball. This is because of the mix of highly flammable alcohol with oxygen inside the container.
- Increase the science: Have the students form think tanks to figure out why the experiment works. Appoint a group leader to present these ideas to the full group and have them work it out until they get it right. Hopefully that will take about ten minutes because that

is how long you need until the smoke clears out of your container and it reoxygenates.

- Approximate costs: Used water cooler container $0, 90 percent iso-propyl alcohol $6.00, matches (250) $1.50 = $7.50 for at least twenty demonstrations

Water Spout

Another showpiece from Jolivette (2012), this experiment gets more dangerous (but more impressive) the hotter your water is. Have the kids stand back, and be cautious with your water temperature because you will get wet.

- What you need: warm water in a pot, canned air (keyboard clean-er), empty two-liter bottle, small cup.
- What you do: cut off the top of the 2-liter bottle. Hold the canned air upside down and spray into the 2-liter bottle to collect 1/4 of a cup of its liquid. This will probably take most of the can of air, so chat as you are doing this. Pour the liquid into the small cup. Pre-pare yourself and rapidly turn the cup upside down into the warm water.
- What happens: Water explosion! The cold liquid from the canned air reacts with the warm water to create a big spray of energy upward.
- Approximate cost: Canned air $6, everything else is reusable.

Ongoing Experiments

Growing Plants

Long-term experiments are a lot of fun, if you have a space that kids can visit to observe them. These experiments can include growing plants like an avocado or a piece of potato. The avocado should be stuck with toothpicks and balanced partially submerged in a container of water while the potato should be planted in soil and watered regularly. Both will need sunlight.

Growing Crystals

Crystals can be grown in a container or through a clean egg shell. Carefully knock the top off several eggs, drain the contents, and clean the eggs carefully. Place the egg shells, hole side up, in an egg carton. Dis-solve several teaspoons of salt in warm water until it won't dissolve anymore, and add some food coloring. Pour the solution inside the egg shells, filling as close to the top as possible. Over the next few weeks, the salt crystals will form inside and outside the shells. This experiment can be tested with all sorts of water-soluble substances like sugar, borax, alum, or cream of tartar.

Discovery Bottles

Discovery bottles are another way to have some hands-on science without an official program. These bottles can be aimed at the younger crew with magnetic bottles or aged up to demonstrate things like viscosity and density.

To make a discovery bottle, you need a clean, empty, clear plastic bottle, some hot glue, and whatever you want to fill the bottle with. For a magnetic bottle, you will need several magnetic items (such as paper clips, pieces of pipe cleaners, or nails) and several noniron items (like a puff ball, rubber band, or button). Put them in your bottle, seal up the lid with hot glue, and then use a magnet to see which items are magnetic.

Viscosity needs at least two bottles to test, but you can have as many as you want. You will need a different substance for each bottle like water, hair gel, dishwashing soap, corn syrup, or anything that has a different viscosity (and is on sale at the dollar store). Fill each bottle with your substance of choice and three marbles before you seal them up (hot glue the lid on tight.) Then, let kids predict how the marbles will move through each substance and explain that viscosity is the resistance of a fluid to movement.

Use small experiment forms that ask the kids to predict what will happen and answer questions about the bottles. Then, add a few definitions or explanations on the forms along with some cool resources for them to check out.

TECHNOLOGY

This aspect of STEM can be tricky to implement on a budget. Technology is expensive. Yet, there are a few ways to use what you or your customers already have to make it work.

Next time one of your library computers bites the dust, ask your administrator if you can have it. With some printed out diagrams from the internet, this dead computer could be your next STEM program. Kids love to take things apart, and observing how a computer is put together is a great way to learn its components.

One great program implemented by Dustin Jolivette (2012) in his branch is a Technology Club. This is run with the help of local computer programming volunteers using LEGO MINDSTORMS kits. The kits are expensive, but they often can be funded through corporate donations, technology non-profits, and educational funds. Look for grant opportunities or send requests to the charitable arms of science, research, technology, and engineering companies. If you can network at conferences, technology fairs, or through listservs, you can find a number of resources that may help provide funding for more in-depth programs.

However, to get started, you can do a technology exercise that doesn't need any technology. Jolivette opens his tech club with a simple demonstration from Tech Corps, a non-profit focused on K–12 technology education, using only a bag of bread and jars of peanut butter and jelly (approximately $8). Have kids, working in teams, write explicit directions for making a peanut butter and jelly sandwich. Emphasize that they need to write down every single step like it is a computer program. Once the first team is done, act out their instructions, but you have to take everything literally. If the first instruction says, "Put the peanut butter on the bread," pick up the jar of peanut butter and place it on the bag of bread. Kids will be amused and a little frustrated, but you can explain that a computer needs every step laid out because it can't think for itself. This serves as a great introduction to writing programming code.

One program that I personally have never tried but think would be great is making an app for an iPhone or Android. This would have to utilize existing computer spaces and customers' smart phones, but the only expense will be your time. There are a number of user interfaces that let you use their programs to make apps, but I would pick one ahead of time to familiarize yourself with it.

ENGINEERING

Engineering has some of the most fun programs because you are building stuff.

Build a Tower

One of the famous ones is the tower experiment where students are challenged to build a tower out of straws, popsicle sticks, and tape.

- What you need: a certain number of straws or popsicle sticks per table/group/individual child, a roll of tape (any kind works) per group, a timer (which can just be a clock on the wall).
- Whoever builds the biggest tower in the specified amount of time wins! However, there are several variations on that. For example, add some paper for a platform and whoever builds a tower that can hold a nickel up the highest wins. Each group just has to have the same materials. Twenty straws is a fairly standard number, but you can increase this number to add to the challenge. Also, popsicle sticks are sturdier than straws, but they often cost a little more. If your budget is really challenged, you could hold a popsicle stick drive during the summer, but be prepared to sanitize those sticks in some boiling water.

Build a Boat

Another fun one is building a boat out of aluminum foil.

- What you need: aluminum foil, something to weigh down the boats like a few rolls of pennies or a container of washers, a bucket or kiddy pool filled with water.
- What you do: divide everyone up into teams or they can work individually. Everyone gets a certain amount of aluminum foil and is challenged to build the sturdiest boat. As they finish their boats, they take them to the pond (bucket or pool) to float them. Most of them should float without anything in them, but you will put weights one-by-one in each boat until it sinks. At that point, you pull up the boat from the bottom (take out the one weight that made it sink) and count the number of weights. The boat that holds the most weights wins.

Build a Bridge

This is a variation on the other two challenges, except you are now taking your straws or popsicle sticks across a space.

- What you need: equal number of straws or popsicle sticks for each group, tape, paper clips, washers, and a timer.
- What you do: each team or individual will build a bridge across a specified distance. While building, they should have a tester space, but the final test should be between two tables (or chair backs) where the judges are. Otherwise, it becomes a contest of who can tape the bridge to the table the best. When the bridges are built, unfold the paper clips to form S-hooks. One side hangs on the middle of the bridge, and the other holds progressively more washers to test the strength of the bridge. The bridge that holds the most washers wins!

This one is also fun to pair with an online bridge building game. There are several out there, although I like the one on http://www.smart-kit.com. This way, kids can try building online bridges and adapt their skills to larger scale projects.

Finish each of the above programs with questions about what worked and what didn't. If kids are able to test each product throughout the time period, they can learn from their mistakes and think of creative solutions.

MATH

Many kids find math intimidating. That means that it is important to incorporate it in a fun way.

Money Matters

A fun way to incorporate math is through money manipulation. This works better for younger kids, but even some teens are fairly clueless about money.

- What you need: play money, things for kids to buy (this can be real things that you want to give out like notebooks and erasers or it can be paper or laminated pictures of items).
- A fun way to do a money program is to set up stores around the library or a meeting room and have a list of things kids need to get. Store options include grocery stores, restaurants, a farmers' market, toy stores, a car dealership, a clothes store, a shoe store, a computer store, a pet store, a book store, and a library. Then, give each child a shopping list asking them to get an outfit, entertainment, a car, dinner for their family, and whatever else you would like to include. They will only have a certain amount of money and a variety of objects that range from cheap to expensive. They have to make sure they get at least one of everything on the list, plus any add-ons they choose. They will use their "money" to buy things and figure out how much they need for everything. They may also need to budget their other choices if they want to get the fanciest items.

Puzzles

Setting up math puzzles and logic puzzles pulls on kids' math skills without necessarily alerting anyone that they are doing math. If you set up these puzzles interspersed with physical challenges or obstacle courses, it becomes a big event.

Water Puzzle

- What you need: a hose or water source, buckets that hold a certain amount of water (or are marked at whatever measurement you decide), and containers that hold different amounts of liquid.
- What you do: each child or team will get a bucket and various containers to carry water that are larger and smaller than their bucket. For example, one team might have a two-gallon container, a one-gallon container, and a seven-gallon container. With one trip to the water source, how can they fill up their five gallon bucket? Each group should have different sizes of containers, so everyone will be able to switch for a few rounds.

Mass Puzzle

- What you need: scales (mass scales are ideal), objects with varying mass (can be anything, as long as it fits on the scale; works best if you have some big objects that don't have much mass, small objects with a large mass, and objects in between).
- What you do: kids (teams or individuals) must get their scale to read a particular number with objects that have different amounts of mass. Whoever gets their number first wins that round, and then everyone switches to a different scale.

Hopefully, one of these ideas strikes your fancy, but you can use them as springboards to develop your own programs. Veteran STEM programmer, Becky Ellis (2012) says, "Don't be afraid to make a mistake or have an experiment not go the way you expect. That's why it's called an experiment. Some of my best programs have 'complications.' Sometimes what looks really cool in a book doesn't work, and I think that's okay. It's a way to bring more into the experiment when you question why the results were not as expected." If you have fun, the kids will too.

ADDITIONAL RESOURCES

The STAR_Net project has two traveling exhibits that libraries can claim, but my favorite STEM resource from them is their online Community of Practice. This includes librarians around the country who are sending messages about STEM opportunities and programs to do in the library. Search "Discover Exhibits Community of Practice."

To add to a handout or even increase your own STEM knowledge, there are a number of YouTube channels with some great educational videos like minutephysics or crashcourse. Watch the whole video before recommending it because some of them may be aimed at different age levels.

Another great resource is the National Girls Collaborative Project. It is geared toward STEM projects aimed at working with girls. Their website has resources including mini-grants and newsletters with information on how to get started.

WORKS CITED

Ellis, Becky. Personal Interview. 18 September 2012.

Hopwood, Jennifer. "Initiating STEM Learning in Libraries." *Children & Libraries*. 10.2 (2012): 53–55. Web. 5 September 2012.

Jolivette, Dustin. Personal Interview. 4 September 2012.

"National Museum and Library Services Board Meeting Role of Libraries, Museums in STEM Education." *US Fed News Service*. 13 Oct. 2010. Web 5 September 2012.

Index

About the Contributors

Vera Gubnitskaia, a manager at the Orange County Library System, Florida, obtained her library degrees from Moscow Institute of Culture (Russia) and Florida State University. Vera worked in public and academic libraries in Russia and United States. She coedited *Marketing Your Library* (2012) and *Continuing Education for Librarians* (2013). Her chapters appeared in the *Librarians as Community Partners* (2010) and in *Library Management Tips that Work* (2011). Her reviews were published by the *Journal of International Women's Studies* and *Small Press Review.*

 Carol Smallwood received a MLS from Western Michigan University, MA in history from Eastern Michigan University. *Librarians as Community Partners: an Outreach Handbook; Bringing the Arts into the Library* are recent ALA anthologies. Others are *Women on Poetry: Writing, Revising, Publishing and Teaching* (2012); *Marketing Your Library* (2012); *Library Services for Multicultural Patrons: Strategies to Encourage Library Use* (Scarecrow Press, 2013). Her library experience includes school, public, academic, special, as well as administration and being a consultant; she's an American Library Association member.

 Paula M. Storm (MILS, University of Michigan) is assistant professor and science librarian at Eastern Michigan University, and supports biology, chemistry, mathematics, physics, clinical medicine, astronomy, and engineering. Previously she was assistant director of the Science and Engineering Library at Wayne State University and competitive intelligence coordinator for the National Center for Manufacturing Sciences. Her memberships include the Special Libraries Association, the American Society of Engineering Education, the National Association of Scholars, International Society of Teaching and Learning. She's appeared in *Library Journal, College & Research Libraries*; her research includes STEM.

ABOUT THE CONTRIBUTORS

Giovanna Badia, MLIS, has been working at McGill University's (Montreal, Quebec) Schulich Library of Science and Engineering since October 2011. She is the liaison librarian for the departments of chemical engineering, earth and planetary sciences, and mining and materials engineering. Her responsibilities include answering reference questions, providing instructional services, and collection development. She previously worked as a medical librarian at the Royal Victoria Hospital in Montreal. She also summarizes and critically appraises published articles in library and information science for the journal, *Evidence Based Library and Information Practice.*

Keary Bramwell, youth collection specialist librarian at Mount Prospect Public Library, Mount Prospect, Illinois since 2007, obtained her MLS from the University of Wisconsin–Madison. Keary is a member of the American Library Association, the Association of Library Services to Children, and the Illinois Library Association. She presented a paper at the Association of College and Research Libraries National Conference in 2005 entitled "Alone at the Reference Desk." Keary also presented a program at the 2012 Illinois Library Association Conference about creating and running science programs in public libraries.

Michael Cherry, teen and youth librarian at the Evansville Vanderburgh Public Library (EVPL), Evansville, Indiana since 2011, obtained his MLIS from the University of Pittsburgh. Michael received a 2012 Young Adult Library Services Association and Dollar General Literacy Foundation grant for the design of an outstanding summer reading program. He is an active member of the American Library Association, Young Adult Library Services Association, and Indiana State Reading Association. In addition to working for the EVPL, Michael has worked at the Crafton Public Library and Andy Warhol Museum in Pittsburgh, Pennsylvania.

Carissa Christner, youth services librarian at Madison Public Library, Madison, Wisconsin since 2006, obtained her MLIS from the University of Wisconsin–Madison. She was awarded the James Krikelas Award for Innovative Use of Information Technology in 2012. Carissa has also worked in smaller libraries and in larger youth services departments, which gave her a broad experience base with different types of library environments. Carissa contributed chapters for two *Collaborative Summer Library Program Manuals* (2009 and 2010) and currently writes a library blog athttp://librarymakers.blogspot.com.

Kathleen J. Clauson is the unit coordinator of the Physical Sciences Library at Western Illinois University, known for her highly successful forensic series, Mock Crime Scene, and outreach to local children in the community. Clauson has a BA in German and an MA in economics. She spent many years as an editor, feature writer, book review columnist, and has published numerous short stories and a novella, *Eva Galuska and the Christmas Carp.* Currently Clauson is planning future STEM outreach for girls, completing her second novella, and a children's book about bullying.

Susan P. Cordell is an assistant professor in instructional leadership and support at the University of West Alabama. Dr. Cordell teaches graduate courses in school library media, educational research, and social foundations of education. She holds a BA degree in English, Spanish, and Secondary Education from Middle Tennessee State University. In addition, she received the MLIS, EdS and PhD from The University of Alabama. Dr. Cordell is a National Board Certified Teacher in PreK–12 Library Media. Before joining UWA, Dr. Cordell was a K–12 teacher and school librarian for twenty years.

Kelly Czarnecki is a teen services librarian at ImaginOn with the Charlotte Mecklenburg Public Library in North Carolina. She has served on many ALA committees including YALSA Teen Tech Week as chair and ALA Councilor-at-Large. She was a Library Journal Mover and Shaker in 2007. She wrote and edited the Gaming Life column for *School Library Journal* from 2006–2012 and has published many articles in professional magazines. She has written one previous book and a manual *Gaming in Libraries* (2010) and *Digital Storytelling in Practice* (2009).

Barbara Fiehn, MS, EdD, is an assistant professor, Library Media Education, Western Kentucky University. Following thirty years as a school librarian, consultant, and media services coordinator, Barbara taught library media education at Minnesota State University at Mankato and Northern Illinois University. She has published articles in *MultiMedia and Internet@schools, Tech Trends, Dragon Lode,* and other journals; chapters in *Educational Media and Technology Yearbook, Library Management Tips That Work,* and *Tips for Librarians Running Libraries Alone.* A member of ALA, Barbara has served on the Intellectual Freedom committee.

Linda M. Galloway is the biology, chemistry, and forensic sciences librarian at Syracuse University, where she received her MS in library and information science. Her professional interests include citation metrics and analysis, altmetrics, and instruction. She has presented at national conferences and has contributed a chapter to *Emerging Roles in Academic Librarianship* (forthcoming). Linda is active in the Upstate New York Chapter of the Special Libraries Association and recently received the Chapter Merit Award. Linda is also president of the Pi Lambda Sigma chapter of Beta Phi Mu.

Barbara J. Hampton has served since 2007 as a reference librarian at Sacred Heart University, Fairfield, Connecticut, which is designated a Patent and Trademark Resource Center for the US Patent and Trademark Office. She earned her MLS at Southern Connecticut State University and her JD at the University of Connecticut School of Law. From 2007–2010, she served as library director for Talcott Mountain Academy, Avon, Connecticut, a K–8 school offering an accelerated mathematics and science curriculum. She has presented and written on curriculum and enrichment resources for able students.

Heather Groves Hannan has led the Mercer Library team on the Prince William Campus of George Mason University (Manassas, Virginia) since September 1997. Prior to that, she was a Corporate Reference and Instruction librarian for MCI in Washington, DC. She has been a presenter at the Virginia Libraries Association's Annual Conference as well as a session volunteer and facilitator. Heather holds a master of science in library science degree from Catholic University in Washington, DC and a bachelor of arts in management degree from Earlham College in Richmond, Indiana.

Eileen G. Harrington is the health and life sciences librarian at the Universities at Shady Grove, Rockville, Maryland. Previously, she oversaw the Naturalist Center at the California Academy of Sciences. Eileen has over fifteen years of experience as an educator both in the United States and Latin America She has a BA in environmental studies and biology from Macalester College, a MES from York University, Toronto, and a MA in LIS from the University of Wisconsin–Madison. Her book Exploring *Environmental Science with Children and Teens* will be published in 2013 by ALA.

Jennifer Hopwood has worked in libraries for over twelve years, currently as a library training coordinator. She holds a MLIS from Florida State University. She is an active member of ALA, ALSC, and YALSA. Her written contributions have appeared in *Children and Libraries: the Journal of the Association for Library Service to Children Marketing Your Library: Tips and Tools that Work* (2012), the Florida Library Youth Program's FLYP Forward and Bookends publications; as well as the websites The Gatekeepers Post, No Flying No Tights, and the ALSC Blog.

Cynthia Houston is an associate professor in the library media education program at Western Kentucky University. She holds an MLS from Clarion University and a PhD in curriculum and instruction from Southern Illinois University Carbondale. She has published in a wide range of journals on a variety of topics in library science including alternative classification, Web 2.0, regional children's literature, and fotonovelas. Her most recent works are a textbook on reference and information services for ABC-CLIO and a chapter on fotonovelas for an edited volume published by Scarecrow Press.

Melanie E. Hughes, MLS, MBA, is an associate librarian, coordinator of Automation and Technical Services, and library liaison to the School of Education at the Indiana University Southeast Library in New Albany, Indiana, where she is developing a graphic novel collection to support student learning. She previously served as an elementary school librarian in Louisville, Kentucky and an English teacher in Japan where she was first exposed to manga. She also serves on the school board for Community Montessori, a public charter school. She recently started scripting her first graphic novel.

Jeanine M. Huss is an associate professor at Western Kentucky University. She teaches preservice elementary science methods, diversity, and graduate curriculum courses. Because environmental education is her passion, she teaches students a love of the environment through an overnight educational experience to Mammoth Cave National Park where they learn about karst topography and an appreciation of the aesthetics of nature. Jeanine has served on Oklahoma Association for Environmental Education and Kentucky Association for Environmental Education boards. She is also active in the North American Association for Environmental Education.

Alvin Hutchinson manages scholarly communications and information technology at the Smithsonian Libraries (Washington, DC) where he has worked for twenty years. Before moving to the digital services division, which operates the Smithsonian Research Online program, he served as a zoology subject specialist both at the National Museum of Natural History and later at the National Zoological Park. In the past he has taught a course in science librarianship and lectured at the School of Library and Information Science at the Catholic University of America in Washington.

Nastasha Johnson is an assistant professor and reference librarian at the F. D. Bluford Library at North Carolina Agricultural and Technical State University. She is the chair of the library faculty assembly, public programs, and library student advisory council committees. She is the liaison to the mathematics, electrical engineering, computer science, computational engineering, and liberal studies departments. Her research interests include faculty training and development and student engagement in urban settings. She received her MLS from North Carolina Central University, and is a former teen librarian.

Fred Kirchner works for the Dayton (Ohio) Metro Library as teen librarian at the Wilmington Stroop Branch. In addition to Homeschool Science Lab, he hosts a weekly middle school chess club, occasional creative writing workshops, and acts out Greek myths whenever possible for middle and high school English classes. Prior to earning his master of library science degree from Kent State University, Fred taught elementary and middle school in Central Ohio. He earned both a bachelor's degree in English literature and a master's in education from The Ohio State University.

Karla Steege Krueger, EdD, is assistant professor of school library studies at the University of Northern Iowa. Her MA is in school library media studies. She has worked in elementary and high school libraries. She is a member of the American Library Association, American Association of School Librarians, the Iowa Library Association, and the Iowa Association of School Librarians. Her recent article, "The Status of Statewide Subscription Databases," appeared in *School Library Research* (2012). Her research interests include online reference and the influence of school library resources on student learning.

Karen Lauritsen is the communications and public programs coordinator at the Robert E. Kennedy Library at California Polytechnic State University, San Luis Obispo. She leads Cal Poly Science Café and other public programs and content development for the library's social media.

Karen has an MA in Education from UC Berkeley in multicultural urban secondary English, and completed the conservatory program at the Second City, the world's premier school of improvisation. She is a member of the American Library Association.

Shawn V. Lombardo, associate professor, joined the library faculty at Oakland University, Rochester, Michigan in 1998. She received her MLIS from Wayne State University and an MA in English literature from Michigan State University. Shawn's research on information literacy, library instruction assessment, student research preferences, and outreach to university populations has appeared in *College and Research Libraries, Reference Librarian, RSR: Reference Services Review,* and *Library Hi Tech.* Currently, she serves as the library's coordinator of collections and the liaison to students and faculty in engineering, computer science, biology, and chemistry.

Carol Patterson McAuliffe has been the head of the Map & Imagery Library at the George A. Smathers' Libraries at the University of Florida (Gainesville, Florida) for almost six years and specializes in geoliteracy, geography, and GIS education, and the educational role of the geographic information librarian. In 2007, she organized the first ever GIS Day on the University of Florida campus and each year the library-hosted event continues to grow and improve. In November 2012, UF will be celebrating its seventh annual GIS Day.

Janna Mattson is the social sciences liaison librarian at George Mason University Libraries, Mercer Library, Prince William Campus, Manassas, Virginia. She has published in Virginia Libraries and has been a presenter at the Virginia Libraries Association's annual conference. She has also coordinated fundraising events for various charitable organizations that promote childhood literacy and higher education for at-risk youth. Janna holds a master of library science degree from Queens College and a bachelor of the arts degree in music from Virginia Commonwealth University.

Laura Munski, executive director of the Dakota Science Center, Grand Forks, North Dakota since 2004, obtained a PhD in teaching and learning from the University of North Dakota. Laura is a member of the National Science Teachers Association, the American Evaluation Association and the North Dakota Council for Social Studies. Laura received the North Dakota State Forest Service Environmental Educator Award in 2012, the University of North Dakota Community Engagement Partner Award in 2007 and the National Wildlife Federation Presidential Stewardship Bronze Award for Community Environmental Education in 2006.

Rosalia Petralia, an instruction librarian at Florida Institute of Technology's Evans Library (Melbourne, Florida), teaches research sources and systems, a for-credit undergraduate information literacy course. She received her MLIS, with an emphasis on instruction, from Florida State University. With a strong background in teaching and technical writing, she is using the Standardized Assessment of Information Literacy Skills test to assess the effect of library instruction on the information literacy of undergraduate students. She is the Evans Library's liaison to the departments of biological sciences, chemistry, and marine and environmental systems.

Gary Pinkston, PhD, is an associate professor of educational technology at Indiana University Southeast in New Albany, Indiana. He has taught courses on the hero's journey in graphic novels and incorporating graphic novels into the classroom. He enjoys creating and teaching teachers about digital storytelling and the importance of art and technology in the classroom. Gary has lengthy teaching experience with the Navajo Nation and in Saudi Arabia. In his spare time he enjoys taking photographs of his Australian shepherd dogs and making them into comic book heroes.

Anne Rauh is the engineering and computer science librarian for Syracuse University Library. She obtained her MA in Library and Information Studies from University of Wisconsin–Madison in 2007. Anne is an active member of the American Society for Engineering Education, the Eastern New York Chapter of Association of College and Research Libraries, and Beta Phi Mu. She has presented at conferences throughout the country and has published in the proceedings of the American Society for Engineering Education.

Reenay R. H. Rogers is currently an assistant professor in instructional leadership and support at the University of West Alabama. She also serves as the principal investigator and codirector of Project Engage, a minority science and engineering improvement program grant from the US Department of Education for STEM education. Degrees include a bachelor of science degree in microbiology, master of arts in secondary science education, and a doctor of philosophy degree in instructional leadership with emphasis in instructional technology, and a minor in educational research from the University of Alabama.

Tiffany B. Russell is an assistant professor and collection management librarian at North Carolina A&T State University. She received a BA from the University of North Carolina at Chapel Hill and a MLIS from the University of North Carolina at Greensboro. She is responsible for the efficient and effective allocation of the entire library budget for all library materials and supplies. Her research interests include digital curation and preservation, diversity in librarianship, and technical services transformation.

Barbara A. Shipman joined Oakland University's Kresge Library, Rochester, Michigan, as a special lecturer in 2009. She received her MLIS from Wayne State University. Barbara is the librarian liaison to the university's Department of Mathematics and Statistics and, in addition to her liaison responsibilities, she provides information literacy instruction and reference services. She has also created numerous online tutorials and interactive learning objects to support the library's instructional mission. Her research interests include faculty and college students' information-seeking behaviors, information literacy instruction, emerging technologies, and embedded librarianship.

Aaron Stefanich has been a children's librarian at Grand Forks Public Library, Grand Forks, North Dakota, since 2009. Prior to this position he was an elementary school media specialist in Minnesota. Aaron obtained his MLIS from San Jose State University. He is a member of the American Library Association and North Dakota Library Association. Aaron is a FIRST LEGO League coach. Other than contributions to *The Good Stuff* (the official magazine of the North Dakota Library Association), this is his first published work.

Kathy Turner, director of research instruction at Florida Institute of Technology's Evans Library (Melbourne, Florida), earned her MLIS from University of Oklahoma. For years, she has taught research sources and systems, a one-credit-hour information literacy course. She serves on the university's undergraduate curriculum committee and as the library's liaison to the Departments of Physics/Space Sciences, Mathematical Sciences, and Education and Interdisciplinary Studies. In 2011, she received funding to measure the impact of instruction on undergraduate information literacy using the Standardized Assessment of Information Literacy Skills test. This study continues.

Sarah Wright, homework help center coordinator at the Hilltop branch of the Columbus Metropolitan Library System (Columbus, Ohio) since 2011, received her MLIS from Kent State University and her MA in geography from Ohio State University. She is a member of the American Library Association, Ohio Library Council, Young Adult Library Services Association, and Association for Library Services to Children. She is also a contributor for the graphic novel review website, No Flying No Tights, and likes to combine her diverse interests with fun library programs for kids.